Paul Gavrilyuk is Assistant Professor of Historical Theology, University of St Thomas, St Paul, Minnesota.

OXFORD EARLY CHRISTIAN STUDIES

General Editors

THE OXFORD EARLY CHRISTIAN STUDIES series includes scholarly volumes on the thought and history of the early Christian centuries. Covering a wide range of Greek, Latin, and Oriental sources, the books are of interest to theologians, ancient historians, and specialists in the classical and Jewish worlds.

Titles in the series include:

Asceticism and Anthropology in Irenaeus and Clement
John Behr (2000)

The Old Latin Gospels
A Study of their Texts and Language
Philip Burton (2000)

Paulinus Noster
Self and Symbols in the Letters of Paulinus of Nola
Catherine Conybeare (2000)

The Cult of Saint Thecla
A Tradition of Women's Piety in Late Antiquity
Stephen T. Davis (2001)

Eunomius of Cyzicus and the Nicene Revolution
Richard Paul Vaggione, OHC (2001)

Ambrose: *De Officiis*
Edited with an Introduction, Translation, and Commentary
Ivor J. Davidson (2002)

St John Damascene
Tradition and Originality in Byzantine Theology
Andrew Louth (2002)

Augustine's Commentary on Galatians
Introduction, Translation (with facing Latin text), and Notes
Eric Plumer (2002)

The Ancient Traditions of the Virgin Mary's Dormition and Assumption
Stephen J. Shoemaker (2002)

The Early Development of Canon Law and the Council of Serdica
Hamilton Hess (2002)

The Commentaries of Origen and Jerome on St Paul's Epistle to the Ephesians
Ronald E. Heine (2002)

Grace and Christology in the Early Church
Donald Fairbairn (2003)

Evagrius of Pontus: The Greek Ascetic Corpus
Translation, Introduction, and Commentary
Robert E. Sinkewicz (2003)

Gregory of Nyssa and the Grasp of Faith
Union, Knowledge, and the Divine Presence
Martin Laird (2004)

The Suffering of the Impassible God

The Dialectics of Patristic Thought

PAUL L. GAVRILYUK

UNIVERSITY PRESS

OXFORD
UNIVERSITY PRESS

Great Clarendon Street, Oxford OX2 6DP

Oxford University Press is a department of the University of Oxford.
It furthers the University's objective of excellence in research, scholarship,
and education by publishing worldwide in

Oxford New York

Auckland Bangkok Buenos Aires Cape Town Chennai
Dar es Salaam Delhi Hong Kong Istanbul Karachi Kolkata
Kuala Lumpur Madrid Melbourne Mexico City Mumbai Nairobi
São Paulo Shanghai Taipei Tokyo Toronto

Oxford is a registered trade mark of Oxford University Press
in the UK and in certain other countries

Published in the United States
by Oxford University Press Inc., New York

First published 2004

British Library Cataloguing in Publication Data
Data available

Library of Congress Cataloging in Publication Data
Data available

ISBN 0-19-926982-3

1 3 5 7 9 10 8 6 4 2

Typeset by Kolam Information Services, Pvt., Ltd, Pondicherry, India
Printed in Great Britain on acid-free paper by
Biddles Ltd., King's Lynn.

To William J. Abraham

ACKNOWLEDGEMENTS

WHEN one dares to shed a new light upon the issues of perpetual significance, such as the question of God's involvement in suffering, one is humbled by the thought that one stands on the shoulders of the giants. I found it impossible, however, to keep the acrobatic posture all the time, and have on occasions resorted to dancing on the graves of the great. I was particularly concerned to refute Adolf Harnack's view that in the patristic period the message of the Bible was corrupted by Hellenistic philosophy, taking the issue of the divine impassibility as a limiting case. Further demolition work in this arena is needed, since at least in the assessment of divine impassibility, Harnack's thesis still reigns supreme in the minds of many modern theologians, who in one form or another support the claim that God suffers.

On a positive side, I owe a debt of gratitude to several people, among both the living and the dead. Among the ancients, it is two illustrious Alexandrians, St Athanasius and St Cyril, who have remained my theological beacons through these years. Among those of modern times, the writings of my eminent countryman, Fyodor Dostoevsky, provided the first existential impetus for me to dive into the deep waters of the problem of God's response to suffering.

No written word will adequately capture the profound impact that William Abraham has had upon my life and studies at the Southern Methodist University. This book is a token of gratitude for all the joys of philosophical friendship that we shared at the SMU.

A special word of appreciation goes to William S. Babcock, for supervising my doctoral research and for making numerous invaluable comments on the typescript of the book at various stages of its development.

Further thanks are due to my colleagues at the University of St Thomas: Joseph Hallman, Michael Hollerich, and John Martens, who were most generous with their time and critical observations.

Part of Chapter 6 was published in *Scottish Journal of Theology* 56 (2003), 190–207. I am grateful to the editor of *SJT* for permission to use this material.

Finally, I want to thank Eugenia, my wife, for her unfailing support and loving criticism of my work.

P. G.

Good Friday, April 2003

CONTENTS

ABBREVIATIONS

Ancient Authors and Works

Arnobius, *Adv. nat.*	Arnobius, *Adversus nationes*
Ath.	Athanasius: *Athanasius' Werke*
Ar. 1–2	*Orationes adversus Arianos*, 1–2
decr.	*Ep. de decretis Nicaenae synodi*
Inc.	*De incarnatione Verbi*
Athenag., *Leg.*	Athenagoras, *Legatio*
Basil, *Eun.*	Basil of Caesarea, *Adversus Eunomium*
Cicero, *De nat. deor.*	Cicero, *De natura deorum*
Tusc.	Cicero, *Tusculan Disputations*
Clem., *Paed.*	Clement of Alexandria, *Paedagogus*
Protr.	*Protrepticus*
Strom.	*Stromata*
Cyril, *Ep.*	Cyril of Alexandria, *Epistulae*
Quod unus	*Quod unus sit Christus*, ed. de Durand
Diogenes Laertius, *Vitae*	Diogenes Laertius, *Vitae et sententiae philosophorum*
Epictetus, *Arr.*	Epictetus, *Arriani commentarius disputationum*
Epiphanius, *Haer.*	Epiphanius of Salamis, *Haereses* (or *Panarion*)
Eusebius, *HE*	Eusebius, *Historia ecclesiae*
Prep. evang.	*Preparatio evangelica*
Gr. Naz.	Gregory of Nazianzus
Gr. Nyss.	Gregory of Nyssa: Jaeger, *Gregorii Nysseni Opera*
Eun.	*Contra Eunomium*: all references are to the 2nd edn. (1960) = *J*
Hippolytus, *Ref.*	Hippolytus, *Refutatio omnium heresium*: GCS 26
Ignatius	Ignatius of Antioch, *Letters*: ed. Holmes
Eph.	*Ephesians*

Polyc.	*Letter to Polycarp*
Rom.	*Romans*
Smyrn.	*Smyrnaeans*
Trall.	*Trallians*
Iren., *haer.*	Irenaeus of Lyons, *Adversus haereses*
Justin, *Apol.*	Justin Martyr, *Apologia*: ed. Krüger
Dial.	*Dialogus cum Triphone*: ed. Goodspeed
Philo, *Cher.*	Philo of Alexandria, *De cherubim*
Conf.	*De confusione linguarum*
Leg.	*Legum allegoriae*
Mut.	*De mutatione nominum*
Op.	*De opificio mundi*
Plant.	*De plantatione*
Post.	*De posteritate Caini*
Quod deus	*Quod deus sit immutabilis*
Sac.	*De sacrificiis Abelis et Cain*
Somn.	*De somniis*
Philostorgius, *HE*	Philostorgius, *Historia ecclesiae*
Ps.-Ath.(?), *Ar.* 3	Pseudo-Athanasius (?), *Orationes adversus Arianos*, 3
Ps.-Ath., *Ar.* 4	Pseudo-Athanasius, *Orationes adversus Arianos*, 4
Pusey	Cyril of Alexandria, *Commentary on the Gospel according to S. John*, i.
Randell	T. Randell (trans.), Cyril of Alexandria, *Commentary on the Gospel according to S. John*, ii.
Smith	R. Payne Smith (trans.), *Commentary On the Gospel of Saint Luke by Saint Cyril, Patriarch of Alexandria*
Socrates, *HE*	Socrates, *Historia ecclesiae*
Sozomen, *HE*	Sozomen, *Historia ecclesiae*
Tertullian, *Adv. Marc.*	Tertullian, *Adversus Marcionem*
Adv. Prax.	*Adversus Praxean*
Adv. Valent.	*Adversus Valentinianos*
Theodoret, *HE*	Theodoret, *Historia ecclesiae*

Other Abbreviations

ACO	*Acta Conciliorum Oecumenicorum*, ed. Schwartz
ANF	Ante-Nicene Fathers, ed. Schaff and Wace
CSEL	*Corpus Scriptorum Ecclesiasticorum Latinorum*
FC	The Fathers of the Church (Washington: The Catholic University of America Press)
GCS	Die griechischen Christlichen Schriftsteller (Leipzig)
Hanson, *Search*	Richard P. C. Hanson, *The Search for the Christian Doctrine of God*
HTR	*Harvard Theological Review*
JEH	*Journal of Ecclesiastical History*
JTS	*Journal of Theological Studies*
LCL	Loeb Classical Library
McGuckin, *Christological Controversy*	John A. McGuckin, *St. Cyril of Alexandria: The Christological Controversy: Its History, Theology, and Texts*
NPNF	A Select Library of Nicene and Post-Nicene Fathers of the Christian Church, ed. Ph. Schaff and H. Wace
PG	*Patrologiae Cursus Completus*, Series Graeca, ed. J.-P. Migne
PL	*Patrologiae Cursus Completus*, Series Latina, ed. J.-P. Migne
Russel, *Cyril*	Norman Russel, *Cyril of Alexandria*
SC	Sources chrétiennes
SJT	*Scottish Journal of Theology*
Sorabji, *Emotion*	Richard Sorabji, *Emotion and Peace of Mind*
Vaggione, *Eunomius*	Richard P. Vaggione, *Eunomius: The Extant Works*
Wickham, *Cyril*	L. R. Wickham, *Cyril of Alexandria: Select Letters*
Winston, 'Philo's Conception'	David Winston, 'Philo's Conception of the Divine Nature'

Introduction

The Dominant Interpretation of Divine Impassibility: The Theory of Theology's Fall into Hellenistic Philosophy

WITH a few significant exceptions,[1] modern theologians advocate the claim that God suffers. Scholarly opinion shows a remarkable consensus on this issue, despite the variety of qualifications, the difference in approaches and topics addressed. Theologians representing various trends, such as theology of the cross, kenotic, biblical, liberation, feminist, process, openness, philosophical, and historical theologies have voiced their opinions in defence of divine passibility. Almost a century ago Maldwyn Hughes noted with approval a tendency among British theologians of his day to 'find the clue to the meaning of the cross in the suffering of God' and emphasized that this trend ran against the traditional teaching of the church.[2] Sixty years later, as the number of the advocates of divine passibility was growing, Ronald Goetz announced the 'rise of a new orthodoxy'.[3] The conviction that divine impassibility is

[1] In the field of philosophical theology Richard Creel has made a case for a carefully qualified divine impassibility in conversation with process thought. Defining impassibility as 'imperviousness to causal influence from external factors', Creel argues that while God is impassible in his nature and will, he is passible in his knowledge of the events in the world. See *Divine Impassibility*. R. A. Muller, H. McCabe, B. Davies, William J. Hill, J.-H. Nicolas, von Hügel, and G. Hanratty likewise argue for retaining a version of the divine impassibility. See their works in the Bibliography.

[2] H. M. Hughes, *What is the Atonement?* Hughes's observation was prompted by the work of the British Kenoticists such as C. Gore, F. Weston, A. M. Fairbairn, C. A. Dinsmore, and others. These thinkers were in turn inspired by two nineteenth-century schools of German Kenoticism, one represented by G. Thomasius and F. Rohmer, the other, more radical one, by W. Gess and F. Godet. For a survey see A. B. Bruce, *The Humiliation of Christ*; I. A. Dorner, *Divine Immutability*; T. Weinardy, *Does God Change?*, 110–23.

[3] R. Goetz, 'The Suffering God: The Rise of a New Orthodoxy'. While Goetz, broadly speaking, agrees with the case made by the contemporary passibilists, he provides a fairly

untenable on philosophical, exegetical, and broadly religious grounds, reigns supreme in the minds of a considerable number of modern theologians.

It is against this background that the allegedly impassibilist patristic heritage is received. It has become almost commonplace in contemporary theological works to pass a negative judgement upon the patristic concept of the divine impassibility. Superficial criticism of the divine *apatheia* on purely etymological grounds, without any serious analysis of its actual function in the thought of the Fathers, has become a convenient polemical starting point for the subsequent elaboration of a passibilist position. Such a dismissive attitude towards the patristic heritage is guided far more by the contemporary climate of opinion on the issue of divine suffering than by any serious engagement with the theology of the Fathers.

A standard line of criticism places divine impassibility in the conceptual realm of Hellenistic philosophy, where the term allegedly meant the absence of emotions and indifference to the world, and then concludes that impassibility in this sense cannot be an attribute of the Christian God. In this regard, a popular dichotomy between Hebrew and Greek theological thinking has been elaborated specifically with reference to the issues of divine (im)passibility and (im)mutability. On this reading, the God of the prophets and apostles is the God of *pathos*, whereas the God of the philosophers is apathetic.[4]

Without exception, biblical authors ascribe to God strong emotions. God becomes angry and repents, feels sorrow and rejoices. Above all else, he is the God of self-sacrificial love and self-giving compassion. He hears prayers and responds to them. The God of the Bible is deeply involved in history. The prophetic writings speak of him as actually suffering with and for humanity.

In contrast, the God of the Greek philosophers, according to this reading, takes no interest in human affairs and is entirely immune from suffering. This deity cannot be influenced by anything external. It is useless to pray to it, except for the psychological benefit of moral exercise. Being incapable of feelings and emotions, such a God is also incapable of love and care.

balanced discussion of the difficulties the affirmation of unqualified divine passibility presents. Cf. Donald Baillie, *God Was in Christ*, 199; D. D. Williams, *What Present Day Theologians are Thinking*.

[4] See Appendix.

All the major Greek philosophical schools have been singled out as possible sources of the idea of divine impassibility in Christian theology. As early as 1924, William Temple wrote: '[W]e have to recognize that Aristotle's "apathetic God" was enthroned in men's minds, and no idol has been so hard to destroy.'[5] The judgement of E. T. Pollard is equally uncompromising: 'Among the many Greek philosophic ideas imported into Christian theology, and into Alexandrine Jewish theology before it, is the idea of the *impassible* God (*apathes theos*), and this idea furnishes us with a particularly striking illustration of the damage done by the assumption of alien philosophical presuppositions when they are applied to Christian theology.'[6]

The mind of the early Fathers, according to this commonly accepted view, was held captive to the Greek philosophical concept of divine impassibility and simply failed to recognize that it stands in stark contradiction to the Christian revelation. Uncritical endorsement of divine impassibility by the early Fathers led to subsequent difficulties and inconsistencies in the understanding of the divine involvement in history and especially in the articulation of the doctrine of the incarnation.

This interpretation of the relationship between Christian theology and Greek philosophy is an offshoot of Adolf von Harnack's (1851–1930) theory of the development of dogma in terms of chronic Hellenization.[7] The process of Hellenization for Harnack had a negative connotation: it implied a deterioration of the originally unadulterated gospel into a rigid doctrinal system. Every time Christian theologians borrowed ideas from philosophers they corrupted and distorted the gospel. It should be noted that a version of this theory was not unknown to the early Fathers and had been around since Hippolytus of Rome (170–235), who argued that the heretics did not derive their doctrines from the scriptures and apostolic tradition, but rather from Greek philosophers.[8] Hippolytus took pains to trace the teachings of individual Gnostic groups to various philosophical schools. Tertullian of Carthage (160–225) seized upon the

[5] W. Temple, *Christus Veritas*, 269. Temple, to his credit, emphasized God's victory in and through suffering. What he missed completely, however, was that impassibility could express precisely this victorious aspect of divine suffering.

[6] E. T. Pollard, 'The Impassibility of God', 356; emphasis in the original. Pollard, it should be noted, rightly recognized that the thought of the Fathers revolved around a paradox of the impassible God who suffered in the incarnation. Pollard quite inconsistently concluded that this paradox was a way of getting rid of the alien philosophical idea of divine impassibility. Cf. Tyron Inbody, *The Transforming God*, 165.

[7] A. Harnack, *What is Christianity?*, 207, 211–12; *History of Dogma*, i. 227–8.

[8] Hippolytus, *Ref.* Proem. 3.

rhetorical potential of this argument and branded Greek philosophy with the title of the mother of all heresies.[9]

Harnack, it would appear, turned the ancient argument against both traditional heretics and the church Fathers. According to him, Gnostic teachings represented an acutely Hellenized distortion of the gospel by philosophy, whereas the orthodox position exhibited the same kind of distortion, only worked out more gradually.[10] The sad result of this process was the transformation of the pure and simple message into a 'speculative philosophical, cultish-mystical and dualistic-ascetic'[11] system. For Harnack, the heroic role of the historian of dogma consisted of exposing this harmful development and of subsequent emancipation of the church from its corrupting influence.[12] Although this theory is a classical example of the genetic fallacy, it has had a permanent grip upon post-Reformation theologians and historians. Despite the fact that Harnack's understanding of Hellenization as corruption of the gospel has come under devastating criticism in many areas,[13] its validity is still implied in the discussion of divine (im)passibility.

A more elaborate version of this standard assessment of the patristic position adds the following consideration. Although the major part of the tradition asserted divine impassibility, there was a minor theme, running through the patristic period, that portrayed God as suffering. This theme can be discerned, for example, in numerous theopaschite expressions that belong to Fathers of unquestionable orthodoxy. In addition, two heretical movements—Modalist Patripassianism and Theopaschite Monophysitism—advocated the claim that God suffers. Therefore, according to this version of the theory, there was a minority voice that asserted the suffering of God in the face of the prevailing opposition. This view is advocated, for example, by J. M. Hallman: 'In spite of the dominant philosophical understanding, there is a faint dissonant chorus in the Christian tradition made up of minor voices. For them the God of Jewish and Christian faith is a fellow-sufferer.'[14]

[9] Tertullian, *De prescr.* 7.

[10] Harnack, *Outlines of the History of Dogma*, 66–7.

[11] Ibid. 61. [12] Ibid. 7.

[13] An important critique of this theory is offered in Alois Grillmeier, *Christ in Christian Tradition*, i. See also W. V. Rowe, 'Adolf von Harnack and the Concept of Hellenization', 69–98; M. Hengel, *Judaism and Hellenism*; W. Pannenberg, 'The Appropriation of the Philosophical Concept of God as a Dogmatic Problem of Early Christian Theology', ii. 119–83; W. E. Helleman (ed.), *Hellenization Revisited*; J. Danielou, *Gospel Message and Hellenistic Culture*, 303.

[14] J. M. Hallman, 'The Seed of Fire', 369.

Hallman's position is in line with the dominant interpretation, not a departure from it. The major elements of this widely accepted interpretation are as follows: (1) divine impassibility is an attribute of God in Greek and Hellenistic philosophy; (2) divine impassibility was adopted by the early Fathers uncritically from the philosophers; (3) divine impassibility does not leave room for any sound account of divine emotions and divine involvement in history, as attested in the Bible; (4) divine impassibility is incompatible with the revelation of the suffering God in Jesus Christ; (5) the latter fact was recognized by a minority group of theologians who affirmed that God is passible, going against the majority opinion. I will refer to this position taken as a whole as the 'Theory of Theology's Fall into Hellenistic Philosophy'.[15]

It will be the burden of this study to show that this widely accepted view is a misinterpretation that stands in need of a thorough revision. The first point is as true as it is platitudinous, with one proviso: I will show in the first chapter that the role of divine impassibility in classical Greek philosophy (as distinct from later Hellenistic views) is exaggerated by contemporary interpreters. The constructive criticism of points 2 and 3 occupies Chapters 1 and 2 of the present study. Points 4 and 5 are taken up in the rest of the work as I develop a rival account centring on the doctrine of the incarnation as the crucial focus for the assertion of both the qualified passibility and the impassibility of God.

Problems with Unqualified Divine Passibility

As I have noted before, in the contemporary theological climate impassibility is so universally presented in an unfavourable light that it is quite often ignored that the notion of unrestricted divine passibility is also fraught with many difficulties. The divine impassibility has so often been caricatured as an alien Hellenistic concept that important religious sensibilities at work in retaining divine impassibility in the Christian context are simply neglected. A few scholars acknowledge that unrestricted divine passibility presents as many theological difficulties as does unrestricted divine impassibility.[16]

One important thing to be grasped from the very beginning is that the choice between an unrestrictedly impassible and an unrestrictedly

[15] See Appendix.

[16] For a survey of this issue see Thomas Weinandy, *Does God Suffer?*. See also an important but neglected book by B. R. Brasnett, *The Suffering of the Impassible God*, 12.

passible God implied in the modern theopaschite consensus presents a false dilemma. This becomes more or less obvious if we realize that all the contemporary advocates of theopaschitism would agree that significant qualifications apply to their assertion that God suffers and has emotions. The following general considerations are designed to illustrate some of the difficulties which arise from attributing unrestricted passibility to God.

First, if God has emotions at all, it is clear that not all human emotions may be ascribed to him. Even the most radical passibilists will concur that the Christian God is not subject to greed, lust, fear, or anxiety. They would grant, for example, that God is not overwhelmed by helpless grief. Unlike human beings, God totally controls his emotions. Therefore, merely to say that God has emotions does not represent any theological achievement whatsoever. On the contrary, it is quite appropriate to be cautious about ascribing emotions to God, since some of them prove to be unworthy of him. As we shall see, the intention to purify theological discourse of unworthy divine emotions is one of the points that is at stake in the patristic endorsement of divine impassibility.

Second, it is equally clear that if God is capable of suffering at all, his suffering is in many respects different from human suffering. For example, it would seem that in order to experience bodily suffering and pain, God would have to have a body and a soul, or some analogue of such a constitution. A significant number of contemporary theopaschites, with the exception of process theologians and some others, do not deal with this problem in any systematic way. No matter how the issue is resolved, it is more fitting for God to acquire a human constitution in order to experience the things typically associated with it. In the language of the Fathers, in order to suffer humanly God must make human nature his own.

Third, in human experience we distinguish between suffering that comes against our will and that which is accepted voluntarily. Not many contemporary passibilists would admit that God is subject to undesired and unforeseen suffering. The admission of such 'accidents' in divine life would be equivalent to denying that God is omnipotent and omniscient. This would lead, in turn, to a thoroughgoing revision of classical theism.[17] The problems with such a radical move are numerous. To name

[17] Developing A. J. Heschel's position, T. E. Fretheim argues that, from the standpoint of biblical theology, divine suffering entails real limitations of the divine power and knowledge of the future. See his *The Suffering of God.* Harold Kushner popularized the argument against divine omnipotence in his *When Bad Things Happen to Good People,*

just two of the most obvious: if God is not omnipotent, is he capable of keeping his promises? If God's power is finite, then how much power precisely does God have? The majority of theologians who today sympathize with passibilism would not be prepared to give up other divine perfections. Less problematic appears to be the claim that, if God suffers at all, his suffering is always voluntary. As I will show, this is precisely what the Fathers maintained with regard to the suffering of God in the incarnation.

Fourth, not every kind of voluntary suffering is praiseworthy. God's voluntary suffering has to have a purpose. Clearly, a view that God suffers incessantly without any purpose whatsoever—what we might call the Perpetual Heavenly Masochist option—is either nonsensical or immoral. An obvious correction would be to see divine suffering as directed towards a redemptive goal. It has been rightly pointed out by Paul Fiddes that God suffers with the kind of suffering which is not passive, but active, salvific, and victorious over all the misfortunes of the human predicament.[18] The latter statement involves a paradox: it acknowledges suffering that is at the same time a redemptive action. I will show that this insight, shared by modern passibilists, was expressed by the early Fathers in the paradoxical statement that God suffered impassibly.

Fifth, perhaps the archargument against the divine impassibility states that it is incompatible with the nature of divine love, providential care, and compassion.[19] It is often urged that compassion entails suffering with the sufferer. Compassion seems to rule out dispassion. Etymological considerations, rather than serious philosophical analysis, have played the same misleading role in the case of compassion as they did in the case of dispassion, or impassibility. It is pointed out that the English noun 'sympathy' is a transliteration of the Greek συμπάθεια, just as 'compassion' is a transliteration of the Latin *compassio*. Since both the Greek and the Latin terms may be literally rendered as 'suffering-with', it is claimed that suffering-with is the essence

113–31. Kushner is hesitant to speak of God who suffers because of the problem of anthropomorphism that divine suffering entails. See ibid. 85–6.

18 See Paul Fiddes, *The Creative Suffering of God.*

19 Consider, for example, the following categorical declaration of H. M. Hughes, *What is the Atonement?*, 94: 'It is of the very nature of love to suffer when its object suffers loss, whether inflicted by itself or others. If the suffering of God be denied, then Christianity must discover a new terminology and must obliterate the statement "God is love" from its Scriptures.' Cf. Dennis Ngien, 'God Who Suffers: If God Does Not Grieve, Then Can He Love at All? An Argument for God's Emotions', 38–42.

of compassion.[20] Thus, as early as Tertullian, the rhetorical question was raised: '*Quid est enim compati quam cum alio pati?*'[21] Modern passibilists sound strikingly like Tertullian when they present the following dilemma: 'Either God sympathizes and then he suffers, or God does not suffer and then he does not sympathize or care.'[22] The Whiteheadian 'fellow-sufferer who understands' is among the most deeply cherished ideas of modern passibilism.

This understanding of compassion leads to several difficulties. Some philosophers have granted that compassion literally means suffering-with and concluded that it leads to the multiplication of suffering. Immanuel Kant held that compassion was a form of emotional contagion irrelevant to and potentially harmful to moral agents. Following the Greek Stoics, Kant argued that compassion, along with other emotions, had no constructive role to play in his deontological ethics. It was duty, not compassion or any other emotion, that rendered any action meritorious.[23]

Friedrich Nietzsche went further than Kant in his criticism of compassion. Under the same assumption that compassion meant literally suffering-with, he argued that acts of compassion only multiplied human misery.[24] Compassion for Nietzsche was a mark of emotional weakness, a degrading emotion unworthy of a superman. A person concerned with the suffering of others became emotionally dependent upon them and inevitably submitted to the destructive influence of suffering. As we will see in Chapter 1, the Epicureans also held that compassion multiplied anxiety and was harmful to a philosopher's well-being.

Both ancient Greek and modern German objections to the moral worth of compassion may be met by rejecting their premise that compassion means literally suffering-with. The following examples will show that suffering-with is neither necessary nor sufficient for every compassionate action.

[20] Cicero, *De nat. deor.* 3. 28 renders συμπάθεια as *consensus*, which may be in turn translated as 'harmony' and 'interaction', not as *compassio*. This is a good example of how precarious are conclusions based upon etymology alone. On the philosophical use of cosmic *sympatheia* see Karl Reinhardt, *Kosmos und Sympathie*.

[21] Tertullian, *Adv. Prax*. 29.

[22] Baron F. von Hügel quotes this statement in 'Suffering and God', 191, and calls it a 'sorry rationalist alternative'.

[23] *Groundwork of the Metaphysics of Morals*, iv. 398; *Religion Within the Limits of Reason Alone*, 26. On the Stoic ban of pity and compassion as *pathē* see Richard Sorabji, *Emotion*, 389–90.

[24] F. Nietzsche, *Human, All too Human*, 38.

Many compassionate actions do not require emotional identification with the sufferer. Consider the case of a compassionate doctor who needs to perform a sophisticated surgical procedure that may have fatal consequences for the patient. What is required from such a doctor is his ability to improve the situation of his patient. The sufferer himself would protest if such a doctor became a copy of his sufferings, if he turned into another helpless patient. Clearly such behaviour would not be judged as the expression of compassion, but rather as a case of nervous breakdown. What emotions the doctor goes through and whether he suffers, mentally or otherwise, before the operation is irrelevant. It is essential, however, that his mind is not clouded by grief, that his hands are not shaking with fear as he performs the surgery, that he is emotionally stable, and the like. He must remain who he was, namely, a doctor, and not become a patient. In this sense the doctor must remain impassible, i.e. he must not allow the sufferings of his patient, no matter how intense those are, to overwhelm his capacity to function as a skilled surgeon. It is worth noting that the Fathers often compare Christ to a compassionate physician of souls and bodies. For example, speaking about the way in which Christ heals our passions Gregory of Nyssa observed: 'We do not say that one who touches a sick person to heal him is himself partaker of the infirmity, but we say that he does make the sick man a favor of recovery, and does not partake of the infirmity: for the suffering does not affect him, it is rather he who affects the suffering (οὐδὲ γὰρ ἐκείνου τὸ πάθος, ἀλλὰ τὸ ἔμπαλιν ἐκεῖνος τοῦ ἀρρωστήματος ἅπτεται).'[25]

It is certainly true that some minimal imaginative appreciation of the situation of the sufferer is necessary for any person to be moved by compassion. At the same time, however, a mere reproduction of the sufferer's feelings is not enough for compassionate action. As Max Scheler, to whom I owe much in my analysis of the nature of compassion, poignantly noted: 'It is perfectly meaningful to say: "I can quite visualize your feelings, but I have no pity for you."'[26] For example, a spectator of Greek tragedy may become profoundly emotionally involved in what happens on the stage, without leaving his seat in a theatre. According to St Augustine, such a person is far from genuine compassion since '[a] member of the audience is not excited to offer help, but

[25] Gr. Nyss., *Eun.* 3. 4. 724 (*J* ii. 146), trans. H. A. Wilson, NPNF 2nd ser. v. 186. The same point is repeated in his *Oratio Catechetica Magna* 14, 16; cf. Origen, *Contra Celsum*, 4.14; *Princ.* 2. 10. 6.

[26] M. Scheler, *The Nature of Sympathy*, 9; Sorabji, *Emotion*, 390.

invited only to grieve'.[27] An act of compassion must always go beyond mere emotional reproduction of another person's grief. As Cicero put it, 'we ought not to share distress ourselves for the sake of others, but we ought to relieve others of their distress if we can'.[28]

To make this point clear, consider the case of a house on fire. Several people are unable to exit the building and cry aloud desperately for help. Firemen have been called, but for some reason they do not come. A crowd is gathering around the house. Some stare at the house with a mixture of anxiety, fear, and curiosity. Some attempt to visualize as vividly as possible what the people who are in the house must be going through. These members of the crowd burst into tears, yell, tear their hair; in short, they are greatly emotionally affected. One of them has already had a fit and lies unconscious. Another has become mad and predicts the end of the world. Yet another person decides literally to suffer with those who are in the house and commits suicide by burning himself. Panic grows. A certain man from the crowd, without going through all the emotional pangs that those standing near him are experiencing, being motivated only by his conviction that the people will surely die if there is no one to help them, gets into the house and, at great risk to his own safety, rescues them. If it is asked, who out of all the people that were present at the scene manifested genuine compassion, the answer is obvious.

Let us briefly analyse the experiences through which the compassionate person had to go in order to save those people. First, he had to have at least a minimal understanding of the danger to which the people in the burning house were exposed. To that end, he did not have to try to burn himself. That would be folly, momentous weakness, not compassion. Second, he had to have the courage and resolution to enter the raging fire. Third, he had to be strongly motivated to save those people. Fourth, he had to be prepared to suffer and to die, if the situation made his suffering and death unavoidable. Compassion is first of all an action, which may or may not entail suffering, depending upon the circumstances.

This example shows that any compassionate action requires more than just suffering-with. The compassionate person may indeed suffer by entering the situation of the sufferer, but his suffering must never simply be the same as that of the sufferer. He suffers voluntarily, as a

27 Augustine, *Confessions* III. ii. 2, trans. Henry Chadwick, *Confessions*, 36.
28 *Tusc.* 4. 56.

consequence of his compassionate intention, whereas the victim suffers unwillingly. The compassionate person is not conquered by suffering, whereas the sufferer is weak and helpless. The compassionate person is able to help precisely because he is not susceptible to suffering to the degree to which the victim is. In this sense the compassionate person must remain impassible, unconquered by suffering.[29]

To conclude, the person who acts out of compassion must be both impassible in order to be able to help and be potentially ready to suffer, if required by the situation. This analysis of human compassion applies by way of analogy to the case of divine compassion in the incarnation. Divine compassion presupposes both impassibility and passibility. It is the main contention of the patristic understanding of the incarnation that God, remaining fully divine, became human, accepted the limitations of human existence, subjected himself to voluntary suffering for the salvation of the world and triumphed over sin, death, and corruption in the end. God is impassible inasmuch as he is able to conquer suffering and he is passible inasmuch as he is able to suffer in and through human nature.

Those who favour unqualified passibilism may still contend that there are prior religious and moral intuitions that override these philosophical arguments or any other logic, however tight it may be, that suggests that compassion does not necessitate suffering-with, and certainly requires more than suffering-with. These thinkers claim that the existence of the suffering and oppressed world demands that God suffer with it. Such a God is the only consolation, the only real solution of theodicy. In the words of Richard Bauckham, 'only the suffering God can help'.[30] There is no doubt that some people may find these words very meaningful and consoling, when they face situations in which social injustice acquires demonic proportions. However, it has not been sufficiently acknow-

[29] It may be objected that we have shifted the meaning of the term 'impassible' from 'unemotional' to 'resilient in the face of suffering'. As the present study will show, this shift is within the range of meanings that patristic authors give to the term 'impassible'.

[30] The expression is taken from the title of Bauckham, 'Only the Suffering God Can Help'. Along similar lines, Kenneth Surin argues that theodicy may be resolved only by postulating a God who is able to suffer sympathetically in 'The Impassibility of God and the Problem of Evil', 97–115. Similarly, Sallie McFague observes: 'God as lover suffers with those who suffer... God as lover takes the suffering into her own being; God feels the pain in his own body in an immediate and total way,' *Models of God*, 142. Cf. also Brian Hebblethwaite's statement that 'only a suffering God is morally credible' in 'Incarnation and Atonement: The Moral and Religious Value of the Incarnation', 87–100. It should be noted that Hebblethwaite advocates a substantially qualified passibilism.

ledged that many religious people in similar circumstances would find this statement problematic.

Many believers would find it immoral and openly offensive to their piety to expect God to be a perpetual sufferer, while at the same time they deeply cherish God's love, mercy, and compassion. For it is downright egoism to want another person to suffer just as I suffer. François de La Rochefoucauld (1613–80) once observed that 'in the misfortunes of our best friends there is something which is not altogether displeasing to us'.[31] Whether we are impressed with this insight of the French *philosophe* is beside the point. One thing appears intuitively clear: it is morally wrong to desire our friends to suffer. (Unless we want them to receive some educational punishment for grave sins. But in the latter case we do not desire their suffering as suffering; what we intend rather is their moral improvement.)

Now, in the case when we ourselves suffer and encounter human indifference it may be a pardonable weakness to wish that someone else were in our shoes. Peter Abelard (1079–1142) observed in the Foreword to his *Historia calamitatum*, that unsurpassable monument to male egoism, that he recounted the story of his misfortunes so that 'in comparison with my trials you will see that your own are nothing, or only slight, and will find them easier to bear'.[32] It is true that we sometimes feel relieved when we find that someone fares no better than we do. However, this attitude to our neighbours, to say nothing about God, is morally objectionable. Most of us would agree that we wish our neighbours to be compassionate and caring. This is very different, however, from wishing them to be afflicted with the same misfortunes that happen to afflict us personally.

It may be objected that the moral problem arises here simply because the order of our wishing God to suffer and God's actual action on our behalf is reversed. We do not first desire God to suffer, and then he answers our selfish petition. Rather God is the one who takes the

[31] François de La Rochefoucauld, *Maximes*, 583: 'Dans l'adversité de nos meilleurs amis, nous trouvons toujours quelque chose qui ne nous déplaît pas.' Quoted from Kant, *Religion Within the Limits of Reason Alone*, 29.

[32] P. Abelard, *Historia calamitatum*, Praef. trans. B. Radice, *The Letters of Abelard and Heloise*, 57. It is noteworthy that some of the early manuscripts of the *Historia* had the title *Abaelardi ad amicum suum consolatoria*. Unfortunately Abelard's lament did not produce the intended effect upon Héloïse. Having read the *Historia* she wrote to Abelard: 'my own sorrows are renewed by the detail in which you have told it [the story of your misfortunes], and redoubled because you say your perils are still increasing', Héloïse, *Ep.* 1, trans. B. Radice, 110.

initiative and suffers for our redemption, and then we respond to him in gratitude. Be that as it may, the basic point remains valid: we should desire divine compassion for its own sake and for our own sake, yet we should not desire divine suffering for its own sake, but only for the sake of some higher redemptive goal. Divine compassion may or may not require divine suffering. At any rate, it certainly entails a measure of impassibility, which in this case means God's ability to vanquish our misery. According to St Augustine, divine compassion far surpasses human compassion precisely because God is not overpowered by our suffering: 'You, Lord God, lover of souls, show a compassion far purer and freer of mixed motives than ours; for no suffering injures you.'[33] Far from being a 'fellow-sufferer who understands', a God who is a mere replica of suffering humanity (as he was for Ludwig Feuerbach[34]) is incapable of being a redeemer.

Some of the points discussed above, and many other problems arising from ascribing unreserved suffering to God, have received considerable attention in the writings of contemporary passibilists.[35] The discussion has now become rather complex and tangled. The limitations of this historical study do not permit us to enter it in detail. Nevertheless, our brief analysis has two important implications for a historical assessment of the problem of divine (im)passibility.

The first implication is that there is no prima facie case for the concept of an emotional and suffering God over against that of an unemotional and non-suffering God. Far from being a barrier to our understanding of divine action, or an axiom to be destroyed, impassibility proves to be an indispensable concept in articulating a sound doctrine of the incarnation.[36] Rhetorical allegations against divine impassibility will not help to further the discussion at all. Until the appropriate qualifications of divine

[33] *Confessions* III. ii. 3, trans. Chadwick, *Confessions*, 37.

[34] See the chapter entitled 'The Mystery of the Suffering God', 59–64.

[35] For a good overview of several contemporary arguments against unqualified divine passibility see Marcel Sarot, *God, Passibility and Corporeality*, 31–66. Sarot agrees that some of the objections to unqualified passibility are valid and admits qualified divine immutability (pp. 65–6). Less successful is the discussion in Lee, *God Suffers for Us*, 23–45. See also M. Jarrett-Kerr, *The Hope of Glory*, 65–75.

[36] Contrary to what F. House argued in 'The Barrier of Divine Impassibility' and to Eberhard Jüngel, who wrote in *God as the Mystery of the World*, 373: 'By orienting this distinction between God and God to the Crucified One we have significantly corrected the classical doctrine of God. For this distinction between God and God based on the cross of Jesus Christ has destroyed the axiom of absoluteness, the axiom of apathy, and the axiom of immutability, all of which are unsuitable axioms of the Christian concept of God.'

suffering and impassibility are made, one must try to remain neutral, no matter how difficult it is, given the modern tendency towards theopaschitism. Note that the neutrality to which I appeal here is a theological claim, not an indefinite obligation of a historian to be objective.[37]

The second implication is that buried in this discussion are fundamental issues related to the nature of religious language and to divine action that may be informed, but cannot be solved solely by a painstaking exegesis of pertinent scriptural passages that suggest divine (im)-passibility, or by rival metaphysical accounts of reality borrowed either from Plato or Whitehead. The Fathers preferred to formulate the problem as the quest for a language worthy of God (*theoprepes, dignus Deo*). We will explore patristic arguments for a fitting interpretation of select emotions and actions ascribed to God in the biblical narrative. Contemporary passibilists argue that a tenacious retaining of the divine impassibility led to absurdities and inconsistencies in the patristic accounts of divine emotions and involvement.[38] Unquestionably, assertions of the type: 'God is both loving and impassible' and 'the impassible one suffered' played a pivotal role in patristic thought. Many passibilists would object that such apparent contradictions are unnecessary and avoidable. They argue that an uncompromising rejection of divine impassibility is a viable way of dissolving all the contradictions involved.

The allegation that the Fathers were inconsistent is serious and, in my judgement, has not been addressed adequately. Are those scholars who offer a sympathetic assessment of patristic sources justified in designating the contradictions involved paradoxical? There is a thin line between a plain contradiction and a paradox, a line that has to be drawn more carefully than it has been in previous studies. Several questions are pertinent to this investigation: are the propositions 'God is both loving and impassible' and 'the impassible one suffered' paradoxes *sui generis*, or are they a part of a larger family of paradoxical statements? How do they function in patristic theology? What ideas are these paradoxes intended to convey? Is there just one type of paradox involved here, or are there at least two? Is it possible to make finer distinctions between different uses of (im)passibility, some for which the paradoxical form of the statement is in principle dissoluble and others for which, on the contrary, it is fundamentally unavoidable? What were the actual attempts to dissolve

[37] J. K. Mozley's pioneering survey of patristic thought, *The Impassibility of God*, is a case of properly exercised historical neutrality.

[38] F. House, 'The Barrier of Impassibility', 413; R. Edwards, 'Pagan Dogma', 313.

the paradox? How were these attempts received? Such and related questions will be systematically addressed in this study.

A Summary of the Book

The major contours of my argument are as follows. In the first chapter I will question the sharp distinction between the Hellenistic God who is apathetic and the biblical God who has emotions and is involved in human affairs to the point of suffering. I will argue that this standard view misrepresents both the philosophers and the biblical authors. On the one hand, the diversity of conflicting accounts of divine nature, emotions, and intervention in the Hellenistic philosophies and the Hellenistic religions at large does not yield a picture of a single impassible philosophical deity, disinterested in the world. This picture is a scholarly caricature, a convenient strawman put together by the modern proponents of the Theory of the Fall into Hellenistic Philosophy. On the other hand, the biblical authors were keenly aware of the fact that to ascribe emotions to God was to raise the problems of anthropomorphism and anthropopathism. I will show that the question of worthy and unworthy divine emotions was not generated by alien philosophical convictions, but by the biblical idea that God, as creator, is different from everything created.

In the second chapter I will contend that the second point of the Theory of the Fall into Hellenistic Philosophy—that the divine impassibility was adopted by the early Fathers uncritically—does not square with the historical evidence. Although there was some overlap in meaning, various functions of impassibility in the Christian sources were quite different from those in the Hellenistic philosophies. Impassibility was not baptized without conversion. On the conceptual level I will show that more is involved in the Christian understanding of divine impassibility than God's immunity from suffering. For the Christian theologians impassibility, as applied to human beings, meant (1) the state enjoyed by the blessed after the resurrection, consisting in freedom from bodily suffering and incorruptibility, and (2) the virtuous state attained by monastic discipline and expressed in true love for God and transfiguration of the passions and freedom from evil inclinations and demonic influences.

With reference to the Christian God impassibility meant that he does not have the same emotions as the gods of the heathen; that his care for human beings is free from self-interest and any association with evil; that since he has neither body nor soul, he cannot directly have the experiences typically connected with them; that he is not overwhelmed by emotions and in the incarnation emerges victorious over suffering and death. I will argue that divine impassibility functioned as an *apophatic qualifier* of all divine emotions and served to rule out those passions and experiences that were unbecoming of the divine nature.

If my criticism of the second point of the Fall into Hellenistic Philosophy Theory is successful, the flaws of the third point will be obvious. The third point states that divine impassibility, as understood by the Hellenistic philosophers and used indiscriminately by the early Fathers, conflicts with the revelation of a caring and loving God, as attested by the Bible. I will show that for the Fathers, divine impassibility was fully compatible with God's providential care for the world, with direct divine involvement in history, and with praiseworthy emotionally coloured characteristics, such as love and compassion.[39]

The analysis will be carried out both on the micro-level of those passages in the early Christian writings where (im)passibility is ascribed to God and on the macro-level of broader developments. I will contend that a theology of martyrdom, the beliefs associated with the sacraments of the Eucharist and baptism, and the tradition of paschal sermons contributed to patristic reflection upon the question of the divine (im)passibility.

I will trace the logic of selected Christological debates from the first five centuries and show how the affirmation of divine impassibility, in a qualified sense, was regarded by the Fathers as fully compatible with the claim that, having become incarnate, God the Son suffered. The question whether, in what sense, and under what circumstances suffering may be ascribed to God runs as a golden thread through the patristic controversies about the person of Jesus Christ. I will argue that this development may be viewed as an attempt to secure both the historical involvement of God in human history, the apex of which is the coming of the Son of God, and the irreducible divinity of God, which transcends the limitations of temporal existence and remains undiminished by God's engagement in history.

The dialectic of this development may be traced through the major theological controversies of early Christianity: Docetism, Patripassian-

[39] According to G. L. Prestige, 'There is no sign that divine impassibility was taught with any view of minimizing the interest of God in his creation or his care and concern for the world that he had made,' *God in Patristic Thought*, 11.

ism, Arianism, and Nestorianism. Second-century Docetists claimed that since Christ was a divine figure, the experiences of birth, suffering, and death were not worthy of his divine status. It would be shameful and degrading for a divine being to be involved in them. On these grounds the Docetists concluded that Christ suffered only in appearance. Ignatius of Antioch and Irenaeus of Lyons, among others, rejected this view, along with the cosmological and soteriological framework upon which it depended, and argued that the birth, suffering, and death of Christ were real and historical. The second-century Fathers stressed that those experiences were God-befitting, since the natural processes of growth and suffering to which all creation was subject were not evil in themselves.

In addition, the Fathers pointed out that it was precisely because the suffering of Christ was real that martyrdom opened a way of imitation and participation in Christ's passion. They also stressed that it was because Christ possessed real flesh that the Eucharist could function as the medicine of immortality for those who in faith partook of Christ's body and blood.

In the third century, Modalist Patripassians claimed that since the Father and the Son were united as aspects of one divine being, the sufferings attributed to the Son had also to be ascribed to the Father. Unlike the Docetic groups, Patripassians accepted that suffering can be ascribed to God in reality, but they were tempted by the opposite extreme and conceived of the Father as of actually becoming or changing himself into the Son for the purpose of the incarnation. They did so in a way that failed to protect the full divinity of God, his undiminished transcendence over the limitations of temporal existence. The church did not accept this view, and affirmed instead that the Father and the Son participated in the incarnation in different ways and that only the Son was involved in the suffering of Christ.

Turning to the fourth century, I will consider five leading interpretations of Arianism, focusing on the interpretation offered by Richard Hanson and Maurice Wiles. According to these scholars, divine suffering was at the very heart of Arian soteriology. Their hypothesis is based on a few theopaschite expressions used in the allegedly Arian sources and the Arian and neo-Arian use of the 'psilanthropic' argument, or the argument that the one who suffered for the salvation of the world had to be more than a mere man. I will point out that a crucial piece of evidence for the Hanson–Wiles interpretation, the anonymous *Homilies on the Psalms*, cannot be decisively shown to be Arian. I will show that the psilanthropic argument was also deployed by the pro-Nicenes, by Apollinaris, and in later controversies with widely different results, and therefore is not tight enough to pass for a distinctly Arian claim. Far from being theopaschites, the Arians appealed to the involvement of the Logos in suffering to prove his unlikeness to the impassible High God. The pro-Nicene theologians, in contrast, affirmed that human salvation required that Christ be fully and truly divine; as God, he voluntarily assumed the human condition with all its limitations. The Nicene theology successfully retained the tension between Christ's fully divine status and his human experiences.

Thus, prior to the Nestorian controversy the church had opposed three extreme misinterpretations of the person and work of Christ: (1) Christ was a divine being and therefore he could not suffer (Docetism); (2) God the Father was temporally changed into the suffering Son, at the expense of his full divinity and transcendence (Patripassianism); (3) Christ was involved in change, birth, suffering, and death, therefore he could not be fully divine (Arianism). Having ruled out the three extreme options, the church asserted that the Son of God suffered in reality and not in mere appearance; that it was the Son who became incarnate and suffered, not the Father; that the Son's involvement in suffering did not diminish his divine status, because the incarnation was a supreme act of divine compassion and as such it was most appropriate and God-befitting.

The justification of the incarnation as an act worthy of God is a common theme of Christian apologetic against philosophically minded pagans, whose understanding of God did not allow for the possibility that God could empty himself, assume the human condition, and suffer the consequences. The very fact that the Fathers quite self-consciously understood their argument for the God-befitting character of the incarnation to be directed against Hellenistic philosophers puts into question the assumption that the Fathers asserted divine impassibility simply as a result of their uncritical acceptance of the conceptuality of Hellenistic theological thought.

It is in the Nestorian controversy that the debate about the involvement of God in the suffering of Christ came fully into focus. Nestorius of Constantinople (d. *c.*451), following his teacher Theodore of Mopsuestia (*c.*350–428), claimed that since God is impassible, the divine subject cannot be involved in the suffering of Christ. According to Nestorius, it is possible to distinguish two subjects in Christ, one human and one divine; the human experiences of Christ are to be ascribed to the former and not to the latter. For Nestorius, the divine impassibility entailed that under no circumstances could God be the subject of birth, suffering, and death on the cross.

Cyril of Alexandria (d. 444) contested this view, arguing that it is wrong to separate Christ into two subjects, ascribing one set of actions to his divinity and the other one to his humanity. For Cyril, it was the divine agent who, without ceasing to be fully divine, emptied himself, assumed human nature, and became the one subject of all the actions and sufferings that are ascribed to Christ in the gospels. Cyril acknowledged that God could not undergo bodily sufferings without assuming a human body, just as God could not have such human emotions as fear and grief without assuming a human soul. The Alexandrian theologian insisted that it is most appropriate to speak of the suffering of God incarnate, of the God who made a human body and soul his own. Cyril sealed the thought of the Fathers when he denied any unqualified notion of God's 'naked' suffering outside the incarnation and at the same time affirmed the free and salvific suffering of the incarnate God, who had accepted the limitations of human existence for the sake of salvation, had triumphed over suffering and death, and had bestowed resurrection and immortality upon the human race. In contrast to Nestorius, Cyril held that impassibility did not make God withdraw to the heavenly realm and supervise the death of Christ from above, but guaranteed that it was God himself who participated in the experiences of human nature, such as birth, suffering, and death, making them his very own.

Cyril's own contribution to the debate includes his elaboration of kenoticism, i.e. the theme of God's self-emptying, especially on the basis of the exegesis of Philippians 2; his further spelling out of the patristic idea of the divine appropriation of human nature, according to which the Son made a human soul and body his own, which Cyril developed with special reference to the church's sacramental practices; and his discussion of traditional analogies of divine–human union, among which I will focus on the analogy of soul–body union. Each of these plays an important role in his understanding of the impassible Word's suffering in the flesh.

I chose to crown the present study with Cyril's theology and to go no further, because I believe that it was Cyril's vision that determined the key questions in the discussions of divine (im)passibility in the centuries that followed. In emphasizing Cyril's role I by no means intend to discount later developments, especially the theopaschite controversy and the contributions of such theologians as Severus of Antioch,

Philoxenus of Mabbug, and Maximus the Confessor. Further research is needed to fill in the details of the picture the main contours of which were painted by Cyril.[40] It is noteworthy that considering the question 'Whether Christ's passion is to be attributed to his Godhead' in *Summa Theologiae*, Thomas Aquinas supported his case by quoting from Athanasius, Cyril, and the acts of the council of Ephesus.[41] In choosing his authorities Aquinas faithfully reflected the mind of the church, which canonized Athanasius' and Cyril's answers to the problem.

The central conclusion that follows from my analysis is that the picture of an essentially impassibilist account of God in patristic theology, varied only by the minority voices that advocated divine suffering, is incorrect. I will argue instead, that the patristic tradition professed that God, remaining fully divine, freely accepted all the consequences of his becoming man, including suffering and death on the cross. God freely chose this method of salvation out of his infinite compassion and love for the human race. Herein lies a permanent contribution of the Fathers, and of Cyril in particular, to Christian doctrine.

I will also conclude that contemporary theopaschitism represents an unnecessarily restrictive theological perspective, which has as many conceptual flaws as the unqualified impassibilism, wrongly ascribed to the patristic authors. The most noticeable flaw of the theopaschite theory is that if God is, without qualification, capable of suffering without assuming human nature, then both the divine transcendence is put at risk and the assumption of the human nature in the incarnation is rendered superfluous. I will suggest that passibility and impassibility are correlative concepts, both of which must have their place in any sound account of divine agency.

40 Severus' dependence on Cyril was especially strong: see Iain R. Torrance, *Christology After Chalcedon*.

41 Aquinas, *Summa Theologiae*, 3. 46. 12.

1

The Case Against the Theory of Theology's Fall into Hellenistic Philosophy

THE standard approach to the issue of the divine (im)passibility in the writings of early Fathers is to draw a sharp distinction between the unemotional and uninvolved God of the Greek philosophers and the passionate God of the Bible. The allegedly biblical vision of an emotional and suffering God is then taken as a norm by which the whole development of patristic theology is judged. The verdict is that on the whole, patristic theology was a departure from this vision. I will argue in this chapter that this approach, the attraction of its simplicity notwithstanding, is fundamentally flawed and misleading both with regard to the opinions of the philosophers and with regard to the biblical material.[1]

Divine Emotions and Divine Involvement in Hellenistic Philosophies: A Variety of Accounts

The first crucial point that has not been recognized by the proponents of the Theory of Theology's Fall into Hellenistic Philosophy is that there is no one unified account of the divine emotions and of the divine involvement advocated by major Hellenistic schools of philosophy, let alone the

[1] T. G. Weinandy is one of only a few scholarly voices that have recently challenged this commonly accepted dichotomy. Weinandy argues that the concept of the divine impassibility must not be understood as an illegitimate import from a Greek philosophical conceptuality, but rather as a natural way of expressing the scriptural idea of the divine transcendence. See *Does God Suffer?*, 199. Cf. also F. J. van Beeck, '"The Weakness of God's is Stronger" (1 Cor 1: 25)', 18.

Hellenistic religions at large.[2] I will treat the issues of the divine emotions and involvement together, in order to expose most vividly the diversity of philosophical proposals.

The comment of Cicero (106–43 BC) at the beginning of his *De natura deorum* reveals that the divine involvement in the world was a hotly disputed topic in the middle of the first century BC:

> Many views are put forward about the outward form of the gods, their dwelling places and abodes, and mode of life, and these topics are debated with the widest variety of opinion among philosophers; but as to the question upon which the whole issue of the dispute principally turns, whether the gods are entirely idle (*nihil agant*) and inactive (*nihil moliantur*), taking no part at all in the direction and government of the world, or whether on the contrary all things both were created and ordered by them at the beginning and are controlled and kept in motion by them throughout eternity, here there is the greatest disagreement of all [. . .] There is in fact no subject upon which so much difference of opinion exists, not only among the unlearned but also among educated men; and the views entertained are so various and so discrepant, that, while it is no doubt a possible alternative that none of them is true, it is certainly impossible that more than one should be so.[3]

So concludes Cicero with a touch of dispassionate scepticism. Sextus Empiricus (AD 160–210) attests in his *Outlines of Pyrrhonism* that the dispute among the philosophers still had not come to any definite

[2] The evidence from the Hellenistic philosophers that both Frohnhofen and Nnamani bring out in their monographs should naturally lead them to this conclusion. It is surprising that both of them conclude that the philosophers were basically united in their understanding of the nature of divine emotions and of the divine involvement. See *Apatheia tou theou*, 90, 115; *The Paradox of a Suffering God*, 34. For a recent criticism of Harnack's assumption that there was a single 'spirit of Greek philosophy' see Rowe, 'Adolf von Harnack and the Concept of Hellenization', 88. Rowe emphasizes profound differences between various Hellenistic schools of philosophical thought. Along similar lines, Roy Kearsley issued the following note of caution: 'The question "What is God in ancient Greek philosophy?" would furnish the perfect title for someone wishing simply to write a really long book. Aristotle, Plato and Zeno would each give a different answer, even if you were fortunate enough to get only one answer from any of them! We should therefore be a little suspicious of sweeping statements to the effect that Christians have grafted "the Greek view of God" on to a simple, pristine and pure Christianity. Just as the philosophical schools of the early Christian centuries were eclectic within a broad spirit and rationale, so Christian "philosophical theologians" did not import entire systems of thought from any particular philosopher or school,' 'The Impact of Greek Concepts of God on the Christology of Cyril of Alexandria', 308. I must stress that Rowe's and Kearsley's positions represent largely neglected protests against the prevailing misconception.

[3] *De nat. deor.* 1. 1. 2–3; 1. 2. 5. Trans. H. Rackham, *Cicero*, 3, 5.

resolution in the second century AD. Some believe, he says, that human affairs are controlled by providence, whereas others think that they are not.[4] There are at least three distinct and competing views held by the philosophers of the Epicurean, the Stoic, and the Middle Platonist schools. Finer distinctions are undoubtedly possible. Since I am merely illustrating the diversity of philosophical proposals, these three will suffice. Besides, the syncretistic spirit of the Hellenistic age should discourage any historian of ideas from drawing too artificial lines of distinction between the teachings of the schools. I will assume that the Middle Platonists had absorbed into their own teaching much of what the Peripatetics and the Neopythagoreans had to offer. The Sceptics did not put forward anything constructive on this issue, although their doubts did serve a positive end of stimulating the discussion.

Each philosophical school came up with its own revision of popular religious beliefs. In the case of later Platonism this revision amounted to a rival metaphysical system. The relationship between folk piety and philosophical sensibilities was far too complex to be seen entirely as that of opposition. The Stoics, for example, tended to preserve as much material from myths and tragedies as possible, while at the same time allegorizing traditional sources rather freely. The Epicureans accepted the traditional belief that gods possessed immortal bodies and were anthropomorphic. They taught that divine happiness consisted in not being influenced by anything external. According to Epicurus, gods are 'strangers to suffering; nothing can cause them any joy or inflict on them any suffering from outside'.[5] The gods are not subject to experiences judged on the basis of hedonistic ethics as negative, such as anxiety, fear, grief, anger, envy, fatigue, and pain.

Criticizing the emotions ascribed to gods in myths as unworthy of the divine nature, the Epicureans frequently spoke of divine emotions in negative terms. At the same time they did not hesitate to ascribe to the gods emotionally coloured experiences regarded in their moral theory as positive. This theory was based upon the principle of the greatest possible pleasure, which they often reformulated in negative terms, as the principle of the least possible pain. The Homeric deities were refashioned to personify the Epicurean moral ideal. They dwelt in

[4] *Outlines of Pyrrhonism*, 1. 151.

[5] τῆι ἀφθαρσίαι δὲ αὑτῶν ἕπεται τὸ ἀπαθὲς ὑπὸ ἅπαντος τοῦ κεχαρισμένον τι ἢ ἄλγος ἔξωθεν ἐπιφέροντος. H. Usener, *Epicurea*, frag. 99, trans. A. J. Festugière, *Epicurus and His Gods*, 58. My exposition of Epicurean thought is much indebted to Festugière.

everlasting joy. The festivals were a way of communicating to humans a measure of divine happiness: 'It is principally through the gods that pleasure springs up in the heart of man.'[6]

While attributing to the gods a limited range of emotionally coloured features, the Epicureans firmly denied any divine–human interaction, which they conceived exclusively along the lines of popular myths. The Homeric deities were torn by the most violent passions and subject to bodily suffering. In visiting humans the gods pursued their selfish ends which often spelled disaster and rarely promised good fortune to mortals. 'Blessed are those whom the gods leave alone,' was a pessimistic beatitude that the tragedians left to posterity.[7]

Granted this traditional picture, the Epicureans wanted to make both sides, human and divine, content by denying divine involvement either in the general government of cosmic phenomena or in human affairs:

> Furthermore, we must not believe that the movement of the heavenly bodies, their turnings from one place to another, their eclipses, their risings and settings, and all such phenomena are brought about under the direction of a being who controls or will always control them and who at the same time possesses perfect happiness together with immortality; for the turmoil of affairs (πραγματε ῖαι), anxieties (φροντίδες), and feelings of anger (ὀργαὶ) and benevolence (χάριτες) do not go with happiness, but all that arises where there is weakness (ἀσθενεία), fear (φόβος) and dependence on others (προσδεήσις τών πλησίον).[8]

> The blessed and immortal nature knows no trouble (πράγματα) itself nor causes trouble to any other, so that it is never constrained by anger (ὀργή) or favour (χάρις). For all such things exist only in the weak (ἐν ἀσθενεῖ).[9]

Epicurus believed that if the gods were to intervene in human affairs, they would become anxious and unhappy. Mingling with mortals would disturb divine tranquillity and infect divine life with ill feelings and favouritism, typical of humans. Caring for another person, so Epicurus taught, one inevitably became psychologically dependent upon that person. Such dependence, he claimed, was a form of weakness, unworthy of gods.

Since gods were perfectly happy they could not have any unfulfilled desires or concerns of their own and therefore had no reason to

[6] *voluptatem in homine a deo auctore creatam adserit principaliter.* H. Usener, *Epicurea*, frag. 385a, trans. Festugière, *Epicurus*, 63.

[7] Aeschylus, *Prometheus Bound*, 978, trans. G. M. Cookson, 50.

[8] Epicurus, *Ep.* 1. 76–7. Usener, p. 28, trans. Festugière, *Epicurus*, 58.

[9] Epicurus, *Sententiae* 1, in *Epicurus*, 94–5. Festugière renders χάρις as 'benevolence', see *Epicurus*, 58.

intervene in human affairs. Epicurus stressed that the major benefit to be derived from the divine indifference was freedom from fear of the gods. The immortals ought to be worshipped in accordance with the customs of the land, but they should not be feared. Since the gods were deaf to prayers, worship became a matter of paying honour to the Epicurean moral ideals. Thus, Epicurus' response to the theological problems engendered by traditional mythology may be summed up as follows: he postulated anthropomorphic, corporeal deities, who were not entirely unemotional to the extent to which they were joyful, and whose existence had no bearing whatsoever upon the world.

It is not surprising that this radical position was deeply offensive to common piety and was contested both on the popular level and by all the other philosophical schools without exception. The widespread opinion was that by denying that the gods were concerned with human affairs Epicurus had effectively abolished not only superstitious fear of the gods, but, in effect, all religion and piety. Fearing that his theory would be ill received, he retained nominal god-talk and even wrote books on holiness and piety.[10] He miscalculated, however. In the circles of the Stoics and the Middle Platonists it became almost a sign of good philosophical taste to level the most crushing criticism against the Epicureans for their denial of providence. Cicero's Cotta voices a common indignation at such thinly disguised Epicurean atheism:

Epicurus, however, in abolishing divine beneficence (*opes*) and divine benevolence (*gratia*), uprooted and exterminated all religion from the human heart. For while asserting the supreme goodness and excellence of the divine nature, he yet denies to god the attribute of benevolence—that is to say, he does away with that which is the most essential element of supreme goodness and excellence. For what can be better or more excellent than kindness and beneficence? Make out god to be devoid of either, and you make him devoid of all love, affection or esteem for any other thing, human or divine (*neminem deo nec deum nec hominem carum, neminem ab eo amari, neminem diligi vultis*). It follows not merely that the gods do not care for mankind, but that they have no care (*neglegantur*) for one another. How much more truth there is in the Stoics, whom you censure! They hold that all wise men are friends, even when strangers to each other, since nothing is more lovable than virtue, and he that attains to it will have our esteem in whatever country he dwells. But as for you, what mischief you cause when you reckon kindness (*gratificatio*) and benevolence (*benevolentia*) as weakness (*imbecillitas*)! Apart altogether from the nature and attributes of deity, do you

[10] See Cicero's repeated remarks on this issue in *De nat. deor.* 1. 76, 85, 115–18, 123.

think that even human beneficence and benignity are solely due to human infirmity? Is there no natural affection (*caritas naturalis*) between the good?[11]

Cotta continued his speech with a moving moral exhortation on the nature of friendship. Philosophical friendship, he suggested, was not based upon profit or self-interest. A true friend seeks the advantage of those whom he loves. In Roman Stoicism the Epicurean contention that benevolence or any expression of care for another person was the sign of weakness was vigorously attacked.

The role of emotions in human relations and in the formation of character was a deeply controversial topic among the various philosophical schools. For the purpose of this study it is only necessary to take note of the diversity of competing proposals on this subject, without entering into a detailed discussion.[12] The Peripatetics defended the ideal of *metriopatheia*, the moderation of passions, which was a quintessential expression of the classical Greek sense of measure and proportion. Their school considered *pathē* as morally neutral, as long as they were kept within limits and ruled by reason.

The early Greek Stoics clashed with the Peripatetics and later Platonists precisely on this point. Against the view that emotions were neutral, the early Stoics argued that all *pathē* were irrational and unnatural perturbations, which should first be curbed and then eliminated. They saw their philosophical school as a hospital in which the soul was cured from four principal diseases: distress (λύπη), pleasure (ἡδονή), fear (φόβος), and desire (ἐπιθυμία).[13] In contrast to the Peripatetic ideal of *metriopatheia* the early Stoics extolled the state of *apatheia*.

It should be noted that the Fathers were quite aware of the existing differences. Jerome in his anti-Origenist moment observed that the doctrine of the soul's *apatheia*

> was the bone of contention between the Stoics and the Peripatetics, that is to say, the Old Academy; for the one school asserted that πάθη, which we read in Latin as *perturbationes*, such as sorrow, joy, hope, and fear, could be completely eradicated and extirpated from the minds of

[11] *De nat. deor.* 1. 121–2. Cf. Ath., *Inc.* 2. Note that the central terms that denote the divine care, which I give in parenthesis, such as *gratia*, *benevolentia*, and *caritas* were baptized by the Christians.

[12] For a comprehensive study see Sorabji, *Emotion*; John M. Rist, 'The Stoic Concept of Detachment', 259–72; M. C. Nussbaum, *The Therapy of Desire*, esp. chap. 10; Michael Frede, 'The Stoic Doctrine of the Affections of the Soul', 93–110.

[13] Cicero, *Tusc.* 3. 7; 4. 23–33. See Brad Inwood, *Ethics and Human Action in Early Stoicism*, 127–45; id., 'Rules and Reasoning in Stoic Ethics'; Sorabji, *Emotion*, 29–32.

men; while the other school held that these disturbances can be restricted and mastered and controlled and kept within proper bounds and checked like bridled horses with certain curbs. Cicero discusses their views in his *Tusculan Disputations* and Origen seeks to blend these views with ecclesiastical truth in his *Stromata*.[14]

The precise meaning of the term *apatheia*, which first became technical in Stoic moral philosophy, was disputed by both ancient authorities and modern scholars. The main issue at stake is whether or not the Stoic *apatheia* literally meant complete eradication of all emotions. Unsympathetic interpreters claimed that this was indeed so. This popular opinion was voiced, for example, by Jerome, who once noted sarcastically that to be impassible one had to become *vel saxum, vel deum*, either stone or God.[15] Whether this widespread opinion was a mere parody or a faithful rendering of the early Stoic position remains debatable.[16]

It is noteworthy that at some stage in the development of their teaching the Stoics refined their uncompromisingly negative attitude towards the *pathē* and admitted the positive role of *eupatheiai*, good feelings, in the formation of character. According to Diogenes Laertius, the Stoics intended the three principal *eupatheiai*—joy (*chara*), caution (*eulabeia*), and wishfulness (*boulēsis*)—to counterbalance the *pathē* of

[14] *Against the Pelagians*, Prologue 1; cf. ibid. 2. 6, trans. J. N. Hritzu, 230. See also Diogenes Laertius, *Vitae*, 7. 110, Cicero's *Tusculan Disputations* provided for the ancients a widely read introduction to this debate. Jerome's confusion of the Old Academy with the Peripatetics suggests that, at least in his mind, the views of the two schools on this subject were very similar.

[15] Jerome, *Ep.* 133. 3. Augustine shared Jerome's reservations, although in a more philosophically reflective and less rhetorically grotesque way. Cf. his warning in *De civitate dei* 14. 9: 'If *apatheia* is the name of the state in which the mind cannot be touched by any emotion whatsoever, who would not judge this insensitivity to be the worst of all moral defects?', trans. H. Bettenson, *St Augustine: Concerning the City of God against the Pagans*, 564–5.

[16] For the view that identifies the Stoic ideal of *apatheia* with the elimination of all emotions see Heschel, *The Prophets*, 252–3. It is interesting that 4 Maccabees, which was so important for the formulation of the Christian understanding of martyrdom and vicarious suffering, specifically emphasized against the Stoics that emotions should be mastered by reason, not eliminated. See 4 Macc. 3: 1; 5: 6. According to Diogenes Laertius, the Stoics distinguished between *apatheia sensu bono*, i.e. absence of evil passions that characterizes a wise man, and *apatheia sensu malo*, i.e. relentlessness or hardheartedness, that characterizes a bad man. See *Vitae*, 7. 117. J. M. Rist argues that the debate between the Stoics and the Platonists on whether the role of *pathē* must be understood as negative or neutral was a matter of definition of *pathē* on which both sides could not agree. See *Stoic Philosophy*, 26–7. Marcia Colish agrees with Rist when she makes the following distinction: 'Stoic *apatheia* is not a state of *anaesthesia* in which the subject feels nothing at all,' *The Stoic Tradition from Antiquity to the Early Middle Ages*, i. 42.

pleasure, fear, and desire respectively.[17] In contrast to *pathē*, *eupatheiai* were more controllable and rational dispositions. The main *eupatheiai* translated into more concrete emotional states such as, rejoicing in virtuous actions of others, parental love, friendliness, and benevolence.

With this provision, the later Stoics continued to opt for *apatheia* as their moral ideal. In later Stoicism *apatheia* referred to a state of mind in which the four principal *pathē*—distress, pleasure, fear, and desire (and those that derive from them)—have been successfully mastered, if not totally stamped out. The Stoics regarded *apatheia* as compatible with philosophical companionship between equally virtuous people. We should note, however, that the attitude towards the moral value of the *pathē* oscillated for the Stoics from neutral to negative. In Stoic ethics the *pathē* were regarded as, among other things, beclouding and distorting the normal human ability to make moral judgements.[18] Quite apart from the influence of Stoicism, the term *pathē* had a negative connotation for the Greek-speaking world, which the term 'emotion' does not have today.

The difference between our modern understanding of emotions and the Hellenistic *pathē* becomes clear if we recall that the ancients extolled mastery over the *pathē* and believed that especially a violent outburst of *pathē*, uncontrolled by reason, is profoundly destructive to human nature. In contrast, an influential Freudian trend in modern psychology, popularized in talk-shows, tends to favour self-expression, a 'speak-it-out' attitude in which the release of emotions is seen as a cure from neuroses, whereas restraint of emotions is viewed with suspicion as repression potentially causing neuroses. Apart from psychologists, existentialist philosophers have made us more aware of the positive role (which most ancient Stoics would deny) that emotions play in the formation of moral judgements.[19]

[17] *Vitae*, 7. 116. See A. A. Long, *Hellenistic Philosophy*, 207; Rist, *Stoic Philosophy*, 25. B. Inwood contends that 'the Stoic ideal of the freedom from passions . . . might be summed up in the slogan "*apatheia* is *eupatheia*"', in *Ethics and Human Action*, 173–5, 305–6 n. 207.

[18] This is only one dimension of the Stoic understanding of relationship between judgement and emotion. The Stoics also held that all emotions (as distinct from sensations) were generated by judgements. I cannot enter into all complexities of this issue here. See Sorabji, *Emotion*, 29–45.

[19] For a spirited, not to say passionate, modern vindication of the positive role of passions in making moral judgements see R. S. Solomon, *The Passions*. For a defence of a cognitive theory of emotions see Martha C. Nussbaum, *Upheavals of Thought: The Intelligence of Emotions*.

The proponents of the Theory of Theology's Fall into Hellenistic Philosophy have inferred from the fact that the Stoics opted for *apatheia* as the philosopher's moral ideal that the Stoic deity was also apathetic.[20] Surprisingly, this inference finds no support in the surviving Stoic sources. Moreover, as I will show below, within the framework of Stoic theology the concept of divine *apatheia* would make little, if any, sense.

The Stoics conceived of the divine realm in two principal ways. First, they spoke of an impersonal deity (usually singular) which they identified either with the fiery breath, or with the world-soul, or with the seminal reason of the world,[21] or even with the world itself.[22] This deity was an active, sentient, rational material principle inherent in, pervading, and operating in passive matter. This deity was subject to all the changes that the world underwent in the Stoic cosmology, particularly those of expansion and contraction. As one fourth-century theologian observed, the Stoics made their God passible by claiming that the changeable world was his body.[23] In contrast, the Christian God does not contract and expand with the world and in this sense is impassible. For the Stoics themselves the issue whether this impersonal deity had emotions or not would be largely irrelevant.[24] The moral ideal of *apatheia* is never applied to God in the Stoic writings.[25]

Second, the Stoics deployed the traditional terminology of the mythical gods (usually plural). Allegorizing the ancient myths the Stoics developed their poetic astronomy. Some of them resisted anthropomorphism to the degree of transforming the gods of the myths into impersonal powers operating in the world. The question of emotions again could not arise with respect to these powers.

[20] Mozley's observation that the Stoic ethical ideal of complete control over the passions was realized in God may have contributed to the spread of this misconception. See *Impassibility of God*, 38.

[21] Diogenes Laertius, *Vitae*, 7. 136.

[22] Cicero, *De nat. deor.* 2. 36; Diogenes Laertius, *Vitae*, 7. 137, 148.

[23] Ps.-Ath., *Ar.* 4. 13. On the authorship of this treatise see R. P. C. Hanson, 'The Source and Significance of the Fourth *Oratio contra Arianos* Attributed to Athanasius', 257–66.

[24] Cf. the comment of John Dillon: 'In terms of Stoic theory, the attribution of *eupatheiai* to God would make no sense, since God is not a person but an impersonal force, and there is naturally no evidence of any such attribution in the sources,' 'The Nature of God in *Quod Deus*', 223–4.

[25] *Pace* Winston, 'Philo's Conception', 24–32.

It would be an oversimplification to say that *all* Stoic descriptions of God were impersonal. Due to their general inclination to retain as much traditional material as possible, the Stoics did not produce a single coherent account of the divine nature. They used both personal and impersonal descriptions rather indiscriminately. Some Stoics had their private devotions, as Cleanthes' hymn to Zeus attested. To give another example, Epictetus had a very strong sense of quasi-personal divine guidance in human life.[26] According to Epictetus, the soul of a man who is of one mind with God is 'free from anger, envy and jealousy'.[27] Assuming a personal description of the deity, Seneca pondered the question whether the deity could repent or change its decisions and came to a negative conclusion on both these issues.[28]

Let us note also that the Stoics joined others in their criticism of the literal understanding of myths and folk superstition.[29] Among the most popular beliefs was the view that gods were easily provoked to anger by humans who dishonoured them or violated their interests in any way. Cicero's observation that 'it is the unanimous teaching of all philosophers that God is never angry (*nec irasci*), nor does he injure anyone (*nec nocere*)'[30] must be taken in the light of the criticism of popular superstition. Still, the evidence does not allow us to speak of the Stoic deities as impassible, either in the sense of unemotional, or in the sense of unaffected by anything external.

The Stoics were the first to develop in considerable detail a theory of divine providence (πρόνοια).[31] They contended against the Epicureans that the order and design observable in the world could not be the result of a fortuitous collision of atoms. The Stoics argued that intelligent causes were responsible for the dispensation of natural phenomena, such as the cyclical rotation of planets, the change of seasons, and the

[26] See Epictetus, *Arr.* 3. 1. 37; 3. 5. 8–11; 3. 21. 12; 3. 22. 53–4; 3. 24. 64–5, 95–7, 110; 3. 26. 28–30; 4. 1. 89–90; 4. 1. 99–102; 4. 3. 9–12; 4. 6. 21; 4. 7. 17; 4. 10. 14–17; 4. 12. 11–12; 4. 13. 24.

[27] Ibid. 2. 19. 26–7.

[28] *De beneficiis*, 6. 23. 1. See the helpful discussion in Micka, *Problem of Divine Anger*, 7–8.

[29] Cicero, *De nat. deor.* 2. 70.

[30] Cicero, *De officiis*, 3. 28. 102; cf. Lactantius, *De ira dei*, 2. 27. 1.

[31] The Stoic proof of providence occupies a large segment of the second part of Cicero's *De nat. deor.* 2. 73–153. Cf. Diogenes Laertius, *Vitae*, 7. 147: 'They say that the deity is immortal, rational, perfect or intelligent in happiness, free from all evil, (κακοῦ παντὸς ἀνεπίδεκτον), non-anthropomorphic (μὴ εἶναι μέντοι ἀνθρωπόμορφον) living being, taking providential care of the world (προνοητικὸν κόσμου) and all that is in the world'.

like. The deity sustains the order and secures the harmony of the universe.

Divine beings also care for the whole human race in its entirety and for each individual in particular. Diogenes Laertius notes that the Stoics 'hold that there are demons (δαίμονες) who are in sympathy (συμπάθεια) with mankind and watch over human affairs'.[32] Divine care for the world was devoid of self-interest and partiality. Gods may be contacted in prayers. The Stoics argued that the prediction of the future, oracles, and divination were possible precisely because the gods hear prayers and respond. They were prepared to admit the possibility of divine visitations in the mythological past. The Sceptics vigorously attacked many of the traditional beliefs that the Stoics relentlessly tried to retain. To conclude, the Stoics held two distinct views: (1) God is material and impersonal, and guides the world as an immanent seminal reason; (2) gods are non-anthropomorphic powers who care both for the operation of the world and for humans. The problem of divine emotions was largely irrelevant to both views.

While the Middle Platonists joined the Stoics in their criticism of Epicurean ethics and theology, they criticized with equal zeal the inconsistent terminology by means of which the Stoics described the divine realm. Having revived and developed the speculative, rather than the sceptical side of Plato's teaching, the Middle Platonists proposed a complex metaphysical system which was at odds with Stoic materialism. Following 'divine Plato' they held that beyond the world of things available to the senses there exists the world of ideas, grasped by intellectual contemplation alone. The two worlds were related in a complex way. Metaphysically, the sensible world derived from and was an imperfect expression of the self-sufficient and perfect intelligible world. Epistemically, the world of becoming could not be known without the prior knowledge of the forms, populating the world of being.

This conceptualization of reality involved several pairs of antithetical oppositions: sensible and intelligible, becoming and being, material and formal, corporeal and incorporeal, visible and invisible, temporal and eternal, mutable and immutable, passible and impassible. Correspondingly, the universe had the following basic structure: the highest levels were occupied by the invisible, immaterial, and intelligible things, or ideas; the lowest levels were populated by visible, material, and sensible entities; whereas the intermediary levels were assigned to the objects to

[32] *Vitae*, 7. 151.

which both sets of descriptions could be applied. The whole system was tightly structured so that within every level there were sub-levels with varying degrees of perfection. The divine realm was identified with the world of ideas. In this hierarchical system the divine realm admitted of degrees of perfection. The supreme God, differently identified by various thinkers, was at the very top of the scale of being. The supreme God was the source of all being, goodness, beauty, and truth. The divine perfection was expressed both by superlatives and by carefully ordered negations.

In the system of Plotinus, for example, the method of negation, the so-called apophatic theology, was stretched to its logical limits. The supreme God of Plotinus, the One, lies beyond all rational conceptualization, beyond negation and assertion of any qualities, even those taken from the intelligible world. The One is known to be ineffable in mystical experience. The One infinitely surpasses everything there is. No description applies to the One in a literal sense. The One cannot even be said to be thought or to exist, since it is beyond all that can be thought or that exists. Given this view of the divine transcendence, to say that such a God was impassible was simply to acknowledge that he transcended the distinction between passible and impassible, just as he transcended everything else.

In the third Ennead Plotinus argued that the whole intellectual realm was impassible since it was bodiless. His major concern was to protect the divine world from evil passions and ignorance which the Gnostics had introduced into discourse about aeons.[33] As the inhabitants of the divine realm, the bodiless souls were impassible in the sense of not being subject to the modifications and changes that are typically associated with bodies. Here Plotinus plunged head on into a centuries-old debate in Greek psychology, which by his time had become very technical. The debate addressed the following series of questions: How is the soul united to the body? Do passions arise from the body or from the soul? Do they form a separate part (Plato) or a faculty (Aristotle) of the soul? Can the passionate faculty operate in the soul without the body, or is it activated only through the body?[34] There was no agreement

[33] *Enneads*, 3. 6. 1–5. See the discussion of this issue in R. T. Wallis, *Neoplatonism*, 74.

[34] Plato's hesitations in *Phaedo*, where he attributed desires to the body and in *Philebus*, where he ascribed them to the soul, provided a starting point. Major options are nicely laid out by the anonymous author of the so-called Tyrwitt's Fragments *De libidine et aegritudine* and *Utrum pars an facultas animi affectibus subiecta sit*. In *Plutarch's Moralia*, XV. 38–71.

among different philosophical schools on these issues, which fact is also registered by the Fathers.[35]

Plotinus' own answer was very intricate. He claimed that the body alone could be called passive and affected in a strict sense. The soul is the source of judgements, and mental images about passions, and as such, it is completely in control of these images. Forming those judgements and images the soul acts and is not acted upon, in this sense remaining impassible.[36] The soul knows which part of the body is affected. The soul possesses impassible awareness (*gnōsis apathēs*) of the body's condition.[37]

The Stoics found this whole line of reasoning very problematic: the soul could not both be impassible by its very nature and at the same time be in need of purification from *pathē* in order to attain the state of *apatheia*. Plotinus responded (rather unpersuasively) that purification is equivalent to turning from the things below to the things above, it is 'waking up from inappropriate images and not seeing them'.[38]

While the divine realm is impassible in the sense that it cannot be changed by anything external, the supreme God oversees everything and holds everything under the sphere of his influence. The supreme God governs the world through the chain of his intermediaries. He is indirectly involved in the material world through the hierarchy of subordinate gods. Both the Stoics and the Platonists placed emphasis upon the universality of divine providence. God cares for all nations, he is not predisposed towards a particular one.[39] His providential care would be imperfect and partial if he were to enter a particular state of affairs in the

[35] See e.g. Tertullian, *De anima*, 14, 16–19; Eusebius, *Prep. evang.* 13. 16–17 (with quotation from the treatise *De anima* by Severus the Platonist); Augustine, *De civitate dei*, 14. Gregory of Nyssa in his Christian rejoinder to Plato's *Phaedo* observed that 'the generality of men still fluctuate in their opinions about this [the relationship between the *pathē* and the soul], which are as erroneous as they are numerous', and that Christian theologians could not afford 'the license of affirming what they pleased' and should therefore 'make the Holy Scriptures the rule and the measure of every tenet,' Gr. Nyss., *Dialogus de anima et resurrectione, PG* 46: 49B–C, trans. W. Moore, NPNF 2nd ser. v. 439.

[36] Plotinus, *Enneads*, 1. 1. 4; 3. 6. 1; 3. 6. 4.

[37] Ibid. 4. 4. 18–19. See H. Chadwick's illuminating discussion of this issue in 'Eucharist and Christology in the Nestorian Controversy', 162.

[38] Plotinus, *Enneads*, 2. 9. 9.

[39] Julian, *Contra Galilaeos*, 99E–106E, contrasted the universalistic understanding of the divine involvement in the world, as given by the Hellenistic philosophers, with the jealous and 'particular' (μερικός) God of the Hebrews. Similar arguments were advanced before him by Celsus (see Origen, *Contra Celsum*, 4. 7; 6. 78) and Porphyry (in Augustine, *Ep.* 102. 8; Jerome, *Ep.* 133. 9).

world of becoming. It is both unnecessary and impossible for him to intervene in human affairs directly. It is unnecessary, because the whole world is in some sense his emanation and partakes of him to a lesser or greater degree. It is impossible for him to enter the world of becoming without relinquishing his perfections, such as transcendence, immutability, and impassibility. The supreme God would betray, diminish, and contaminate himself if he entered the order of sensible things.[40] Human souls and other minor divinities may indeed fall from the intellectual world and become embodied. But it would be blasphemous and foolish, according to the Platonists, to ascribe such unworthy actions to the supreme God.[41] To sum up, within the framework of the carefully articulated logic of negative theology, the Platonists claimed that God is supremely transcendent, immaterial, and above passions, that he cares for the world and is involved in it indirectly through the chain of intermediaries. It is true that among educated pagans, whose philosophical views tended towards later Platonism, the divine impassibility did acquire the status of a universally shared opinion.[42]

We must note, however, that this opinion was a relatively new development. Impassibility is not applied to God in the extant writings of the Presocratics (saving Anaxagoras), Plato, and the Stoics. Yet the founder of the Academy and the sages of the Stoa have received an entirely undeserved blame from the proponents of the Theory of Theology's Fall into Hellenistic Philosophy for having corrupted patristic thought with the 'axiom' of divine impassibility.[43] Divine impassibility makes its debut on the philosophical scene in the writings of Aristotle, twice with reference to the opinion of Anaxagoras that the divine mind remains unmixed and in this narrow sense *apathēs*. Building upon Anaxagoras' insight, the Stagirite argued that since the Unmoved Mover cannot be moved by anything else, he remained impassible in the

[40] Plato, *Symposium*, 203a; Apuleius, *De deo Socratis*, 3–4 discussed in Augustine, *De civitate dei*, 9. 16.

[41] See Plotinus, *Enneads*, 2. 9. 9; Porphyry, *Adversus Christianos*, frag. 75–8. I owe these references to Wallis, *Neoplatonism*, 104.

[42] See Sallustius, *Concerning the Gods and the Universe*, 1, 2, 14, ed. A. D. Nock; Julian, *Hymn to the Mother of the Gods*, 11. 3 (170c), in LCL i. 476. Julian also ascribes to the Cynics the view that the attainment of *apatheia* is the goal of human life and that this is equivalent to becoming a god. (Ἀπάθειαν γὰρ ποιοῦνται τὸ τέλος· τοῦτο δὲ ἴσον ἐστὶ τῷ θεὸν γενέσθαι). Julian, Εἰς τοὺς ἀπαιδεύτους κύνας 12. 16. (*To the Uneducated Cynics*, 192A, in LCL ii. 34).

[43] According to Moltmann, 'Since Plato and Aristotle the metaphysical and ethical perfection of God has been described as *apatheia*,' *Crucified God*, 267–8.

sense of not being acted upon.[44] It should be noted that the early patristic authorities show no awareness of this highly technical point of Aristotle's metaphysics. So much for classical Greek philosophy as a source of the 'axiom' of divine *apatheia*.

If we turn to the philosophical schools of the Hellenistic age, we will discover that divine impassibility was by no means axiomatic in them. As the preceding discussion illustrates, amidst the diversity of philosophical voices it is only possible to distil an almost platitudinous conviction that the gods of the poets behave themselves improperly and that an improved account of the divine emotions and divine involvement is in order.

Sextus Empiricus' observation that the philosophers agree that gods are impassible should be interpreted in the light of this generally shared desideratum.[45] Unfortunately, this observation has been tendentiously interpreted by the proponents of the Theory of Theology's Fall into Hellenistic Philosophy to mean that gods are static and unemotional, and therefore unconcerned with human affairs.[46] As we have seen, the Epicurean gods shared pleasurable emotions and remained unconcerned, the Stoic deity was impartial and at the same time extended providential care to the whole cosmos, whereas the Platonist God transcended everything, human emotions included, and was indirectly involved in the world through intermediaries.

To see this complex web of theological views as involving for the Christian Fathers a clear-cut choice between the involved God of the Bible and the uninvolved God of the Hellenistic philosophers is extremely misleading. Enlightenment deism should not be read into the philosophical climate of late antiquity. I repeat there was no *consensus*

44 *Physica*, 256^{b}25, *Metaphysica*, 1072^{a}5, *De anima*, 429^{b}25. In *De generatione et corruptione* 324^{b}5–10 impassibility in the sense of incapacity for being affected is ascribed to the immaterial entities. Interestingly, Aristotle himself was by no means consistent on the subject of the human mind's impassibility. In *De anima*, 429^{b}23–8 Aristotle argues that mind has both passible and impassible aspects. When the mind thinks about itself it is on the one hand passible because it is being thought of and on the other hand impassible because it thinks about itself.

45 *Outlines of Pyrrhonism*, 1. 162.

46 e.g. Heschel, *The Prophets*, 262; Nnamani, *Paradox of a Suffering God*, 34 n. 57. Consider Tomáš Špidlík's categorical identification of the philosophical divine *apatheia* with indifference: 'The God of the great philosophers is absolutely free of passions. There is nothing that could provoke him, because he is utterly disinterested in the world and its human concerns,' *The Spirituality of the Christian East: A Systematic Handbook*, 270–1. Špidlík fails to distinguish between the ideal of human *apatheia* in Stoicism and in Eastern monasticism.

philosophorum amounting to an affirmation of divine indifference and non-involvement. On the contrary, competing philosophical schools were keenly aware of profound differences in these matters. The Fathers could not possibly agree with the philosophers simply because the philosophers did not agree among themselves.

To add to this already complex picture of philosophical thought, there were the suffering and passionate gods of the mystery cults.[47] One may recall, for example, the tragic story of Osiris locked alive in the coffin and thrown into the Nile to be later dismembered by cruel Typhon; or Kore ravished by Adonis and dragged into the underworld against her will; or young Dionysos brutishly devoured by Titans; or Orpheus torn to pieces by his overly enthusiastic fans, the Thracian maenads. It was believed that participation in the sacred rites, in which the sufferings and passions of the gods were cultically re-enacted, bestowed purification of passions upon the initiates.

In this regard Iamblichus wrote:

> [W]hen we see the emotions (*pathē*) of others in comedy and tragedy, we still our own emotions and make them more moderate and purge them, and in sacred rites, through the sight and sound of obscenities, we are freed from the harm that comes from actual indulgence in them. So things of this sort are embraced for the therapy of our souls and to moderate the evils which come to us through the generative process, to free us from our chains and give us riddance.[48]

Those who argue that the adoption of the divine *apatheia* was the result of Hellenization must reckon with the no less prominent Hellenistic idea of the suffering and dying gods of the mysteries. Hellenistic religions too had their passion narratives. The Fathers had to find an adequate language to express the truth of divine revelation, carving out their distinctive account of divine agency in the midst of passion and dispassion narratives of the Hellenistic world, and proposing their own understanding of the divine passibility and impassibility. Our next step is to examine the claim that the Bible, taken as a whole, unequivocally supports the image of a suffering and emotional God.

[47] I will not delve here into the interpretative puzzles surrounding the mystery cults, but restrict my observations to what is common knowledge. See Walter Burkert, *Ancient Mystery Cults*; *Greek Religion*, 276–304.

[48] Iamblichus, *On the Mysteries of the Egyptians*, 1. 11, trans. Sorabji, *Emotion*, 286. For a discussion of Aristotle's theory of catharsis of emotions through fear and pity experienced by watching Greek tragedy see Sorabji, ibid. 288–92.

Anti-anthropomorphic and Anti-anthropopathic Tendencies in the Bible

It must be admitted that the Bible ascribes to God a much wider range of human emotions than any philosophically minded pagan of the Hellenistic period would ever find appropriate. Let us note, however, that the biblical authors themselves see such descriptions as at once illuminating and problematic. The attribution of certain emotionally coloured characteristics to God, e.g. love, compassion, mercy, long-suffering, anger, hatred, jealousy, grief, and joy, among many others, is an illuminating attempt to describe the depth of God's personal concern for his creation, his closeness to his creatures, and the directness of the divine involvement in their affairs. At the same time, if understood along the lines of purely human analogies, these emotionally coloured characteristics become problematic. For only a particular kind of love, jealousy, anger, and so forth are ascribed to God in the Bible. For example, God loves without becoming emotionally dependent upon the object of his love. God does not seek gratification of his own desires in love, but pursues only the welfare of his creatures.

Or, to give another illustration, God does not become arbitrarily angry. Divine anger in the Bible expresses God's judgement upon human sin and rebellion.[49] Divine anger is inseparable from divine judgement: God's righteous indignation at human disobedience. It is obvious that not all expressions of anger imply moral judgement. Anger in the form of uncontrolled passion may blind conscience, instead of expressing its insights. The Bible portrays God as being in full control of his emotions, anger included. He is not subject to mindless and capricious rage.

As it is clear from the examples of love and anger, select emotionally coloured characteristics do not apply to God in the same sense as they do to human beings. There are further constraints upon all divine emotions. Such descriptors must be compatible, for example, with God's holiness and lordship over history. The Old Testament stresses the fact that both direct and indirect manifestations of the holy God have a numinous character (e.g. Exod. 33: 20). To protect humans from direct encounter

[49] B. E. Baloian, *Anger in the Old Testament*, 156–9. Walter Brueggemann shows in his *Theology of the Old Testament* that the Old Testament passages that speak of God's arbitrary anger and unrestrained rage, if taken literally, present considerable moral problems. See also Brian Rice McCarthy, 'Response: Brueggemann and Hanson on God in the Hebrew Scriptures', 615–19.

with his power, God reveals himself indirectly through intermediaries in the form of his angel (Gen. 16: 7; Num. 22: 24; Gal. 3: 19), or his glory (Lev. 9: 6, 23), or his name (Lev. 24: 11, 16), or his presence (Deut. 4: 37). The fact that God sometimes uses intermediaries accentuates divine transcendence without ruling out the possibility of direct divine intervention.

Biblical authors also emphasize the difference between the living God of the Hebrews and lifeless idols. Yahweh is not subject to death, in contrast, for example, to the Western Semitic god of fertility Tammuz, whose periodic suffering, death, and resurrection were commemorated in a ritual (Ezek. 8: 14).

In addition, there is an imposing number of biblical passages that present conflicting views about divine (im)passibility and (im)mutability. God in the Bible is said to repent (Gen. 6: 5–7; Exod. 32: 12–14; Deut. 32: 36; Judg. 2: 18; 1 Sam. 15: 11; Ps. 90: 13; 106: 45; 135: 14; Jer. 42: 10; Hos. 11: 8–9; Jonah 3: 9–10; 4: 2) and to be incapable of repenting (Num. 23: 19; 1 Sam 15: 29; Hos. 13: 14); he is said to change his mind and to be unchangeable (Ps. 102: 26–7; Mal. 3: 6; Heb. 1: 11–12; Jas. 1: 17; Heb. 6: 17); he is said to walk in the garden of Eden (Gen. 3: 8) and to dwell in 'thick darkness' (Exod. 20: 21) and in 'unapproachable light' (1 Tim. 6: 16). It is important to note that the tensions created by these conflicting descriptions of God arise within the biblical narrative itself.[50] They are not tensions between the Greek and the Hebrew ways of thought.

The tensions mentioned above arise only when various theological strands of the biblical canon are considered together, as a unified whole. Some scholars object to the appropriateness of such an enterprise on the grounds that different literary sources of the Bible were produced under diverse historical circumstances; hence their conflicting theological standpoints were never meant to be reconciled. While the premise of this argument is both correct and platitudinous—surely the documents in question were written by different people in different times and places—the conclusion is entirely unsatisfactory and question-begging. The Church had its theological reasons (into the complex array of which we need not enter here) for carefully selecting and canonizing a list of ancient writings as authoritative and thereby making it a special task of its teachers to bring various theological proposals put forward in them into

[50] In 'The Concept of God after Auschwitz: A Jewish Voice', 6. Hans Jonas admits that contemporary philosophical proposals about divine suffering (which he himself supports) clash with the biblical conception of divine majesty.

a coherent whole. Thus, an attempt to draw together various biblical representations of divine agency is not only appropriate, but also theologically inescapable, once the biblical materials are treated as the church's canon.[51]

One of the traditional ways of interpreting the passages that affirm divine immutability and imply divine impassibility is to regard them, among other things, as cautions against anthropomorphism. That the Bible openly protests against anthropomorphism by denying select forms of visual representation of God as leading to idolatry is undeniable (Exod. 20: 4–6). The failure to deal extensively with the problem of anthropomorphism as posited by the biblical authors themselves is a serious flaw in contemporary passibilist theologies that appeal to the biblical sources.[52]

Unlike some modern passibilists, the ancient translators of the Hebrew Scriptures into Greek were keenly concerned about the problem of anthropomorphism. A tendency towards anti-anthropomorphism and anti-anthropopathism is clear in the Septuagint. Charles Fritsch's study of the Pentateuch addresses this issue.[53] Fritsch showed that when the Alexandrine translators considered descriptions of divine emotions or actions theologically problematic they either replaced them with less explicitly anthropomorphic descriptions, or omitted them altogether. The Septuagint renders several passages in which Yahweh is said to repent by different verbs that downplay the idea of change in the divine mind. For example, the Hebrew text of Exod. 32: 14 expresses the result of Moses' successful intercession in the following way: 'and Yahweh repented (√נחם) of the evil that he planned to bring on his people'. In contrast, in the Septuagint this verse was translated: 'and the Lord was moved with compassion (ἱλάσθη)'.[54]

The same holds for the divine emotions of anger and grief. For example, the Hebrew text of Gen. 18: 30 says: 'Oh, let not the Lord be angry (√חרה), and I will speak,' whereas the translation eliminates the reference to the divine anger in the following way: 'let it be nothing

[51] See Brevard S. Childs, *Old Testament Theology in a Canonical Context.*

[52] 'In the OT we find no anti-anthropomorphic tendencies at all', declares Hoaas in 'Passion and Compassion of God', 143. D. E. Cook makes a point similar to mine in 'Weak Church—Weak God: The Charge of Anthropomorphism', 69–92. E. Burnley also issues an important note of caution in 'The Impassibility of God', 90–1.

[53] See C. T. Fritsch, *Anti-anthropomorphisms.*

[54] A similar softening of the idea of change in the divine mind is evident in the LXX trans. of Exod. 32: 12 and Num. 23: 19. See Fritsch, *Anti-anthropomorphisms*, 17–18.

(μή τι), O Lord, if I speak'. Or, to give another example, the Hebrew phrase 'that there be no wrath (√קצפ) upon the congregation of the children of Israel' is changed by the Septuagint into 'that there be no sin (ἁμάρτημα) among the children of Israel' (Num. 1: 53). Any translation involves a measure of interpretation. Since wrath is the expression of the divine judgement upon sin, it was logical, from the standpoint of the translators of the Septuagint, to render the meaning of the passage in this way.

Likewise, several passages that suggest that God has a body, that he moves or occupies a particular place have been carefully rephrased by the Greek translators. For example, in the account of Passover in Exodus 12, the Septuagint renders the Hebrew verb פסח, to 'pass over' or to 'hop', by the Greek σκεπάζω, to 'cover'.[55] It must be noted that the anthropomorphisms and anthropopathisms in the Greek translation were not eliminated consistently. In many cases boldly anthropomorphic and anthropopathic expressions were retained in the Greek translation.[56]

Nevertheless, the anti-anthropopathic tendency is definite and visible. In addition to the passages noted by Fritsch in his study of the Pentateuch, there are other significant anti-anthropopathic changes that the Septuagint makes. Let me give two examples, which loom large in the contemporary argument for divine suffering. The passage from Isaiah 63: 9 reads in the reconstruction of the original Hebrew version (which is by no means secure): 'in all their afflictions he [Yahweh] was afflicted (if we read לוֹצָד instead of לאצָד), and the angel of his presence saved them: in his love and in his pity he redeemed them' (KJV, NAS). The Septuagint gives a considerably different version that may very well go back to the original text: 'And he [God] became to them deliverance out of all their affliction (καὶ ἐγένετο αὐτοῖς εἰς σωτηρίαν ἐκ πάσης θλίψεως): not an ambassador, not a messenger, but he himself saved them, because he loved them and spared them.' As we see, the Septuagint does not mention the divine affliction at all, while it affirms that God is a compassionate and loving redeemer. It is important to recognize that the early Christian theologians simply did not have before them

[55] Exod. 12: 13, 27. For the discussion of these and other passages see Fritsch, ibid. 28–35. The meaning of the original is retained in Exod. 12: 23.

[56] e.g. Judg. 10: 16; Ps. 95: 10; Jer. 4: 19; Hos. 11: 8–9; Jon. 4: 2. One of the most striking examples is Jonah 3: 9 where 'God may repent (√שוב) and change his mind (√נחמ) from his fierce anger' is rendered in Greek by εἰ μετανοήσει ὁ θεὸς καὶ ἀποστρέψει ἐξ ὀργῆς θυμοῦ αὐτοῦ.

the version of the text to which the modern theopaschites appeal. For them Isa. 63: 9 expressed the idea of the redeeming compassion of God without suggesting any divine affliction.

The second example of the anti-anthropopathic tendency in the Greek translation of the prophets is in Jeremiah 31: 20 (LXX Jer. 38: 20). The Hebrew text says: 'my bowels are troubled (√המה) for him'. The Septuagint, in contrast, eliminates the reference to the divine digestive system: 'therefore I made haste (ἔσπευσα) to help him'. Examples of such softening of the emotive aspect of the divine action may be multiplied.[57]

Fritsch concludes that there were two parallel traditions in which anti-anthropomorphic tendencies were expressed in pre-Christian Judaism:

> There appear to be then two streams of anti-anthropomorphic development in Jewish history. One goes its own way through the Old Testament into the rabbinical period, confined to the Hebrew and Aramaic languages and guided by ritualistic and theological developments within Judaism. The other, resulting from contact with Greek thought and idiom, continues until it becomes identified with the abstractions of Alexandrian philosophy.[58]

It is crucial that the anti-anthropomorphic impulse was not solely an external Hellenistic influence, but was also an internal development within pre-Christian Judaism. Although the tendency towards anti-anthropomorphism and anti-anthropopathism was by no means consistently followed in the Greek translation, Fritsch thinks that it was 'strong enough to give to the LXX a unique and a somewhat different conception of God from that which is found in the Hebrew Old Testament'.[59] This tendency made a permanent imprint upon Christian theology when the Septuagint, not the Hebrew text, became the scripture of the early church. The apocryphal *Kerygmata Petrou*, which forms a part of pseudo-Clementine corpus, gives a good illustration of how pronounced the anti-anthropopathic tendencies became in heterodox Jewish-Christian circles. The author of *Kerygmata Petrou* claims that the passages of the OT that speak of divine grief, jealousy, and repentance are spurious and were

[57] e.g. Ps. 78: 40 cf. LXX 77: 40; Jer. 42: 10 cf. LXX 49: 10; Judg. 2: 18 cf. LXX 2: 18; Exod. 32: 12–14 cf. LXX 32: 12–14.

[58] Fritsch, *Anti-anthropomorphisms*, 65. Fritsch's point of view is supported by U. Mauser, 'Image of God and Incarnation', 337–8. See also E. M. Yamauchi, 'Anthropomorphism in Hellenism and in Judaism', 212–22. Regarding the emergence of negative theology in Hellenistic Judaism, Gnosticism, Platonism, and Christianity see J. Daniélou, *Gospel Message and Hellenistic Culture*, ii. 323–43.

[59] Ibid. 65.

inserted by the seventy elders to whom Moses delivered oral Law.[60] Although the church at large did not embrace such frivolous 'redaction criticism' of the OT, it shared the concern to interpret the anthropopathic passages in a God-befitting manner. Later lapses into naïve anthropomorphism and anthropopathism in rabbinic thought did not have any observable influence upon the theology of the early Fathers.[61]

In the light of the preceding discussion it becomes pivotal how to evaluate the role of such a seminal figure as Philo of Alexandria (25 BC–AD 45). Is Philo a dangerous Hellenizer who subverted the substance of the Hebrew Old Testament, made it serve pagan philosophy, and led the Christian exegetes astray from the idea of the passible God of the scriptures? This is a common reading of Philo which is given by the proponents of the Theory of Theology's Fall into Hellenistic Philosophy.[62] Or should he be regarded as the one who expressed, systematized, and developed already present anti-anthropomorphic and anti-anthropopathic tendencies that arose within Judaism itself? These questions cannot be answered without undertaking an excursus into Philo's basic theological convictions and exegetical method, as well as his understanding of the divine emotions and the divine involvement in the world.

For Philo God is first of all the universal agent: 'God never ceases to act. As it is the property of fire to burn and that of snow to chill, so it belongs to God to act. Even more so, for God above all else is the principle of action.'[63] All activity belongs to God as the creator and sustainer of the world. Philo develops his understanding of divine power by means of the two Aristotelian categories, action (ποίησις) and suffering (πάθος).[64] He parts ways with Aristotle, however, when he applies the categories to the distinction between creator and creature, rooted in the Bible:

> For some men, admiring the world itself, rather than the Creator of the world, have represented it as existing without any maker, and eternal; and as impiously as falsely have represented God as existing in a state of complete inactivity, while it would have been right on the other hand to marvel at the might of God as the

[60] *Kerygmata Petrou* H II. 43. 2, Schneemelcher and Wilson (eds.), *New Testament Apocrypha*, ii. 120. Cf. Ptolemy, *Letter to Flora* (in Epiphanius, *Haer.* 33. 4).

[61] See on this issue M. L. Klein, *Anthropomorphisms and Anthropopathisms in the Targumim of the Pentateuch*. The text is in Hebrew with an introduction in English.

[62] This case is made, for example, by R. B. Edwards and H. Kraft. See Appendix. For a comprehensive survey of competing theories of influence upon Philo see D. Winston, *Logos and Mystical Theology in Philo of Alexandria*, 9–42.

[63] *Leg.* 1. 5. Cf. *Cher.* 77. See Winston, 'Philo's Conception', 22; Weinandy, *Does God Suffer?*, 77, 79.

[64] *Op.* 8.

creator and father of all, and admire the world in a degree not exceeding the bounds of moderation...[65]

Wolfson suggests that the vague expression 'some men' in the first line of this passage refers to Peripatetics, and contends that 'Philo specifically rejects... the theism of Aristotle, in which God is conceived as an incorporeal form which from eternity existed together with the world as the cause of its motion.'[66] It is very likely that Philo's attack upon those who represent God as 'existing in a state of complete inactivity' is directed against the Epicureans, who, as we recall, were almost universally criticized for making the gods idle and inactive. The world, Philo argues, must not be made an end in itself, for it owes its existence to the benevolent and loving creator.

Philo is aware of the fact that the divine action in the world is vividly described in the Bible by means of anthropomorphisms and anthropopathisms. He admits that such descriptions are inescapable, since human beings for the most part are incapable of freeing their minds from the ideas associated with familiar fields of discourse.[67] However, for Philo, as for the translators of the Septuagint, it is the overarching theological vision of the Bible itself, not just philosophical arguments, that makes it difficult to accept the anthropomorphisms at face value. He observes: '[T]here are two principal positions laid down with respect to the great cause of all things: one that God is not as a man [Num. 23: 19; cf. Hos. 11: 9]; the other that God is as a man [Deut. 8: 5].'[68] Scholars agree that this passage provides the clue to Philo's understanding of the function of religious language as applied to God.[69] Philo stressed that while the Bible amply deployed anthropomorphic descriptions of God, it also properly cautioned against too literal an understanding of them. Philo proposed to treat these descriptions of God as analogies that are helpful pedagogically for admonishing and educating simpler minds.[70]

[65] Ibid. 7, trans. Yonge, *Works of Philo*, 3.

[66] H. A. Wolfson, *Philo*, i. 175. Wolfson later admits that Philo never explicitly condemned the Aristotelian conception of God as entirely incompatible with the scripture. See ibid. 177.

[67] *Sac.* 95.

[68] *Quod deus*, 53; cf. ibid. 69, trans. Yonge, 162.

[69] J. C. McLelland observes: 'Philo is guided by two Mosaic maxims.' See *God the Anonymous, A Study in Alexandrian Philosophical Theology*, 39. Cf. Wolfson, chap. on 'Scriptural Presuppositions', in *Philo*, ii. 98, 126; 'Negative Attributes in the Church Fathers and the Gnostic Basilides', 145–56, esp. 145; Dillon, 'The Nature of God in *Quod Deus*', 221; Winston, 'Philo's Conception', 24.

[70] *Somn.* 1. 232.

Anthropomorphic analogies were permissible, if proper negative qualifications were made. Philo observed that God could not be divided into parts;[71] divine reality was not available to the ordinary senses;[72] divine nature was comprehensible only to the extent it was disclosed in revelation. Philo cautioned against ascribing to any assertion or negation regarding divine nature a complete certainty. Only God knows his own nature fully and accurately.[73]

Far from being a pioneering Hellenizer, Philo stood in a respectable Jewish tradition of interpretation that tended to downplay the literal force of anthropomorphisms. To begin with, Philo drew upon a translation that already showed an anti-anthropomorphic tendency. Let us note that the Hebrew text of Numbers 23: 19, to which Philo did not have access, says: 'God is not a man,' whereas the Septuagint, cited by Philo, adds a comparative particle 'as': 'God is not *as* a man.' The Hebrew text asserts that God is not literally a human person, whereas the Septuagint translation emphasizes the dissimilarity by saying that God cannot even be compared to a human being, suggesting more forcefully that the language of analogy is fraught with difficulties.

Philo's discussion of the issue of divine repentance in Genesis 6: 6–7 is already based upon the anti-anthropopathic Greek translation of the Hebrew text.[74] The Hebrew text says: 'And the Lord repented that he had made man on the earth, and he grieved at his heart. And the Lord said, I will destroy man whom I have created from the face of the earth; both man, and beast, and the creeping thing, and the fowls of the air; for I repented that I had made them.' The Septuagint, from which Philo quotes, renders this text in the following way: 'God considered in his mind (ἐνεθυμήθη) that he had made man upon the earth, and he thought upon it (διενοήθη); and God said I will destroy man whom I have made from off the face of the earth.' As we see, the translators of the Septuagint have already eliminated all explicit references to emotional states—grief and repentance—and rendered them in Greek by emotionally colourless mental acts—deliberation and reflection.

Philo's extended interpretation of this passage follows and develops the logic of the translators of Septuagint. He notes that there are 'careless inquirers' who interpret the text to mean that God actually repented (μετέγνω) of the creation of the human race when he saw its impiety.

71 *Leg.* 2. 1–3; *Mut.* 184.
72 *Mut.* 7–10.
73 *Leg.* 3. 206–7; *Post.* 13.
74 *Quod deus*, 20.

Philo objects to this interpretation which takes one back from the Septuagint translation to the original Hebrew text. His point is that change of mind in God would entail divine ignorance and is incompatible with divine foreknowledge. But God is the maker of time and no human thought is hidden from him. God does not change his judgement depending upon the human situation, because God knows what will come to pass before it happens. Creatures are morally unstable and changeable, but God is unlike them.[75]

Having established the point that divine judgement is unchangeable, Philo quotes the rest of Gen. 6: 7 (LXX Gen. 6: 8): 'I will destroy man whom I have made from off the face of the earth, from man to beast, from creeping things to the fowls of the air, because I was wroth (ἐθυμώθην)[76] in that I made him.' In this case the Septuagint renders the divine repentance in the Hebrew text anthropopathically as the divine anger. The Greek text forces Philo to consider the issue of divine emotions, instead of keeping to that of divine repentance. The question that he addresses next is whether God may literally be said to be subject to anger and other passions:

> Now, some persons, when they hear the expressions which I have just cited [i.e. LXX Gen. 6: 8], imagine that the living God is here giving way to anger (θυμοῖς) and wrath (ὀργαῖς); but God is utterly inaccessible to any passion (πάθει) whatever. For it is the peculiar property of human weakness (ἀσθενεία) to be disquieted by any such feelings, but God has neither the irrational passions (ἄλογα πάθη) of the soul, nor do the parts and the limits of the body in the least belong to him.[77]

Philo, following the Stoics, saw no virtue in anger and on those grounds dismissed anger as a passion unworthy of God. As we will see in the next chapter, for the early Fathers the issue was not quite as clear-cut as for Philo and warranted an extended discussion.

While Philo recognized only a pedagogical role for divine repentance, anger, envy, and grief, he did not eliminate all emotions from the life of God indiscriminately. God is the source of all joy and blessedness, which he freely shares with his people without a shadow of envy. Philo recognized that such emotionally coloured characteristics as mercy,

[75] *Quod deus*, 70. For a helpful discussion of the divine immutability in Philo see Hallman, *Descent of God*, 24–9.

[76] Philo gives ἐθυμώθην which is a better attested reading than a repeated and less colourful ἐνεθυμήθην.

[77] *Quod deus*, 52, trans. Yonge, 162; slightly modified. Cf. *Leg.* 2. 1–3.

kindness, care, unmixed joy, and blessedness were God-befitting.[78] His admission of divine compassion (ἔλεος) marks an apparent departure from the Stoics, for whom pity was a form of distress to be extirpated from the soul of a wise man.[79] Philo's God is a loving creator whose care for the world could be metaphorically expressed by means of anthropomorphisms. Philo's approach is in harmony with the general tendency of the Greek translators towards the mitigation and elimination of anthropomorphisms and anthropopathisms in the Hebrew text of the Bible.

Taking into account this interpretation of Philo, as well as the general anti-anthropopathic tendency in the scriptures of the early church, it is misleading to think of the patristic theological dilemma as involving a choice between the unemotional and uninvolved God of the Hellenes and the emotional and suffering God of the Hebrews. This is a false dilemma that fails to reckon with the variety of understandings of the divine emotions and divine involvement offered by the Hellenistic world and the qualifications of anthropomorphic representations of God that appear in the Greek and even in the Hebrew biblical text, as well as in its early non-Christian interpreters. No matter how far one presses the difference between *le Dieu des philosophes et des savants* and the God of the prophets, between Greek ways of thought and the 'Hebrew experience of God' (Heschel), this contrast simply does not do justice to the vast panorama of proposals in which both divine passion and divine dispassion found their expression. The Theory of Theology's Fall into Hellenistic Philosophy must be once and for all buried with honours, as one of the most enduring and illuminating mistakes among the interpretations of the development of Christian doctrine.

[78] *De Abrahamo*, 202; *Quod deus*, 108; *Cher.* 86; *Plant.* 91.

[79] See Winston, 'Philo's Conception', 31.

2

The Christian God *v.* Passionate Pagan Deities: Impassibility as an Apophatic Qualifier of Divine Emotions

THIS chapter offers a preliminary analysis of the function of the divine impassibility in select patristic sources without special reference to the christological debates on the incarnation. The first point to be observed about the divine impassibility in the ante-Nicene theology is that the early Fathers did not make much of this concept. The description of God as impassible fades in importance before the emotionally coloured divine characteristics of mercy, love, goodness, and compassion. One finds nothing amounting to a doctrine, or to a universally endorsed body of teaching.[1] Instead, one discovers scattered remarks here and there. Bearing this in mind one must beware of overinterpretation and of inflating the issue to undue proportions. As I noted in the introduction, much of contemporary criticism of the divine impassibility suffers precisely from superficial philological overinterpretation.

Our guiding question is this: what is the function of the concept of the divine impassibility in patristic accounts of divine emotions and involvement? The proponents of the Theory of Theology's Fall into Hellenistic Philosophy uncritically identify divine impassibility with apathy and

[1] The only treatise specifically dedicated to our subject is *Ad Theopompum de passibili et impassibili in deo*. The work, attributed to Gregory Thaumaturgus, survives only in a Syriac translation from the Greek original. L. Abramowski's objections against the Gregorian authorship are quite compelling. See 'Die Schrift Gregors des Lehrers "Ad Theopompum" und Philoxenus von Mabbug', 273–90.

indifference. Negatively, I will argue in this chapter that this claim finds no support in the relevant patristic sources. Positively, I will try to establish three things. First, I will show that by calling the Christian God impassible the Fathers sought to distance God the creator from the gods of mythology. In this debate the major goal was to rule out popular pagan modes of imaging the divine realm as unworthy of the Christian God.[2] Second, the Fathers viewed impassibility as compatible with select emotionally coloured characteristics, e.g., love, mercy, and compassion. Especially revealing in this regard is the patristic treatment of divine anger, an issue that first came to the fore in the debate with Marcionism. Third, I will locate the divine impassibility in the conceptual sphere of apophatic theology. I will show that in apophatic theology impassibility was first of all an ontological term, expressing God's unlikeness to everything created, his transcendence and supremacy over all things, rather than a psychological term implying the absence of emotions. In this conceptual framework divine impassibility safeguarded God's undiminished divinity and transcendence.

Divine Impassibility Entails that the Christian God is Free from the Unworthy Passions of Pagan Deities

The differences between pagan and Christian understandings of the divine involvement and emotions are most vividly expressed in Christian polemic against traditional pagan beliefs about gods and, in turn, in pagan attacks upon the God of Christian revelation. The myths spoke of the gods as being endowed with human passions and weaknesses. Happily, Christians were not the only ones who understood the impropriety of ascribing human, all too human, characteristics to gods. Many philosophically minded pagans and Jews shared the same sensibility. Charges of anthropomorphism against the traditional polytheism became commonplace among philosophers from the time of Xenophanes (sixth century BC). In the ages that passed, various philosophical schools developed moral theories that either converted passionate mythical deities into antiheroes, or allegorized them into impersonal natural forces.

Materially, the Christian apologists added little to the negative side of the polemic. They drew upon the sceptical claims that the ancient myths

[2] Cf. Weinandy, *Does God Suffer?*, 89.

were pure fables, as distinct from *historia*, accounts of events that really happened. They accepted reductionist theories, set forth by the Sceptics, according to which the traditional gods were prominent men or heroes of the past, divinized and immortalized after their death.[3] Some apologists also endorsed a psychoanalytical insight that the gods of Homer were personifications of extreme and violent human passions. In this context the role of the Christian apologists was to add fuel to the glowing coals of already existing philosophical dissatisfaction with traditional beliefs. Nevertheless, one Christian innovation stands out in this otherwise traditional critique: the harmless *daimones* who occupied a sublunary space between gods and humans were converted into nasty, malevolent, and malodorous fallen beings who were believed to oppose God and to use every occasion to bring ills upon humans. Christians did not hesitate to identify all the immortal inhabitants of Olympus with these unseemly creatures, the demons.[4]

The acceptance of Christianity entailed a radical change, a break with the past worship of the demons. Those who considered entering Christian catechetical schools had to abandon the false gods along with their vile passions, and serve the true God instead. Justin Martyr describes this change of allegiance in the following way:

> [B]ecause we, who out of every race of men used to worship Dionysus the son of Semele, and Apollo the son of Leto, who in their passion with men did such things of which it is shameful even to speak, and Persephone and Aphrodite, who were stung to madness by love for Adonis and whose mysteries you also celebrate, or Asclepius, or some one or other of those who are called gods—have now, through Jesus Christ, learned to despise them, though threatened with death for it, and have dedicated ourselves to the unbegotten and impassible (ἀπαθεῖ) God; we are not persuaded that He was ever goaded by lust for Antiope, or such other women, or of Ganymede, nor was He delivered by that hundred-handed monster, whose aid was obtained through Thetis, nor, on this account, was anxious that her son Achilles should destroy many of the Greeks because of his concubine Briseis. We pity those who believe these things, and we recognize those who invented them to be demons.[5]

Justin, as this passage shows, was eager to demarcate the character of the Christian God from that of the passionate Homeric deities. The God of Christians is impassible, free from passions, in the sense that, unlike

[3] Athenag., *Leg.* 26–30; Ath., *Contra Gentes*, 12. 2.

[4] Justin, *Apol.* 1. 5; Athenag., *Leg.* 23–5; Clem., *Exhortatio*, 2–3.

[5] Justin, *Apol.* 1. 25. 1–3, trans. Barnard, 40. For the discussion of the function of the divine impassibility in Justin see W. C. Placher, 'Narratives of a Vulneralde God', 137.

Dionysius, he is not prone to debauchery; unlike Apollo, he is not a woman-hunter; unlike Persephone and Aphrodite, he is not engaged in rivalry over the handsome Adonis; unlike Zeus, he neither corrupts young boys (Ganymede), nor shows partiality towards his illegitimate sons (Achilles). In this context divine impassibility means that God is above the passions of envy, lust, and all selfish desires.[6] To ascribe these passions to God the creator was to obliterate important distinctions between him and his fallen creatures.

According to the poets, the Olympians took an impassioned interest in the affairs of mortals. The problem was that such involvement often meant peril and destruction for mortals. As Clement of Alexandria observed: 'The demons love men in such a way as to bring them to the fire [of hell].'[7] The issue between the Christians and popular pagan piety was not whether the gods were involved at all (this was accepted on both sides), but rather *how* were they involved? What manner of divine involvement was most appropriate? What intentions, emotions, and actions may fittingly be ascribed to God? Early Fathers and poets gave very different answers to these questions.

Since the Homeric gods were the slaves of violent passions, it was natural for the poets to explain their intentions in terms of irrational outbreaks of rage, lust, revenge, ambition, domination, anger, and aggression. In this picture of divine emotions love (*eros*) was a blind, all-consuming outburst of desire. The idea of divine justice was distorted by the conflict of competing divine wills and interests.[8] Mercy and love, devoid of justice, were reduced to arbitrary expressions of divine favour.[9]

In the context of polemic against this picture of divine emotions and involvement another second-century apologist, Athenagoras, noticed in passing that gods, properly thought of, 'neither fall in love, nor experience passion (οὐκ ἐρῶσιν, οὐ πάσχουσιν)... For the divine needs nothing and is above lustful desire (κρεῖττον ἐπιθυμίας τὸ θεῖον).'[10] Along the same lines Irenaeus observed that 'the Father of all is far removed from those affections (*affectionibus*) and passions (*passionibus*) which have their place in humans'.[11] If emotions can be ascribed to God

6 Gr. Naz., *Or.* 28. 11; John of Damascus, *Expositio accurate fidei orthodoxae*, 1. 1.

7 Clem., *Protr.* 3.

8 As pointed out by Plato in *Euthyphro*, 7a ff.

9 Stauffer, 'Ἀγαπάω, ἀγάπη, ἀγαπητός', *TDNT* i. 36–7.

10 Athenag., *Leg.* 21. 4; 29. 3; cf. Iren., *haer.* 2. 12. 1; 2. 17. 3, 8.

11 Iren., *haer.* 2. 15. 3.

at all, they are not violent irrational perturbations, unrelated to God's thoughts and plans. God, as the creator of all, is in total control of his actions and emotions. For Athenagoras, 'God did not create the world as if he were in need of it.'[12] Later Fathers underlined that the creation of the world was a free act of divine will, not a necessary expression of God's nature.

By calling God 'impassible' Justin and other Apologists were clearing the decks of popular theological discourse in order to make space for God-befitting emotionally coloured characteristics such as mercy, love, and compassion. The world of the Fathers, not unlike ours, was full of theological charlatans. Hence such purging of discourse about God was indispensable. The divine impassibility meant first of all that God is in total control of his actions and that morally objectionable emotions are alien to him.

The Limiting Case of Divine Anger

When it came to their own understanding of divine emotions and involvement, the Fathers had to meet the same criticism that they mounted against myths from the side of their cultured despisers, the philosophers. The major target of attack and derision was the doctrine of the incarnation—a scandal to philosophical piety and an offence against the best metaphysical proposals of the Hellenistic age. This doctrine, in relation to the issue of divine (im)passibility, will be treated in detail in the chapters that follow. Here we will explore a relatively minor theme, i.e. select philosophical objections to the biblical portrait of divine emotions and Christian attempts to meet these objections.

Many philosophers were puzzled by the fact that Christians, while decrying the Homeric myths with remarkable passion, accorded such a great place in their religion to certain barbaric books in which God was described in the most naïve, anthropomorphic, and anthropopathic terms. Pagan readers of the Bible could justifiably ask, was not the God of the prophets afflicted with the same kinds of passions as the gods of the poets? So, for example, emperor Julian, whose private sympathy for Christian morals and asceticism was surpassed only by his public disdain of Christian theology and worship, argued that the deity portrayed in Scripture fared no better before the moral critique of

[12] Athenag., *Leg.* 16, trans. E. R. Hardy, 313.

the philosophers than the passionate gods of Homer. Discussing certain instances of divine anger in the Old Testament, Julian observed:

> The philosophers bid us imitate the gods so far as we can, and they teach us that this imitation consists in the contemplation of realities. And that this sort of study is remote from passion (δίχα πάθους) and is indeed based on freedom from passion (εὐ ἀπαθέιᾳ κεῖται), is, I suppose, evident, even without my saying it. In proportion then as we, having been assigned to the contemplation of realities, attain to freedom from passion (εὐ ἀπαθέιᾳ), in so far do we become like God. But what sort of imitation of God is praised among the Hebrews? Anger and wrath and fierce jealousy (ὀργὴ καὶ θυμὸς καὶ ζῆλος ἄγριος).[13]

Julian's strategy is very typical of any philosophical critique of divine emotions. He starts from a human moral ideal, in this case from *apatheia*, and deploys it as a criterion for judging whether a given divine attribute is God-befitting. Expressed more formally, the argument runs as follows: if emotion E is either (1) morally objectionable, or (2) incompatible with other divine attributes, E cannot be predicated of God. Julian held that anger is both (1*) morally reprehensible and (2*) incompatible with the divine impassibility, and concluded that anger is unworthy of God.

In the context of polemic with paganism and Gnosticism, when a detailed treatment of the problem of divine anger was not warranted, some early theologians relied without much reflection upon a highly influential Stoic view that anger was as an irrational perturbation unworthy of a true philosopher. According to Seneca, the philosophical schools were in agreement that God was free from anger.[14] Criticizing pagan myths, Athenagoras and Aristides conceded the Stoic view that the passion of anger was intrinsically evil, on a par with the passions of greed and lust. On these grounds they concluded that anger without qualification was unworthy of God.[15]

In the same context, a North African theologian of the third century, Arnobius, refused to give the divine anger any positive function in his theology.[16] In his apologetic work against pagan folk religion Arnobius

[13] Quoted by Cyril, *Contra Julianum*, 171E. Cf. *Fragmentum Epistolae* (Letter to a Priest) 301A–B (LCL xxix. 326). Cf. also Tertullian, *Apologeticum*, 50.

[14] Seneca, *De officiis*, 3. 102. On this issue see Kleinknecht, Ὀργή, *TDNT* v. 386–7.

[15] Aristides, *Apol.* 1; Clement of Rome, *Cor.* 19. 3; Clem., *Strom.* 4. 23: 'God is impassible, free of anger, destitute of desire'; *Strom.* 6. 3. 31. 1; *Paed.* 1. 8. 68. 3; Athenag., *Leg.* 23. 1: 'for in God there is neither anger nor lust and desire nor yet semen for producing offspring'.

[16] See Micka, *Problem of Divine Anger*, esp. 34–5.

wrote: 'You judge that the deities are angry (*irasci*) and perturbed (*perturbati*), and given over and subject to the other mental affections; we think that such emotions are alien from them, for these suit savage beings and those who die as mortals.'[17] Arnobius defined anger as a 'passion which approaches closest to wild animals and beasts, disturbs with misfortune those who experience it and leads to the danger of destruction'.[18] According to him, to be angry is nothing else 'than to be insane, to rave, to be carried away by the lust of revenge and made savage by the loss of reason, to revel in the tortures of another's grief'.[19] Following the Stoics, Arnobius saw anger as an essentially demoralizing and harmful emotion, potentially leading to self-destruction. Given this interpretation, Arnobius' conclusion that 'the gods are not angry at any time' is not surprising.[20] If anger in all cases blinds our moral judgements, then indeed anger is an emotion unworthy of God.

However, the majority of the Fathers would find this popular philosophical treatment of anger one-sided. They would judge Arnobius' definition to be restrictive and to have failed to grasp a significant moral dimension of anger. It was Marcion, in particular, who forced the Fathers to articulate a more discriminating account of divine anger. As it is well known, Marcion objected to the use of the OT in the church primarily on theological grounds. He taught that the deity of the OT was cruel, warlike, inconsistent, merciless, and consumed with the passion of anger.[21] Such a deity, as Marcion believed, was inferior to the God of mercy and compassion revealed in the NT. In Marcion's opinion, anger and mercy could not be the properties of one and the same divine being.

The Fathers, notably Irenaeus and Tertullian, objected that far from being a sign of weakness, divine anger in Scripture was intimately related to divine justice. Far from being a conscience-blinding perturbation of the mind, divine anger in the Old Testament manifests God's righteous indignation at human disobedience. Irenaeus wrote:

> That they [the Marcionites] might take away the vindictive and judicial power from the Father, imagining that to be unworthy of God, and thinking that they had found a god angerless (*sine iracundia*) and good, they taught that the one [god] is a judge and the other is a savior, ignorant of the fact that they were taking away the intelligence and justice of both deities.[22]

[17] Arnobius, *Adv. nat.* 7. 36. [18] Ibid. 7. 5. [19] Ibid. 1. 17.
[20] Ibid. 7. 9. [21] Iren., *haer.* 1. 27. 2.
[22] Ibid. 3. 40. 1, trans. Harvey, ii. 133–4.

As Irenaeus points out, Marcion failed to see that without the emotions expressing God's condemnation of evil, God could be neither just, nor merciful, nor good, nor intelligent. In order to capture this morally significant dimension of divine anger Tertullian introduced an expression 'judicial sentiment' (*judiciarius sensus*).[23] Divine emotions, according to Tertullian, are immediately related to God's 'judicial functions' and express God's intimate concern for human salvation.

In the light of this picture of divine emotions, we must disagree with J. K. Mozley's observation that 'Tertullian's description of the character of the divine feelings reads like a Christianized version of the Stoic exaltation of ἀπάθεια.'[24] On the contrary, Tertullian's *judiciarius sensus* was a quite deliberate departure from the Stoics who held that anger overpowers the mind and obscures judgement, consequently denying to anger any positive function in morality.

The majority of the Fathers recognized that anger was a morally ambiguous, rather than plainly evil emotion. Some expressions of anger may be conscience-blinding, uncontrollable, and evil. However, other instances of anger convey a morally valuable reaction—condemnation of sin.[25] The anonymous author of the Pseudo-Clementine *Recognitions*, written most probably in Syria in the beginning of the third century, arguing against the philosophers, aptly summarizes the double-sided nature of anger:

> [T]he philosophers say that God is not angry, not knowing what they say. For anger is evil whenever it disturbs the mind (*mentem turbat*) so that it destroys right judgment. That anger, however, which punishes the wicked does not bring on disturbance of the mind (*perturbationem menti non infert*), but is, I may say, one and the same affection which allots rewards to the good and punishment to the wicked. For if he should give blessings to the virtuous and to the wicked and bestow similar remuneration on the good and the evil, he would appear unjust rather than good.[26]

23 Tertullian, *Adv. Marc.* 2. 17.

24 Mozley, *Impassibility of God*, 38.

25 It should be noted that the NT, unlike the Septuagint, more or less consistently makes a terminological distinction between the two kinds of anger. Anger in the sense of blind outburst of passion is usually rendered as θύμος and is predominantly ascribed to humans, whereas anger as reaction to sin is conveyed by the more emotionally subdued ὀργή. It is the latter term that is most commonly used for the wrath of God. Θυμός expresses the divine anger only in Rom. 2: 8 and Rev. 14: 10, 19; 15: 1, 7; 16: 1, 19; 19: 15. Stählin, Ὀργή v. 422, rightly cautions against any conclusions based upon rigid linguistic differentiations.

26 *Recognitiones*, 10. 48, trans. T. Smith, ANF xiii. 205. Cf. Iren., *haer.* 3. 40. 1.

The author's argument is basically the same as that of Irenaeus and Tertullian: the unqualified denial of divine anger leads to a morally inadequate concept of God and puts into question God's ability to punish the wicked.

It is in Lactantius' *De ira dei* that we find a mature patristic answer to the philosophical unease with ascribing anger to God. Heavily relying upon Cicero, Lactantius criticized the Epicureans for treating divine care for the world as weakness and a form of emotional dependence.[27] Having dismantled the Epicurean position with the Stoic arguments, Lactantius proceeded to argue against the Stoics themselves. For Cicero and Seneca, as we recall, all expressions of anger were morally objectionable. Seneca objected to the Peripatetic view that anger, if guided by reason, strengthened the virtue of military valour.[28] The Stoics were convinced that anger could never be rationally directed and contributed nothing to the extermination of evil. For them anger only confounded moral judgement, instead of increasing its force. Hence, anger must be eradicated from the soul as completely as possible, not merely controlled by reason.[29] Seneca went so far as to say that even when a horrible crime, like the killing of one's father and the rape of one's mother was committed before the philosopher's very eyes, a true lover of wisdom should remain tranquil and would strive to avenge and protect his relatives without anger.[30]

Lactantius disagreed with the Stoic refusal to admit any morally fruitful application of anger. Some instances of anger, Lactantius argued, have a morally sound teleology: they are directed at punishing the wicked. To support his case, Lactantius uses the analogy of a household. Suppose a slave killed all his master's children, slew his wife, and set his house on fire. Lactantius observes with indignation that 'to pardon deeds of this kind is the part of cruelty rather than of kindness'. Indeed, the absence of emotional reaction to a comparable crime would strike anyone as going against our deeply engrained moral intuitions. Lactantius continues that the world is a household in which the wicked occupy the position of slaves with respect to God. Being a kind and just master of his house, God will not permit such atrocities to go unpunished.

[27] *De ira dei*, 4.

[28] Aristotle, *Eth. Nic.* 4. 11. *Contra* Aristotle: Cicero, *Tusc. Disput.* 4. 43; Seneca, *De ira*, 1. 9. 2; 2. 15. 1–3; 3. 3. 1–5.

[29] *De ira*, 2. 13. 1. Cf. the following categorical statement of Seneca: 'The wise man will have no anger towards sinners,' *De ira*, 2. 10. 6, trans. J. W. Basore, *Seneca: Moral Essays*, 187.

[30] Seneca, *De ira*, 1. 12. 1–2; cf. 1. 16. 1–2.

Lactantius distinguished between just and unjust anger.[31] Only the former could be ascribed to God. Justin, Theophilus, Cyprian, Commodian, and others shared the conviction that anger was a powerful tool for expressing condemnation of sin.[32]

If God can be said to be angry in a qualified sense, how precisely does he experience anger? There was a diversity of opinion on this matter. Does God really feel anger? Some, like the Alexandrians, Clement and Origen, responded that although God himself did not feel anger, humans experienced the consequences of his judgement and punishment *as if* God were indeed angry. They explained that biblical authors ascribed anger, vengeance, and fury to God in order to instill pious fear in simple folk. The use of such language, according to Clement and Origen, is primarily pedagogical and metaphorical.[33]

John Cassian insisted that anger should be ascribed to God not *anthrōpopathōs*, 'anthropopathically', but 'in a sense worthy of God who is a stranger to all perturbations (*digne Deo, qui omni perturbatione alienus est*)'.[34] Cassian followed Evagrius Ponticus in including anger into the catalogue of eight generic passionate thoughts (*logismoi*): gluttony, impurity, avarice, sadness, sloth, vainglory, and pride.[35] According to Evagrius, it was one of the goals of ascetic life to eradicate these thoughts in the process of attaining *apatheia*, freedom from passions.[36] It should be noted that the monastic list of evil thoughts overlaps only partially with the four generic *pathē* of the Stoics—distress, pleasure, fear, and desire. There is a profound difference between monastic and Stoic moral ideals. Evagrius' statement that '*agapē* is a progeny of *apatheia*' would be unacceptable to a Stoic. We must stress that monastic condemnation of

[31] *De ira dei*, 17.

[32] Justin, *Dial.* 39. 257D; 123. 351D, 352A; Theophilus, *Ad Autolicum*, 1. 3; Cyprian, *Ad Demetrianum*, 5; 7; 10; Commodian, *Instructiones*, 1. 2.

[33] Clem., *Paed.* 1. 8. 68. 3; *Strom.* 2. 16; Origen, *Princ.* 2. 4. 4.

[34] *Institutiones*, 8. 4. 3. Since Latin lacked a corresponding term, Cassian transliterated Greek ἀνθρωποπαθῶς. See the discussion of this passage in Colish, *Stoic Tradition*, ii. 121–2.

[35] See *Praktikos*, 81. On interrelationship between *agapē* and *apatheia* see Sorabji, *Emotion*, 388–9, 395. Augustine was the first to distinguish clearly between the Stoic and the monastic moral ideals of *apatheia*. See esp. *De civitate dei*, 14. 9. On *apatheia* as monastic ideal see Robert Somos, 'Origen, Evagrius Ponticus and the Ideal of Impassibility', 365–73; B. Maier, 'Apatheia bei den Stoiken und Akedia bei Evagrios Pontikos', 230–49; T. Ware, 'The meaning of "Pathos" in Abba Isaias and Theodoret of Cyrus', 315–22; Basil Krivocheine, *In the Light of Christ*, 349–60.

[36] Evagrius Ponticus recommended calming anger by the singing of psalms, patience, and alms-giving. See *Praktikos*, 11, 15, 22–3, 25.

the passion of anger depended primarily upon Jesus' interdiction of anger in the Sermon on the Mount, and only secondarily upon the Stoic caution regarding the corrupting effects of this passion.

Evagrius allowed, however, that anger could be useful in fighting other bad thoughts, an idea that no Stoic would find acceptable.[37] Other ascetic writers likewise admitted that anger was a legitimate weapon in spiritual warfare against the devil and his temptations.[38] The ascetic's soul became a battleground at which passionate thoughts waged their war against the spirit. God, for obvious reasons, was not in need of self-correction and, therefore, was entirely free from anger.

Following the Alexandrian tradition, John Cassian held that God in his very being did not experience anger. It is the fear of divine punishment, Cassian proposed, that caused humans to experience divine kindness and justice as wrath and vehement anger.[39] Augustine put the matter in similar terms. For him, divine anger is a function of human reaction: 'The wrath of God is an emotion which is produced in the soul which knows the law of God, when it sees this same law transgressed by sinners.'[40] To speak of God as becoming angry is a common, but not an entirely sound way of expressing the idea of divine punishment: 'God does not suffer perturbation when He visits men in anger; but either by an abuse of the word, or by a peculiarity of idiom, anger is used in the sense of punishment.'[41]

According to Augustine—who, as we will discover later in this chapter, was by no means consistent on this point—what humans perceive as divine anger is not an inherent quality of divine life, but a human emotional reaction to divine judgement. To imagine God as angry is a human way of realizing the gravity of sin and inevitability of divine judgement. Such an understanding of divine anger may be called subjectivist on the grounds that to be angry does not belong to the nature of God, but only to the way in which humans conceive of divine judgement.

[37] Ibid. 24. See Sorabji, *Emotion*, 360–2.

[38] e.g. Gregory of Nyssa argues, presumably against the Stoics, in *De anima et resurrectione, PG* 46: 65A–B: 'If anger (θύμος) is to be extinguished, what arms shall we possess against the adversary?', trans. W. Moore, NPNF, 2nd ser., v. 433.

[39] Cassian, *Inst.* 8. 4. 3.

[40] Augustine, *Enar. in Ps.* 2. 4. Cf. *Ad Romanos*, 9, *De civitate dei*, 15. 25. See the discussion of these passages in Colish, *Stoic Tradition*, ii. 222. Cf. Marius Victorinus, *Adversus Arium*, IA. 44.

[41] Augustine, *Contra Faustum*, 22. 18. For the discussion of Augustine's understanding of divine anger see J. C. Fredouille, 'Sur la colère divine: Jamblique et Augustine', 7–13, and Hallman, *Descent of God*, 114.

In contrast, Tertullian, Lactantius, Novatian, and Cyril of Alexandria would disagree with a purely subjectivist interpretation of divine anger. In their view, God indeed experiences anger, although in a carefully qualified sense. Lactantius explains that divine anger is perpetual in the sense that God does not change his disposition towards unrepentant sinners. Those who do not reform their morals will reap the consequences of God's everlasting wrath. At the same time God is kind, longsuffering, and compassionate to those who repent. God is fully in control of his anger and he never becomes angry arbitrarily.[42]

The ancients believed that uncontrollable passions both disrupted one's emotional life and corrupted one's physical existence.[43] Unlike humans, God is neither emotionally overwhelmed nor physically destroyed by the passion of anger. Novatian aptly expressed this idea:

> A human being can be corrupted by them [passions], since he is corruptible; but God cannot be corrupted by them since he is incorruptible. They [passions] may overpower material which is passible (*passibilis materia*), not impassible substance (*impassibilis substantia*). God becomes angry not out of vice, but for the sake of healing us. He is merciful even when he threatens, because through his menaces humans are recalled to rectitude.[44]

For Novatian the claim that God is impassible did not exclude the meaningful attribution of emotions to God, including anger. Impassibility is a corollary of incorruptibility and as such it prevents God from being overwhelmed by or thwarted by the emotion of anger. In this text divine impassibility functions as a negative qualifier that limits the analogical application of anger to God in a way that is God-befitting. God's anger is rationally directed towards the healing of humans from vice.

Similarly, Tertullian invokes the attribute of divine incorruptibility when he contrasts emotions, as humans experience them, with the divine emotions. He goes so far as to admit that 'human soul has the same emotions and sensations as God', and these emotions are a part of divine image (*imago dei*) in human beings.[45] He immediately qualifies this bold statement, adding that 'such things as, say, anger and exasperation, we do not experience as felicitously as God, for God alone is blessed by

[42] Lactantius, *De ira dei*, 21: 'God is not angry for a short time (*temporalem*), because He is eternal and of perfect virtue, and He is never angry unless deservedly . . . Because He is endued with the greatest excellence, He controls His anger, and is not ruled by it, but He regulates it according to His will.'

[43] See Mozley, *Impassibility of God*, 37.

[44] Novatian, *De trinitate*, 5.

[45] Tertullian, *Adv. Marc.* 2. 16.

virtue of his incorruptibility. He can be angry without [lacuna in the text], can be provoked without endangering himself, can be moved without being overwhelmed ... All these he experiences in his own manner, in which it is fitting for him to experience them.'[46] Tertullian is prepared to speak of a broad range of divine emotions, as long as their precise meaning and application is qualified. Like Novatian, Tertullian emphasizes God's sovereign freedom and total control over his emotions.

Considering the issue of divine patience (*patientia*), Augustine developed the distinction between divine and human emotions along similar lines:

> [A]lthough God cannot suffer [anything evil] (*deus nihil* [*mali*] *pati posit*), and patience (*patientia*) surely has its name from suffering (*patiendo*), we not only faithfully believe in a patient God (*patientem Deum*), but also steadfastly acknowledge Him to be such. Who can explain in words the nature and the quantity of God's patience? We say He is impassible (*nihil patientem*), yet not impatient (*impatientem*); nay, rather, extremely patient (*patientissimum*). His patience is indescribable, yet it exists as does His jealousy, His wrath, and any characteristic of this kind. But, if we conceive of these qualities, as they exist in us, He has none of them. We do not experience these feelings without annoyance (*sine molestia*), but far be it from us to suspect an impassible God (*impassibilem Dei*) of suffering any annoyance. Just as He is jealous without any ill will, as He is angry without being emotionally upset, as He pities without grieving, as He is sorry without correcting any fault, so He is patient without suffering at all.[47]

Here, in contrast to the passages cited above, Augustine does not deny that God can experience anger. Rather Augustine expresses a common conviction of the Fathers that divine impassibility does not rule out all divine emotions. Instead, divine impassibility entails freedom from and control over those emotional states that humans cannot manage easily.[48] God is impassible in the sense of being immune to the negative consequences typically associated with human emotions. Augustine emphasizes that God is not overpowered by anger or by any other perturbation contrary to reason.

[46] *Ita et illas species, irae dico et exasperationis, non tam feliciter patimur, quia solus deus de incorruptibilitatis proprietate felix. Irascetur enim, sed non* [...], *exacerbabitur, sed non periclitababitur, movebitur, sed non evertetur ... quae omnia patitur suo more, quo eum pati condecet*, ibid. 2. 16 (CSEL xlvii. 357–8). See Weinandy, *Does God Suffer?*, 104–6.

[47] Augustine, *De patientia* 1. 1 (*PL* 40. 611). Trans. L. Meagher, *Saint Augustine*, FC xvi. 237.

[48] See Augustine, *De civitate Dei* 14. 7. Augustine's opinion that human *apatheia* is not attainable in this life is shared by Jerome and is typical of Latin authors in general.

Cyril of Alexandria joined the chorus of the Western Fathers in admitting anger as a God-befitting divine emotion. While Cyril recognized that human language could not adequately describe divine emotions, he at the same time insisted that divine anger and longsuffering captured an important dimension of divine punishment:

> The divine nature is exceedingly terrible in uttering reproofs, and is stirred to violent emotion by unmingled hatred of evil, against whomsoever the divine decree may have determined that this feeling is justly due; and this is in spite of immeasurable longsuffering. Whenever therefore the Divine Scripture wishes to express God's emotion against impious designs of whatever kind, it derives its language as on other occasions from expressions in use among us, and in human phraseology speaks of anger and wrath; although the divine essence is subject to none of these passions in any way that bears comparison with our feelings, but is moved to indignation the extent of which is known only to Itself and utterly unspeakable.[49]

Thus, for Novatian, Tertullian, Lactantius,[50] Augustine, and Cyril of Alexandria divine impassibility was quite compatible with certain divine emotions, even with anger. Divine impassibility was an important apophatic qualifier[51] of all divine emotions that ensured that God experiences them in the manner appropriate to him alone.

Divine Impassibility as an Apophatic Qualifier of Divine Emotions

In patristic theology impassibility consistently appears among other negative characteristics that express God's distinction from all creation. For example, Athenagoras spoke of God as being 'uncreated, eternal, invisible, impassible (ἀπαθής), incomprehensible, and infinite...'[52] Divine transcendence was expressed in patristic thought by the

[49] *In Ioannem*, 12. 6, trans. P. E. Pusey, 193. Cf. *In Lucam*, 1; *De adoratione in spiritu et veritate, PG* 68: 153D–155A; 169D; 364C; 378C–D; 381D; 389C. I owe the references from *De adoratione* to Hallman, 'Seed of Fire', 372.

[50] *Divinae institutiones*, 2. 8. 44; cf. 1. 3. 23; 1. 8. 6.

[51] My use of the term 'qualifier' is different from that proposed by Ian Ramsey: for Ramsey qualifiers have primarily an evocative function. See his *Religious Language*, 55–60. Cf. Edward Farley, *Divine Empathy, A Theology of God*, 115–18.

[52] Athenag., *Leg.* 10. 1. Cf. 8. 3; Aristides, *Apologia*, 1, 4, 7, 13; Theophilus, *Ad Autolicum*, 1. 3, 4; Clem., *Eclogae propheticae*, 21. 1. 4; *Protr.* 6; *Strom.* 5. 11–12; Hippolytus, *Contra Noetum*, 8. 3; Frag. 1; Eusebius, *Prep. evang.* 7. 19; Ath., *Ar.* 1. 28; Augustine, *Acta seu disputatio contra Fortunatum Manichaeum*, 3; Gr. Nyss., *Eun.* 3. 4. 723 (*J* ii. 144); John of Damascus, *Expositio accurate fidei orthodoxae*, 1. 8; 1. 14; and hundreds of others.

distinction between created and uncreated. The negative characteristics of the uncreated God followed from this distinction. Creatures are finite, visible, and passible; God, in contrast, is infinite, invisible, and impassible. One should beware of overinterpreting this contrast in the sense of 'detached', 'apathetic', and 'unemotional'. There is no warrant for such an interpretation in the sources. The idea expressed is fairly general and modest: God is unlike everything else, and therefore he acts and suffers action in a manner different from everything else.

Given the context of negative theology, divine impassibility should not be treated as an isolated concept, as is often done by the proponents of the Theory of Theology's Fall into Hellenistic Philosophy. On the contrary, divine impassibility should be located among the predicates of immutability, invisibility, incorporeality, indivisibility, incorruptibility, incomprehensibility, and the like.[53] The interpretative difficulties that arise in the case of divine impassibility have family resemblances to those that arise in the case of other apophatic qualifiers. Correspondingly, the investigation of the function of other apophatic qualifiers may cast light upon the function of impassibility.

How then do other apophatic qualifiers actually function? When considering the apophatic qualifiers it is important not to jump to quick conclusions on purely etymological grounds. For example, the statement 'God is uncreated' may be interpreted as meaning that God is not yet created and therefore non-existent, which is not at all its intended meaning in Christian religious discourse. If one looks more closely at the context within which the qualifier 'uncreated' actually functions, one will discover that this negative adjective means that God the creator has no source or origin and surpasses everything in the created order. In this case negation functions as superlative.

In other cases apophatic qualifiers indicate creaturely limitations. For example, the adjectives invisible, incomprehensible, and inexpressible qualify our ability to see, comprehend, and describe God. These qualifiers do not function in such a way as to rule out God's ability to disclose himself to humans. They rather serve as indicators of the divine transcendence and creaturely limitations.

[53] Most modern discussions of the issue either isolate impassibility altogether or treat it in tandem with immutability alone with the result that the larger context of apophatic theology is neglected.

Likewise, to say that God is impassible is not to prevent any meaningful discourse about divine emotions. We saw earlier in this chapter that divine impassibility restricted the ways in which anger could be predicated to God. While the issue whether God is subject to anger was an issue of contention, most of the Fathers shared the opinion, expressed, for example by John Chrysostom, that the divine impassibility was quite compatible with God's loving-kindness and care:

> For if the wrath of God were a passion, one might well despair as being unable to quench the flame which he had kindled by so many evil doings; but since the Divine nature is passionless, even if He punishes, even if He takes vengeance, He does this not with wrath, but with tender care, and much loving-kindness; wherefore it behooves us to be of much good courage, and to trust in the power of repentance.[54]

It is precisely because God is impassible, i.e., free of uncontrollable vengeance, that repentant sinners may approach him without despair. Far from being a barrier to divine care and loving-kindness, divine impassibility is their very foundation. Unlike that of humans who are unreliable and swayed by passions, God's love is enduring and devoid of all those weaknesses with which human love is tainted.

The function of apophatic qualifications, such as 'God is impassible' is fairly modest: it spells out the truth that emotionally coloured characteristics should not be conceived entirely along the lines of their human analogies. Apart from the incarnation, we can say that no contradiction is involved in affirming that God is in one respect like human beings, i.e. possessing certain emotionally coloured characteristics, and in another respect unlike human beings, i.e. impassible. In this case, the contradiction, if it arises, is easily dissolved by limiting the function and meaning of the apophatic qualifier 'impassible' on the one hand and the meaning and function of the emotions that are ascribed to God analogically on the other hand.

In contrast, when we speak about the incarnation the tension involved goes deeper. The claim is not that God who is otherwise unlike human beings reveals himself *as* a human being. The claim is that God who is otherwise unlike human beings actually takes flesh. In the incarnation the impassible God is no longer *like* a man, but he literally *assumes* human nature, is born of a virgin, and suffers on the cross. Divine incarnation is a peculiar case where the tension between divine transcendence,

[54] Chrysostom, *Ep. ad Theodorum*, I. 4, trans. W. R. W. Stephens, NPNF, 1st ser., ix. 93.

expressed in terms of impassibility, and divine participation in the human condition, expressed in terms of *pathos*, is particularly acute and cannot be dissolved.[55] Just what this vital tension between divine impassibility and Christ's suffering was meant to convey and how the issue played itself out in the major christological controversies will be the subject of the chapters that follow.

[55] W. S. Babcock drew attention to the centrality of this tension for patristic christology in 'The Christ of the Exchange', 330.

3

Docetism Resisted: Christ's Suffering is Real

> He who believes that God was born and suffered (*Qui natum passumque Deum* . . . *credit*) and sought again His Father's throne, and that He will come again from the skies, that on His return He may judge the living and the dead, sees, if he follows the rewards of Christ, that the inner court of heaven lies open to the holy martyrs.[1]

HAVING provided a preliminary assessment of the divine impassibility *remoto Christo,* we are now in a position to look more closely at how both divine impassibility and divine suffering interplayed in the major christological debates of the early church. To remind the reader, the view that dominates the current assessment of this issue splits the Fathers into two camps: the impassibilist majority and the passibilist minority, the former having fallen prey to the philosophical thought of their age, the latter being the harbingers of modern theological achievements. Quite often surprisingly meagre evidence is adduced to qualify a theologian as either impassibilist or passibilist.

In the Introduction I have argued that the approach that sees (im)-passibility as an either/or issue is misleading. Contrary to the view held by the proponents of the Theory of Theology's Fall into Hellenistic Philosophy, boldly theopaschite declarations (found in abundance in second- and third-century[2] and later patristic writings) do not by them-

[1] An epitaph on the grave of the Martyrs Felix and Philip, ascribed to Pope Damasus, *c.*360. H. P. V. Nunn, *Christian Inscriptions*, 60.

[2] Michael Slusser has conveniently assembled the following theopaschite passages in the Appendix to his dissertation: *Barnabas*, 5. 1, 5–6, 12–13; 7. 2–3; 14. 4; *2 Clement*, 1. 1–2; Ignatius, *Eph.* 1. 1; 7. 2; 18. 2; *Rom.* 6. 3; *Smyrn.* 1. 1–2; *Polyc.* 3. 2; *Martyrium Polycarpi*,

selves provide an interpretative key to the doctrine of the incarnation. On the contrary, they raise further questions. In every case when such provocative statements appear, it should be asked: how do they function within the theology of a given author? What do they communicate about the nature of Christ's divinity and about the role of the flesh assumed in the incarnation? Instead of merely assembling theopaschite statements as presumably conveying a biblical idea of divine involvement, we will do better if we consider both impassibility and passibility as corollary terms necessary for an adequate account of the incarnation.

Furthermore, the scholarly discussion of the issue is considerably impoverished by the fact that thus far it has remained only on the micro-level of those passages where (im)passibility is discussed or alluded to. What is neglected in the process is the logic of broader doctrinal developments, as well as the complex web of communal beliefs and practices leading to and feeding those developments.

The Tension between Christ's Divine Status and his Subjection to Human Suffering

Prior to debating the issues of whether and how God was involved in the suffering of Christ that dominated the christological controversies, the early Christians sang hymns to the Crucified, confessed the Crucified in baptism, ate the body of the Crucified in the Eucharist, expelled evil spirits by the power of the Crucified, reorganized their calendar around the events leading to his crucifixion and resurrection, and, in the case of the martyrs, followed the Crucified to the point of death.

As is widely acknowledged, several NT christological hymns, notably Philippians 2: 6–11 and Hebrews 1: 3–4, express in a few succinct statements three major themes: first, Christ's pre-existence, second, his earthly ministry with the emphasis on his suffering and crucifixion, and third, his exaltation and ascension to heaven.[3] Philippians 2 has proved to be a real *crux interpretum* both for the Fathers and for modern biblical

17. 2–3; *Ad Diognetum*, 9. 2; *Apocalypse of Baruch*, 4. 15; *Testament of Levi*, 4. 1; *Sibylline Oracles*, 6. 26; 8. 249–50; Tatian, *Or.* 13; Athenag., *Leg.* 21. 4; Tertullian, *De patientia*, 3. 2. 9; *Ad uxorem*, 2. 3. 1; *Adv. Marc.* 21. 16. 3; 2. 27. 2; *De carne Christi*, 5. 1; Clem., *Protr.* 10. 106. 4–5; *Paed.* 1. 8. 74. 4; *Strom.* 4. 7. 43. 2; 5. 11. 72. 3; 7. 2. 6. 5. To these may be added: Melito, *Peri Pascha*, 46, 66, 69–73, 79, 96, 100; frag. 13; frag. II. 3; II. 13–14; II. 21; Hippolytus, *Contra Noetum*, 18.

[3] Oscar Cullmann, *The Earliest Christian Confessions*; Jack T. Sanders, *The New Testament Christological Hymns*; Kelly, *Early Christian Creeds*, 18–23.

theologians. At the beginning of the hymn Christ is identified as the one who 'existed in the form of God'.[4] The next strophe (vv. 7–8), in sharp contrast to the first, speaks of his 'emptying himself', 'humbling himself', 'being found in human form', and 'becoming obedient to the point of death'. The last strophe, again in sharp contrast to the previous one, starts with a rather abrupt affirmation of Christ's glorification by the Father: 'Therefore God also highly exalted him', and ends with a confessional formula: 'Jesus Christ is Lord!' The tension is created by the fact that the person to whom the first line of the hymn ascribes what can be broadly defined as a divine status is described in the second strophe as undergoing such human experiences as suffering and death.[5]

The third strophe declares that 'at the name of Jesus every knee should bend', i.e. that the invocation of Jesus' name has the same effect as the invocation of the name of God, the obvious implication being that the exalted one has a divine status (broadly defined). The tension is stark and obvious: the person who emptied and humbled himself, suffered and died on the cross, that very person is worthy of worship and adoration.

The church's worship of the Crucified is also expressed in Thomas's confession, 'My Lord and my God!' (John 20: 28) made before the risen Jesus bearing the marks of his crucifixion. In Revelation 5: 12 we find a heavenly choir singing praises to the Crucified who is symbolically portrayed as a sacrificial animal: 'Worthy is the Lamb that was slaughtered to receive the power and wealth and wisdom and might and honour and glory and blessing!' The hymn in Heb. 1: 3–4 does not elaborate the theme of Christ's humiliation and death, alluding to them as 'purification for sins'. Nevertheless the basic structure of the hymn is the same: pre-existence, earthly ministry, and exaltation. Other NT hymns, such as John 1: 1–14 and Colossians 1: 15–20, do not develop the theme of exaltation, whereas 1 Timothy 3: 16 and 1 Peter 3: 18–22

[4] Modern scholarship has exposed several interpretative difficulties involved in this verse. The majority view, which I endorse here, sees this hymn as affirming that Christ was in some sense equal to God. For a good survey of different interpretations see R. P. Martin, *Carmen Christi*, and in R. P. Martin and B. J. Dodd (eds.), *Where Christology Began*. For discussion of the meaning of the hymn in the context of Hellenistic religions see Adela Yarbo Collins, 'The Worship of Jesus and The Imperial Cult', 243 ff. For the contemporary theological significance of various traditional interpretations see Sarah Coakley, '*Kenosis* and Subversion', 82–111.

[5] I use the expression 'divine status' in a sense that may or may not imply the ontological equality of Christ with God the Father, just as it neither implies, nor rules out subordination to the Father.

(also considered by many form critics to be a hymn) do not refer explicitly to Christ's pre-existence. Still, the fundamental tension between Christ's divine status and his subjection to the human experiences of birth and death is retained.

It is precisely because the above-mentioned hymns contain *in nuce* this vital tension that they came to occupy a pivotal role in the centuries-long christological debates that led to the formulation of the major confessional documents of the church. In the early church the hymns, with their emphasis upon Christ's divine status,[6] provided raw material for the creeds. The protocredal statements in turn informed the theological vision of the hymns.

The common features of early Christian hymns and pre-credal confessions have already become the subject of several scholarly works. In this regard, 1 Tim. 3: 16 has been discussed as a credal hymn of the early church.[7] In his study of *homologia* in the NT Vernon Neufeld has drawn attention to the fact that the liturgical hymn in Phil. 2: 5–11 is confessional in nature, ending with a protocredal statement, 'Jesus Christ is Lord.'[8] Along the same lines, Ernst Käsemann argued that Col. 1: 15–20 is a confession that was used in the ancient baptismal liturgy.[9]

More telling still are direct citations from the hymns found in the later creeds and expositions of faith. Thus, for example, an expression from the first strophe of the Colossians hymn, 'the firstborn of all creation', is literally reproduced in a pre-credal statement cited by Justin Martyr, the Antiochean exposition of faith (268), the Caesarean creed (end 3rd c.), and several fourth-century synodal creeds adopted in Antioch.[10] The following expression, 'in him all things in heaven and on earth were created, things visible and invisible... all things have been created

[6] See an observation of the author of *The Little Labyrinth*, quoted in Eusebius, *HE* 5. 28: 'And how many psalms and hymns, written by the faithful brethren from the beginning, celebrate Christ as the Word of God, speaking of Him as divine?' See also, Pliny the Younger, *Ep.* 10. 96. On this issue, see Jaroslav Pelikan, *Christian Theological Tradition* i. 173.

[7] O. R. Wilson, 'A Study of the Early Christian Credal Hymn of I Timothy 3: 16'.

[8] Vernon H. Neufeld, *The Earliest Christian Confessions*, 61, 67, 145.

[9] 'Eine urchristliche Taufliturgie', 133–48.

[10] Justin, *Dial.* 126. 1; Antiochean exposition of faith in Hahn and Hahn, 151; Dedication Council creeds, formula 2 (not in 1, 3, or 4), in Ath., *De synodis*, 23; Antiochean creed of 363, in John Cassian, *De incarnatione*, 6. 3; creed of Ancyra/Antioch (371), in Marcellus, *ekthesis*; Syrian creed of *c.* 380, in *Apostolic Constitutions* 7. 41; creed of Mopsuestia (late 4th c.), in Theodore of Mopsuestia, *A Commentary on the Nicene Creed*, acc. to reconstruction of J. Lebon. The relevant texts are reproduced in Kelly, *Early Christian Creeds*, 74, 186–8, 207, 268, 276.

through him and for him', with slight modifications appears with even greater frequency in the christological article of fourth-century synodal creeds and credal summaries of faith.[11] The same applies to the influence of John 1: 3 and Phil. 2: 5–11.

Even more important than material similarities is the fact that the structure of the second article of many early pre-credal statements and of all later synodal creeds repeats the same pattern of pre-existence, earthly ministry, and ascension. To give some idea of this pattern, let us consider a mid-second-century christological protocredal statement cited by Justin Martyr in his *Dialogue with Trypho* and used, as the context suggests, as an exorcistic formula:[12]

pre-existence	Son of God and 'firstborn of all creation'
earthly ministry	who was born through the virgin and became a man destined to suffer, and was crucified under Pontius Pilate [by our people], and died and rose again from the dead
exaltation	and ascended into heaven

Despite Justin's tendency towards subordinationism,[13] the tension between adjacent clauses is clearly conveyed by this protocredal statement. We will see in Chapter 5 that the addition of the clause 'of one essence with the Father' to the Caesarean creed at the Council of Nicaea further sharpened the already present tension between Christ's divine status and the human experiences and actions ascribed to him.[14]

As I will show in Chapter 6, the dispute between Cyril of Alexandria and Nestorius in part revolved around the interpretation of two key texts: the christological article of the Nicene creed and the Philippians hymn. The choice of Phil. 2 out of all the other passages in the NT was by no means accidental. The second article of the creed and Phil. 2 are twin brothers, exhibiting the same threefold pattern and containing the same tension. Origen paraphrased the tension involved in terms of a concise paradox: 'he who was in the form of God saw fit to be in the form of a servant; while he who is immortal dies, and the impassible

[11] See Kelly, *Early Christian Creeds*, 182–9.

[12] In *Apol.* 2. 6 Justin mentions exorcisms 'in the name of Jesus Christ who was crucified under Pontius Pilate'. The same invocation is twice quoted in the apocryphal *Acts of Peter and Andrew* (4th c.?), ANF xiii. 527.

[13] Justin, *Apol.* 1. 13.

[14] Cf. Daniel Liderbach, *Christ in the Early Christian Hymns*, esp. 83–6.

suffers, and the invisible is seen'.[15] The logical structure of this paradox remained to be spelled out in the christological debates of the next two centuries.

Later in this chapter we will explore the implications of this tension for second-century reflections upon the issue of divine (im)passibility. More specifically, we will trace the major theological contours of the church's resistance to the Docetic attempt to dissolve the tension. Before that, however, let us briefly turn to what may be called the ultimate confession of the Crucified, the confession of the martyrs.

Divine Suffering in the Theology of Martyrdom

The early Christian theology of martyrdom left a permanent imprint upon the liturgical practices of the church, upon the institution of monasticism, and upon the vision of the Christian life as an imitation of Christ.[16] In the words of Irenaeus of Lyons, Christians who die for Christ 'strive to follow the footprints of the Lord's passion, having become martyrs of the suffering One'.[17] Martyrs chose to imitate Christ in the most radical way possible: in suffering, humiliation, and death. St Ignatius of Antioch expressed this choice most powerfully in his letter to the church in Rome: 'Allow me to be the imitator of the sufferings of my God (πάθους τοῦ θεοῦ μου).'[18] This is the earliest patristic statement that makes God the subject of Christ's suffering on Golgotha. It is clear from the wider context of Ignatius' writings that he does not mean that God suffers perpetually.[19] The goal of martyrdom is neither masochistic enjoyment of suffering as such, nor the aspiration that by death one will enter into a condition of ceaseless suffering with Christ. Many exaggerations of modern passibilism would scandalize the ancient martyrs. For them, on the contrary, the imitation of Christ's sufferings

[15] *qui immortalis est, moritur et impassibilis patitur et invisibilis videtur.* Origen, *In Leviticum Homiliae*, 3. 1, trans. G. W. Barkley, *Origen on Leviticus*, 52. Cf. Augustine, *Sermo*, 212. 1; 215. 5.

[16] See W. H. C. Frend, *Martyrdom and Persecution in the Early Church*; Gordon Jeanes, 'Baptism Portrayed as Martyrdom in the Early Church', 158–76.

[17] Iren., *haer.* 3. 18. 5, trans. A. Roberts, ANF i. 447.

[18] Ignatius, *Rom.* 6. 3. Cf. *Eph.* 1. 1: 'Being as you [Ephesians] are imitators of God, once you took on new life through the blood of God (ἐν αἵματι θεοῦ) you completed perfectly the task so natural to you,' trans. Michael W. Holmes, *The Apostolic Fathers*, 137. Cf. Acts 20: 28; Gr. Naz., *Or.* 45. 22.

[19] Ignatius, *Eph.* 7. 2. See Jonathan Bayes, 'Divine ἀπάθεια in Ignatius of Antioch', 27, 29.

guaranteed participation in his glory in which all suffering ends (cf. Rom. 8: 18).

In his letter to the Ephesians Ignatius spelled out the already familiar credal tension between crucifixion and ascension in terms of opposed adjectives: 'There is only one physician, who is both flesh and spirit, born and unborn, God in man, true life in death, both from Mary and from God, first subject to suffering and then beyond it (πρῶτον παθητὸς καὶ τοτε ἀπαθής), Jesus Christ our Lord.'[20] Along the same lines, Justin Martyr wrote that Christ was 'first made subject to suffering, then returned to heaven'.[21]

It was believed that those who became partakers of Christ's resurrection also shared his impassibility. In the theology of martyrdom impassibility acquired the special sense of a state enjoyed by the blessed after the resurrection in which, according to St Paul, 'corruptible is changed into incorruptible' and all persecution and unjust suffering comes to an end. Justin Martyr wrote: 'The unjust and intemperate shall be punished in eternal fire, but the virtuous and those who lived like Christ shall dwell with God in a state that is free from suffering (ἐν ἀπαθείᾳ).'[22]

God will raise Christians 'incorruptible, impassible (ἀπαθεῖς) and immortal'.[23] It is noteworthy that impassibility here appears in tandem with other negative adjectives and conveys the basic idea that the resurrection state is very different from the tribulations of the present age. Justin is careful to distinguish impassibility from mere insensitivity which, as the persecutors contend, awaits every mortal after death.[24] Justin also points out that resurrection impassibility is far from the Cynic ideal of indifference that renders moral performance in this life irrelevant for the life in the world to come.[25]

The description of the resurrection state in terms of impassibility squarely limits Christ's suffering to the temporal framework of the incarnation. Several writers of the NT emphasize that Christ's sacrifice on the cross has a unique and unrepeatable ('once-for-all') character.[26] In addition, many pre-credal statements and all later synodal creeds affirm that Christ suffered *sub Pontio Pilato*, attaching a clearly defined point of historical reference to his death. In the eyes of the ancients, the tag 'in such and such year and month of the reign of such and such a governor'

[20] Ignatius, *Eph.* 7. 2, trans. Holmes, 141. [21] Justin, *Dial.* 34.

[22] *Apol.* 2. 6; cf. Athenag., *Leg.* 10. 5–6, 31. 4. 9; Gregory Thaumaturgus, *Fides non universa*, 2.

[23] *Dial.* 46. 7. [24] *Apol.* 1. 57; cf. 1.45. [25] *Apol.* 2. 3.

[26] Rom. 6: 9–10; 1 Pet. 3: 18; Heb. 7: 27; 9: 12, 26–8; 10: 10.

was a common way of dating events, including one's birth and death. Unlike the gods of the mysteries, Christ does not suffer and rise periodically with the change of seasons or with the arrival of harvest time.

However, the place accorded to Christ's suffering was such that it was bound to break the limitations of history. The theology of martyrdom very quickly linked the idea of imitation to that of participation in the passion of Christ. The difference between imitation and participation is substantial: while it is natural to imitate a past example, it is impossible to participate in a process that is not in some way continuing in the present. If communion in Christ's suffering is open to those who follow him, then Christ's suffering itself must be in some sense an enduring reality, extending beyond the boundaries of his earthly ministry.

We catch several glimpses of this idea in the NT.[27] For example, in Saul's vision on the road to Damascus, Christ implicitly identifies himself with the church in its present persecution: 'Saul, Saul, why do you persecute me... I am Jesus whom you persecute' (Acts 9: 4). To persecute the church is to persecute Christ himself. Converted, Saul once mentioned 'the marks of Jesus branded in his body' (Gal 6: 17), a tantalizing statement that inspired the medieval tradition of stigmata and passion mysticism.

Participation is reciprocal: just as the martyr partakes of the passion of Christ so also Christ shares the tortures of the martyr. Christ suffers in the martyr—this idea had a major impact upon the theology of martyrdom.[28] It is powerfully expressed in early third-century North African martyr-act, *Passio Perpetuae et Felicitatis*. This work tells the story of the martyrdom of five Christians who were apprehended and kept in prison, waiting to fight with the wild beasts in the amphitheatre. One of the arrested, a young woman named Felicitas, was pregnant and delivered unduly three days before the execution. A prison guard watching her birth pangs expressed a doubt about her ability to withstand greater suffering. Which doubt Felicitas met with the following remarkable reply: 'I suffer now myself that which is natural. But then, another will be in me who will suffer for me, because I am about to suffer for him.'[29]

[27] Phil. 3: 10; 2 Cor. 1: 5, 4: 10; Rom. 8: 17; Col. 1: 24. See Joseph Ton, *Suffering, Martyrdom, and Rewards in Heaven*, 138–41, 178–80.

[28] See B. Dehandschutter, 'Le Martyre de Polycarpe et le développement de la conception du martyre au deuxième siècle', 664–5.

[29] *Modo ego patior quod patior; illic autem alius erit in me qui patietur pro me, quia et ego pro illo passura sum. Passio Perpetuae*, 15.

The grandeur of these words lies in their dignified brevity. Christ will give strength to Felicitas on the day of her martyrdom, he will be intimately close to her. Even more, he will be suffering in her and for her. Yet, as Felicitas is keen to point out to the prison guard, Christ does not share in all kinds of her sufferings. If Pilate happened to have a headache on the day of crucifixion, Christ would not suffer in him or for him, since the procurator's suffering would be purely physiological, he would 'suffer what there was to suffer', *patior quod patior.* Likewise, Felicitas' birth pangs are natural and involuntary. Her martyrdom, in contrast, is chosen deliberately and purposefully. Christ suffers in those whose torment has as its ultimate goal the closest possible union with the Lord.[30]

The martyr's attachment to Christ at the point of death is so profound that she is mystically identified with him. This is beautifully portrayed in another account of martyrdom, *The Letter of the Churches of Vienne and Lyons.*[31] The anonymous author describes how the onlookers present at the execution of Blandina, a 'frail and delicate female slave', contemplate with amazement the following transformation:

Blandina was hung up fastened to a stake and exposed, as food to the wild beasts that were let loose against her. Because she appeared as if hanging on a cross and because of her earnest prayers, she inspired the combatants with great zeal. For they looked on this sister in her combat and saw, with their bodily eyes, Him who was crucified for them, that He might persuade those who trust in Him that every one who suffers for the glory of Christ has eternal communion with the living God. When none of the wild beasts at that time touched her, she was taken down from the stake and taken back to prison. She was preserved for another contest. By gaining the victory in more conflicts, she might make the condemnation of the Crooked Serpent unquestionable, and she might encourage the brethren. Though she was an insignificant, weak, and despised woman, yet she was clothed with the great and invincible athlete Christ. On many occasions she had overpowered the enemy, and in the course of the contest had woven for herself the crown of incorruption.[32]

[30] The union with Christ was believed to be achieved at the point of the martyr's death: 'at the very hour of their tortures the most noble martyrs of Christ were no longer in the flesh, but rather the Lord stood by them and conversed with them', *Martyrium Polycarpi*, 2, trans. M. H. Shepherd, 149–50.

[31] The martyr-acts describe a local persecution in south France which took place in 177. Most scholars agree that the letter is authentic. See A. Chagny, *Les Martyrs de Lyon de 177.*

[32] Eusebius, *HE* 5. 1. 41–2, trans. Bruno Chenu *et al.*, 47–8.

So complete is Blandina's identification with the Crucified that those present look at the stake and see the cross, they watch Blandina and Christ appears before them. It is noteworthy that in both cases Christ's suffering has an element of active endurance. Christ does not multiply the suffering of the martyr by adding his own suffering to it. On the contrary, Christ strengthens the martyr by taking her suffering upon himself. He mystically substitutes his body in place of the martyr's body. In Felicitas' words: 'another will be in me who will suffer for me'. In contrast to Whitehead's portrait of God as 'a fellow-sufferer who understands', in the scene of Blandina's death Christ offers more than just a helpless commiseration. His suffering gives the power to withstand torture. Christ fights for the martyr against Satan and helps her to conquer the enemy. Paradoxically, Christ's passion in the martyr turns out to be his victorious action on her behalf.

The same letter preserves another account of remarkable endurance. The deacon Sanctus, arrested by the authorities together with the other Christians, was put through unbearable torture, including the application of red-hot iron to 'the most delicate parts' of his body. The narrator explains how Sanctus was able to endure everything because 'it was Christ who suffered in him and did great wonders, destroying the enemy and showing as a pattern to the rest that there was nothing terrible where there is the love of the Father, nothing painful where there is the glory of Christ'.[33] The author tells us that, to the surprise of the cruel authorities, Sanctus' second torture became a source of miraculous cure for the wounds left by the first one. In this account, Christ's presence in the martyr brings about not just miraculous endurance, but healing.

Thus, the early Christian theology of martyrdom offers the insight that Christ's suffering (in the qualified sense of providing power to endure persecution to those who suffer for his sake) extends beyond the historical limits of the incarnation onto the experience of the martyrs. This idea received its development in the earliest surviving paschal sermon, composed by Melito, bishop of Sardis. According to Melito, the divine Logos suffers not only in the martyrs of the present, but also in the patriarchs and prophets of the past:

It is he who in many endured many things: it is he that was murdered in Abel, and bound in Isaac, and exiled in Jacob, and sold in Joseph, and exposed in Moses, and slain in the lamb, and persecuted in David, and dishonoured in the prophets. It is he that was enfleshed in a virgin, that was hanged on a tree, that

[33] Eusebius, *HE* 5. 1. 23, trans. Chenu, 47.

was buried in the earth, that was raised from the dead, that was taken up to the heights of the heavens.[34]

Here the Logos's suffering with the just of OT times is woven into a description of the key points of the incarnation, which are enumerated in the second article of the early creeds. That the Logos spoke through the prophets and apostles was a common conviction of early fathers.[35] But Melito develops this idea and considers not only the speech acts, but also the sufferings of the Logos as transcending the temporal boundaries of the incarnation and extending out into the whole of salvation history. The theology of martyrdom made a similar move in affirming Christ's suffering in the martyrs. It would be premature to dismiss this move as a piece of poetic imagination.

In Melito's surviving works and fragments divine involvement in salvation history is held in creative tension with the description of God in negative attributes, including immortality and impassibility. Melito is far from advocating an unqualified theopaschitism. According to Melito, the impassible Logos 'accepted the passions of the suffering one through the body which was able to suffer, and dissolved the passions of the flesh'.[36] As in the martyr-acts, the suffering of the Logos occurs in and through the human body.

The Fathers, including Melito, were concerned to point out a crucial dissimilarity between the passion of Christ on the cross that was first and foremost 'for us' and 'for our sins' and the persecution of the saints that bore witness to the passion of Christ, but was not redemptive in the same sense. Augustine, for example, emphasized that 'No martyr's blood has been shed for the remission of sins.'[37] In the later christological controversies, it became expedient to distinguish as sharply as possible between the Logos' indwelling of the saints and prophets of the past without sharing in their experiences and the Logos' becoming incarnate in Christ and participating in the human condition to the uttermost. Thus, for example, Athanasius of Alexandria took pains to correct certain unidentified heretics in his letter to Epictetus written *c.*371:[38]

[34] *Peri Pascha*, 69–70. Cf. *Peri Pascha*, 59; frag. 15. 18–27; new frag. II. 2–3, trans. S. G. Hall (with slight changes), *On Pascha and Fragments*, 37–8.

[35] Justin, *Apol.* 1. 62, 64; Origen, *Princ.* 1. Praef. 1 develops allusion in Heb. 11: 24.

[36] *Peri Pascha*, 66.

[37] Augustine, *Tract. in Joan.* 84; Leo the Great, *Ep.* 84, 97.

[38] For dating see Hanson, *Search,* 420.

Accordingly, it is no good venture of theirs to say that the Word of God came into a certain holy man; for this was true of each of the prophets and of the other saints, and on that assumption He would clearly be born and die in the case of each one of them. But this is not so, far be the thought . . . We are deified not by partaking of the body of some man, but by receiving the Body of the Word Himself.[39]

We may surmise that these legitimate theological concerns contributed to the fact that Christ's suffering in the martyrs and the persecution of the Logos with the prophets and righteous of the past remained somewhat isolated theologoumena in the early patristic writings.

According to a more generally accepted view, the persecution of the OT righteous served as a prefiguration of the passion of Christ.[40] This interpretation does not require an extension of the sufferings of the Logos beyond the limits of the incarnation into the OT history. It was Melito, among many others, who elaborated with painstaking poetic detail a vision that the events of the OT serve as a preliminary sketch, as a model of the things that will become a reality in the NT. The idea of prefiguration, of foreshadowing, rather than that of actual participation became widely accepted in patristic theology. In her worship of the Crucified the church wanted to make one thing clear: God is faithful to his redemptive purposes in history even if that entails assuming fragile humanity and dying the death of a slave on the cross.

Pagan Reactions to Worship of the Crucified God

It is precisely the latter point that proved to be a stumbling block for pagans, simple folk and philosophically minded alike. Even those pagans who knew precious little about Christianity recognized that the figure of the Crucified held a central significance for the members of this strange secret society. Pagan ridicule and disgust at Christians is powerfully expressed by a mid-second-century graffito, discovered in 1857 on the wall in the Palace of the Caesars on the Palatine Hill. This ancient caricature sketchily portrays a boy on his knees before a crucified figure with a donkey's head. The words scratched below the graffito read: 'Alexamenos worshipping his god.' The caricature itself is a fruit of a curious confusion. It was gossiped around among antagonistically disposed pagans that the Jews worshipped an ass and that they used to have

39 Ath., *Ep.* 61. 2. Cf. *Ar.* 3. 31 and *Ep.* 59. 11.

40 Jean Danielou, *From Shadows to Reality*.

a donkey's head hanging in the holy of holies in the Temple.[41] According to Tertullian, later the accusations of onolatry (ass-worship) were directed at Christians.[42] We may surmise that the scribbler of our graffito intended to kill two birds with one stone: Christians were ridiculed together with the Jews for worshipping the Jewish God nailed to the cross.[43]

For more refined tastes a second-century satirist Lucian wrote a lampoon, *The Passing of Peregrinus* in which he mocked the Christian veneration of martyrs. The book painted Christians as naïve and gullible followers of an imposter, Peregrinus. Lucian remarked in passing that Peregrinus was revered by his followers 'as a god... next after that other whom they still worship, the man crucified in Palestine'.[44] The report is again confused. Lucian made Christ into a divinized, martyred hero, despite the insistence of the apologists that worship belongs to God alone, whereas martyrs should be piously remembered—nothing more. But Lucian was not in the least concerned about making such subtle distinctions.[45]

More religiously serious pagans felt that their *pietas* was itself offended by the new sect's object of worship. Minucius Felix recorded such pagan indignation: 'He who explains their ceremonies by reference to a man punished by extreme suffering for his wickedness, and to the deadly wood of the cross, appropriates fitting altars for reprobate and wicked men, that they may worship what they deserve.'[46] Those who worship

41 Tacitus, *Annals*, 1. 5. 3. 4; Tertullian, *Apology*, 16; *Ad nationes*, 1. 14. See John J. Gager, *The Origins of Antisemitism*, 46, 79.

42 Tertullian reports that around 197 an apostate Jew once appeared on the streets of Carthage carrying a figure robed in a toga with the ears and hoofs of an ass, bearing a label: *Deus Christianorum Onocoetes* ('the God of the Christians begotten of an ass'). Tertullian adds with indignation that 'the crowd believed this infamous Jew,' *Ad nationes*, 1. 14.

43 There is a curious Christian (?) amulet with ass and foal, bearing an inscription: *D[ominus] N[oster] Ie[sus] Chr[istu]s Dei Filius*. It could be a symbolic representation of triumphal entrance in Jerusalem. The amulet is dated *c*.400. See Thomas F. Mathews, *The Clash of Gods*, 49–51.

44 *De morte Peregrini*, 11–16. The Basilidean Gnostics endorsed a pagan contention that those who affirm the reality of crucifixion proclaim 'the doctrine of a dead man', *The Second Treatise of the Great Seth*, 7. 60. 22. See also a rather obscure passage from the *Apocalypse of Peter*, 7. 74. 13–15: 'And they [the non-Gnostic Christians] will cleave to the name of a dead man, thinking that they will become pure.'

45 A similar misconception was shared by the pagan authorities who refused to give the body of St Polycarp back to his admirers, fearing that the Christians would 'abandon the Crucified and begin worshipping this one [i.e. Polycarp]', *Mart. Polyc.* 17. 2, trans. Shepherd, 155.

46 Minucius Felix, *Octavius*, 9. 3.

the Crucified deserve to be crucified!—this is the battle cry of a heart burning with piety. The pagans were disgusted with the appalling innovations that the atheistic Galileans introduced into the traditional ways of imaging the divine realm. Many believed in good faith that the Christians provoked the jealous anger of the Olympians (together with the rest of pantheon) by being unreservedly attached to the crucified God.[47]

On the popular level the clash was between the two modes of piety, the old and the new, while on a second, more reflective level, the conflict was between the Christian revelation and divergent philosophical accounts of divine involvement. More discriminating pagans pinpointed exactly where the heart of the offence lay: 'The gods are not hostile to you because you worship the Omnipotent God but because you maintain that a man, born of a human being, and one who suffered the penalty of crucifixion, which even to the lowest of men is a disgraceful punishment, was God ...'[48]

To claim that the Omnipotent God was crucified seemed both impious and inconsistent with the nature of God. The charge of inconsistency, although less popular, was particularly pressed by the philosophers. A curious fifth-century Nestorian fabrication of a letter from the famous Neoplatonist Hypatia to Cyril of Alexandria, furnishes a suitable example of what the common charge of inconsistency could have looked like:

> The pagans, those poorly informed and those who are wise, found an opportunity to accuse this doctrine [Christianity] and call it inconsistent, for the evangelist said, 'No one has at any time seen God.' How, therefore, they [pagans] say, do you say that God was crucified? They say, how was he affixed to the cross, who has not been seen? How did he die, and how was he buried?[49]

This telling observation about a common pagan perception of Christianity could be based upon Nestorius' own complaint that 'the heathen indeed are not content to name Christ God because of the suffering of the body and the cross, and the death'.[50]

47 On this issue, see Robert L. Wilken, 'Pagan Criticism of Christianity', 117–34, esp. 123 and his later book, *The Christians as the Romans Saw Them*, 48–67.

48 Arnobius of Sicca, *The Case Against the Pagans*, trans. G. E. McCracken, 1. 36, p. 84. Cf. Augustine, *Enarrationes in Psalmos*, 40. 4 (38. 451). For a discussion of this point see Babcock, 'Christ of the Exchange', 106 n. 1.

49 In Cyril, *Ep.* 88. 1 (spurious letter of Hypatia to Cyril), trans. J. I. McEnerney, *St Cyril of Alexandria: Letters 51–110*, 130.

50 Nestorius, *Liber Heraclidis*, 1. 1. 1, trans. Driver, *Nestorius*, 7.

The fictional Hypatia admits later in the letter that when she learned about Nestorius' teaching she immediately wrote to him, saying: 'the questions of the pagans are solved'.[51] Presumably, Nestorius' explanation, that it was a man who suffered and was seen on the cross, while the divinity remained invisible and impassible, made perfect sense to the pagan intelligentsia. We should, however, beware of making too much of this forgery.[52]

A straightforward way of taming the offence of the cross was open to the church: as long as Christians did not ascribe a divine status to their founder, they deserved pity at best and ridicule at worst as overly gullible followers of a teacher with an ass's head. If the Christians chose this way, no Roman governor would persecute them as subversive sectarians. If the Christians agreed not to place the Crucified on the same plane as the immortal gods, their claims would cease to threaten pagan piety. Much to the chagrin of pagans, the majority of the Christian schools did not embrace this solution. They kept impiously insisting that 'a man who lived a most infamous life and died a most miserable death was a god'.[53] This dictum of Celsus summarizes a common pagan bewilderment at the theological indecency of Christianity.[54]

Many pagans shared the view of Celsus that Jesus did not handle his crucifixion in a God-befitting manner: 'If he was really so great he ought, in order to display his divinity (εἰς ἐπίδειξιν θεότητος), to have disappeared suddenly from the cross.'[55] Discussing this point, Origen compares Celsus' reaction to that of the Jews who stood near the cross and reviled Christ, shouting at him to come down. It should be noted that Celsus offers a subtle, but significant modification of this same 'divine escapism' motif: in order to 'display his divinity' Christ should have disappeared from the cross, not just dismounted before all who

51 *Ep.* 88. 2.

52 The spurious origin of this letter is betrayed by an obvious anachronism: Hypatia died in 415, thirteen years before Nestorius became the patriarch of Constantinople. See Emilien Lamirande, 'Hypatie, Synésios et la fin des dieux', 467–89; Sarolta A. Takács, 'Hypatia's Murder—the Sacrifice of a Virgin and its Implications', 47–62.

53 Origen, *Contra Celsum*, 7. 53.

54 Ibid. 4. 1–10, 14–16; 5. 1–5. Cf. also emperor Julian's indignant remark: '[T]his his new Galilean God, whom he [Diodore of Tarsus] declares eternal because of a fable, was by his ignominious death and burial destitute of that Godhead which Diodore invents.' Quoted by Fecundus of Hemiane, *Pro defens. trium capit.* 4. 2 (*PL* 67: 621A–B), trans. Grillmeier, *Christ in Christian Tradition*, i. 353.

55 Origen, *Contra Celsum*, 2. 68. Celsus seems to suggest an essentially Docetic solution to the scandal of the cross without being aware of the Docetic strand within Christianity. See ibid. 2. 16, 23.

stood around. The sudden disappearance of the deity from the scene was not uncommon in stories about divine visitation throughout the world. It was precisely a sudden miraculous disappearance that was taken to be revelatory of the true identity of an otherwise incognito divine visitor.[56]

The Function of the Divine Impassibility in Docetism

The 'escapist' way of taming the scandal of the cross found a great number of adherents. Already a century before Celsus the church was pressed to oppose emerging Docetic interpretations of the gospel narratives. Docetism narrowly defined is the view that the founder of Christianity had only an apparent, not a real human body and was subject to the human experiences of birth, fatigue, thirst, hunger, suffering, death, and the like in appearance only, in reality being immune from them. Docetism, understood more broadly, includes views that divide the hero of the canonical gospels into the two subjects, one divine, the other merely human: the title 'Christ' tending to be ascribed to the divine subject, and the title 'Jesus' to the human one.[57] According to this two-subject version of Docetism, 'Jesus' was the subject of the human experiences, reported in the gospels, whereas 'Christ' was either not implicated in those experiences at all or implicated only putatively. Let us note that the broader version of Docetism embraces a variety of speculations about the nature of Jesus' body, including the view that 'Jesus' possessed a real human body (which is precisely what is ruled out by the narrow definition of Docetism). However, as Michael Slusser has pointed out in a definitive essay on the extent and definition of Docetism, there is a fundamental agreement between these two versions of this heresy:

[56] See on this subject Edwin Yamauchi, 'The Crucifixion and Docetic Christology', 1–20; 'Anthropomorphism in Hellenism and Judaism', 213. Curiously, the canonical gospels present us with several examples of disappearance stories. For example, Christ's escaping a sure death by stoning in Luke 4: 29–30. It is important to note, however, that this particular disappearance does not function for Luke as divinity-revealing (although it forms a part of an overall plan of Christ's going to meet his death in Jerusalem). In Luke 24: 13–35 Christ dines incognito with the two disciples and is recognized by them 'in the breaking of the bread' (traditionally interpreted as an allusion to the Eucharistic celebration), and upon being identified, vanishes from their sight. Again, for Luke the breaking of the bread, not the disappearance, becomes identity-revealing.

[57] There were exceptions to this rule. Valentinians, according to Tertullian, held that the heavenly Jesus descended upon Christ in the sacrament of baptism in the likeness of a dove, *Adv. Valent.* 27.

In the view of Irenaeus, the malice of those who taught a 'seeming' Christ lay in their denial that the heavenly Savior was ever really involved in the material and human realities of this creation as we experience them. This denial was no less complete in the case of doctrines which separated the heavenly Christ from the earthly Jesus than it was in the case of doctrines which held that Jesus was a phantom.[58]

We will follow Slusser in classifying the two-subjects Gnostic christology as broadly Docetic, despite the fact that some of those who endorsed this view treated Jesus' body as more or less real.

The origins of Docetic beliefs in Christianity are obscure. Hippolytus knew a Gnostic sect called *Docetae*.[59] Docetic tendencies were widely shared by many (although not by all) Gnostic groups.[60] At the same time Docetic reinterpretations of the gospels were not restricted to the early Christian Gnostics.[61] R. M. Grant argued with great persuasiveness that Docetism, especially its earlier forms, owed as much to heterodox Jewish sectarian thought as to Graeco-Oriental speculation.[62] This observation delivers yet another blow to the interpretation favoured by the Fall of Theology into Hellenistic Philosophy theorists who sharply contrast the God of intertestamental Judaism with the God of the philosophers. The actual interplay of different proposals about the divine involvement, as we saw in Chapter 1, was much more intricate.

Docetism, whatever its origins, posed the fundamental question that concerns us in this study: which actions and experiences ascribed to Jesus Christ in the gospels may be deemed fitting for a divine visitor from the heavenly realms? That Christ was indeed such a visitor was not debated by the Gnostics. Furthermore, the Docetists broadly agreed that certain human experiences of Jesus Christ were not God-befitting and that a thorough reinterpretation of the gospel narratives was in order.

Just how the story of the gospels had to be revised depended partly upon the guiding considerations and partly upon the ingenuity of a given

[58] Michael Slusser, 'Docetism: A Historical Definition', 172; 'Theopaschite Expressions in Second-Century Christianity', 222–8. Slusser has in mind Iren., *haer.* 3. 11. 3; 16. 1; 18. 3–6; 22. 1–2. For a different, but compatible classification of various Docetic strands see Simone Pétrement, *A Separate God,* 144–56.

[59] Hippolytus, *Ref.* 8. 3. 25. Cf. Clem., *Strom.* 7. 17.

[60] e.g. Cainites ((Ps.-?) Tertullian, *Adversus omnes haereses*, 2. The groups that produced the *Tripartite Tractate*, 1. 5, and *The Letter of Peter to Philip*, 7. 2, reflect non-Docetic strands in Gnosticism.

[61] Different Docetic interpretations of the crucifixion were shared by e.g. the Marcionites, Manicheans, some Muslims (*Quran*, 4. 157), the Medieval Bogomils, and the mysterious Aphathartodocetae mentioned by John Damascene (*De haer.* 84; *PG* 94: 754 ff.).

[62] R. M. Grant, 'Gnostic Origins and the Basilidians of Irenaeus', 121–5.

Docetic group. As far as guiding considerations are concerned, no rigid criteria were established. The debate on the authority and content of the apostolic tradition formed a suitable framework. The Gnostics appealed to secret revelations that went back, as they alleged, to the time of the apostles. Most Gnostic teachers rejected the church's rule of faith and claimed to have access to esoteric apostolic tradition.[63] The church Fathers argued that the Gnostics could not offer a reliable evidence of apostolic succession and therefore could not claim the authority of apostolic tradition for their speculations.[64] The details of this debate need not concern us here.

In part, the Docetic reinterpretations were driven by a non-theological concern for the greater acceptance of the Christian message in pagan society. A slave's death on the cross was unanimously regarded as shameful and degrading. There was nothing heroic or inspiring about such a death, so ran a common pagan verdict.[65] These sentiments are expressed, for example, in a Basilidean account of the crucifixion which puts the following confession into the mouth of Christ:

> And the plan which they devised about me to release their Error and their senselessness—I did not succumb to them as they had planned. But I was not afflicted at all. Those who were there punished me. And I did not die in reality but in appearance, lest I be put to *shame* by them because these are my kinsfolk. I removed the *shame* from me and I did not become fainthearted in the face of what happened to me at their hands. I was about to succumb to fear, and I suffered according to their sight and thought, in order that they may never find any word to speak about them. For my death which they think happened, (happened) to them in their error and blindness, since they nailed their man unto their death. For their Ennoias did not see me, for they were deaf and blind.[66]

The writer proceeds to explain how Christ vanished from the scene of the crucifixion 'altering shapes' and how all those who were witnessing the event, in a fit of self-delusion crucified Simon of Cyrene, the bearer of the cross.[67] Meanwhile, the triumphant Christ invisibly present behind the scene, was 'laughing at their ignorance'. It is clear that the

[63] Tertullian, *De prescr.* 19; Ptolemy, *Letter to Flora* in Epiphanius, *Haer.* 33. 7. 9.

[64] Iren., *haer.* 3. 2–5; Origen, *Princ.* 1. Praef. 2.

[65] For valuable quotations from Cicero and Seneca see Martin Hengel, *Crucifixion*, 30–1, 89.

[66] *The Second Treatise of the Great Seth*, 7. 2; emphasis added. Cf. Iren., *haer.* 1. 24. 4.

[67] This motif is corroborated by the account of Iren., *haer.* 1. 24. 4. Let us note that Hippolytus' account is different: he ascribes to the Basilideans a version of the 'two-subject' christology, according to which a bodily part of Jesus suffered, and the spiritual part remained immune from suffering, *Ref.* 7. 20. 9–12.

'divine deception' scenarios were created by the Gnostics to remove the shame of crucifixion. Despite the intricacies of the Gnostic cosmology and Christology, the undergirding conviction, shared by Celsus and the satirists, was clear: God-befitting actions should not overstep the boundaries of social propriety. Such was a minimal, yet unavoidable test that a pagan account of divine involvement had to pass.

Along similar lines, the Docetic segment in the apocryphal *Acts of John* narrates how at the time of the crucifixion the apostle John fled to the Mount of Olives and hid himself in a cave, being unable to bear the sight of Jesus' suffering. John was weeping when he suddenly heard the voice of the Lord, revealing to him the true nature of things: 'John, to the multitude down below in Jerusalem I am being crucified, and pierced with lances and reeds, and gall and vinegar is given me to drink. But to you I am speaking, and pay attention to what I say.'[68] This announcement was followed by a vision of a cosmic 'cross of light', which, according to John's invisible interlocutor, had various names: Word, Mind, Jesus, Christ, Door, Way, Son, Father, Spirit, and so on. The mysterious voice went on to explain that there is a profound difference between the cross of light which 'marked off things transient and inferior' and the illusory wooden cross of Golgotha:

> But this [the cross of light] is not the cross of wood which you will see when you go down here, neither am I he who is upon the cross, whom now you do not see, but only hear a voice. I was reckoned to be what I am not, not being what I was to many others; but they [orthodox Christians] will call me something else, which is vile and not worthy of me... Therefore I have suffered none of the things which they will say of me.[69]

As the passage from the *Acts of John* makes clear, in some Gnostic teachings the cross became a symbol of higher cosmic realities and lost any connection with the historical event of Jesus' humiliating execution. Apart from considerations of social impropriety of crucifixion, there were deeply ingrained theological convictions that made their stamp

[68] *Acts of John*, 97, trans. J. K. Elliott, *The Apocryphal New Testament*, 320. This work was most probably written in late 2nd c. Only chaps. 87–105, which form a self-contained body of material, exhibit clear Docetic influences.

[69] *Acts of John*, 98–9, trans. Elliott, 320–1. Cf. *The (First) Apocalypse of James*, 5. 31. 1–30. We must note, however, that the author of the *Acts of John* makes every effort to reconcile his obviously Docetic account of crucifixion with the reality of persecution and martyrdom. In the same work its apocryphal author, the imprisoned apostle John, assures his readers that the divine Lord 'himself suffers with the sufferers' and speaks about piercing, wounding, death, and blood of the Logos. See *Acts of John*, 101; 103.

upon the Docetic reinterpretations of the passion narrative. In any Docetic system one deals with an intricate web of presuppositions about the Godhead, cosmos, human beings, salvation, and Christology. The theological views of the Gnostic groups defy clear-cut classification partly due to insufficient evidence and partly due to the nature of the writings themselves.[70]

The Gnostics left us the most daring flights of speculative fancy which continue to fascinate the learned.[71] They indulged in the most exalted apophaticism on a par with that of Numenius, Albinus, and Plotinus.[72] Together with the later Platonists, the Gnostics tested the logical limits of the language of negative theology. For Basilides, for example, the supreme God was unoriginate, beyond knowing and beyond being, beyond words and beyond any description. In this context the negative adjective 'impassible' was quite often applied to the divine realm. It was a common dualistic conviction, running through most (but not all) Gnostic writings, that the divine and spiritual entities could not come in direct contact with matter and could not be subject to the decay and corruption associated with bodily substances. It was widely accepted among the Gnostics that matter and body were intrinsically evil and therefore beyond redemption. Gnosticism is characterized by a rift between creation, conceived in emanationist terms and ascribed to the evil activity of an imperfect deity, and redemption, regarded as a work of a higher deity. Given these background beliefs, it was supremely inappropriate and soteriologically pointless for the impassible being to be implicated in the experiences of birth, suffering, and death.

The most radical Docetists claimed that the divine saviour assumed flesh in appearance only, either denying the reality of Christ's body altogether, or questioning the fact that his body was human.[73] According to Origen, it was precisely an overriding concern to protect the absolute divine impassibility that led to the denial of the reality of crucifixion: 'Those who introduced Docetism imagined him [the saviour] to be impassible (τὸ ἀπαθὲς) and superior to such mishaps as humbling

[70] Davies, 'The Origins of Docetism', suggested a classification of the types of Docetism according to one of the four dominant factors: doctrine of the Godhead, cosmology, anthropology, and Christology. This classification accounts well for the variety of grounds on which the reality of Christ's human experiences was denied.

[71] See Richard Smith, 'The Modern Relevance of Gnosticism'.

[72] H. A. Wolfson, 'The Negative Attributes in Plotinus and the Gnostic Basilides', 121–5.

[73] According to Epiphanius, *Haer.* 41, this view was advanced by Cerdo the Syrian.

himself 'unto death' and becoming obedient ever to the cross . . .'[74] The experiences that were predicated of the (broadly defined) divine subject in Phil. 2 were dismissed by the Docetists as putative. Such was the Docetic 'solution' to the tension inherent in the hymn.

Another version of Docetism, mentioned in the beginning of this section, was concerned to preserve the divine impassibility at the expense of dividing the figure of the gospels into two distinct subjects, identified as spiritual and fleshy, heavenly and terrestrial, the impassible and the passible one. The Docetists interpreted the impassibility of the divine subject as entailing a complete separation from the unseemly human experiences of the human subject, particularly those of birth and death.[75] Cerinthus, among others, taught that Jesus was a real human being, born of Joseph and Mary, and that 'after his [Jesus'] baptism Christ descended upon him in the form of a dove, from the power that is over all things, and then he proclaimed the unknown Father and accomplished miracles. But at the end Christ separated again from Jesus, and Jesus suffered and was raised again, but Christ remained impassible, since he was pneumatic.'[76]

The teaching of the Ophites, as reported by Irenaeus, also involved the descent of the heavenly Christ (accompanied by Sophia) upon the earthly Jesus during baptism and Christ's separation from Jesus just before the crucifixion.[77] Certain Valentinians, according to Irenaeus, went further in their speculations and split the subject of the gospels into four parts. They declared that only the psychic and corporeal (also called 'ineffable') parts suffered, whereas the 'spiritual seed' and 'the Soter' parts remained immune from suffering, having separated from the other two parts at the trial of Pilate.[78]

Although each of the four parts of Christ played its own role in the Valentinian cosmology, the four-part christology, as it functions in this account of the crucifixion, is no different from the two-subjects christ-

[74] Origen, *Comment. in evangelium Joannis*, 10. 25(4). Cf. Iren., *haer.* 3. 16. 1: '[Unidentified Gnostics] say that He merely suffered in outward appearance, being naturally impassible.'

[75] Iren., *haer.* 3. 11. 7.

[76] *Christum autem impassibilem perseverasse, existentem spiritalem.* Iren., *haer.* 1. 26. 1, trans. A. Roberts, ANF i. 352. A similar story was spread about Simon Magus by his adherents. *Haer.* 1. 23. 3. Irenaeus, in general, is a fairly reliable source of information about Gnosticism. On Irenaeus' reliability see F. M. M. Sagnard, *La Gnose Valentinienne et le témoignage de saint Irénée*, 94–103.

[77] Iren., *haer.* 1. 30. 12–13; 3. 16. 6; 3. 16. 9; 3. 17. 4; 4. 2. 4.

[78] Ibid. 1. 1. 7–8. Tertullian, *Adv. Valent.* 27. On Valentinian christology see G. A. G. Stroumsa, *Another Seed.*

ology, since it states that two parts remained impassible, while the other two suffered in a rather grotesque manner.

Since our survey is not intended to be exhaustive but only illustrative of the variations in the two-subjects Docetic christology, further examples of this view need not be adduced here. It is crucial for us that the divine impassibility functioned in all these strands of Docetism in a similar way: it led to the denial of any divine association with the unseemly human experiences of birth, suffering, and death.

The Church's Rejection of Docetism

Let us turn our attention to a curious feature of certain brands of Gnostic theology that put substantial limitations upon their use of the term 'impassible' with reference to the divine realm. Gnosticism, particularly in its Basilidean and Valentinian versions, is characterized by a peculiar juxtaposition of two conflicting types of theological discourse. The first type, already discussed at length, was represented by a highly developed form of apophatic theology. The second type was bluntly anthropopathic and drew rather indiscriminately upon Jewish sectarian thought, old Homeric myths, and the stories of the mystery cults. Unfortunately, much of the youthful *gaiété* of the old sagas faded away under the influence of the decadent spirit of the ageing Hellenism! Unlike the heroes of Homer, 'young in their souls',[79] the Gnostic aeons were no longer merrily consorting, artfully stealing, frankly deceiving, and viciously fighting against each other. Instead, the Gnostic deities fornicated, deceived, and schemed against each other in a rather psychopathic manner.[80] Troubled residents of the Pleroma were afflicted with fear, distress, and insatiable desire—a grim, but realistic picture of the subconsciousness of the 'age of anxiety',[81] so profoundly alienated from its youthful pagan past.

Divine *pathē* were not just an archaic rudiment of the Gnostic cosmology, something one could easily dispense with. The existence of gendered aeons was explained in terms of passionate copulation between different pairs of parent deities. According to the Valentinian myth, an aeon called Sophia was liberated from primary evil passions which then generated the substances that constituted the material

[79] Plato, *Timaeus*, 23c. [80] Hippolytus, *Ref.* 5. 26.

[81] The expression is taken from the title of E. R. Dodds's work *Pagans and Christians in an Age of Anxiety*.

world.[82] The belief that different passions, e.g. *phobos* and *eros*, were instrumental in bringing gods into existence, was a part of the Homeric theogony. The Valentinians reworked this belief rather ingeniously and developed a full-blooded cosmology on the basis of it.

By blending the language of the old myths about the passionate escapades of the gods with the apophatic method (the very method that was designed to purge the divine realm from unworthy emotions and to remove gender qualifications!), the Gnostics created a confusion in the rules of proper theological discourse and threatened to deprive God-befitting language of all meaningful application. If the Gnostics had just resorted to the old language of the myths, they would not be so dangerous. But the two types of discourse, jumbled together, created an explosive mixture. Plotinus was scandalized and embarked upon a lengthy treatise in refutation.[83] It was all the more disturbing that some Gnostic ideas appeared to be dangerously close caricatures of Plotinus' own views, a point that A. D. Nock summarized in an aphorism that Gnosticism was 'Platonism run wild'.[84]

Irenaeus was the first to point out an inconsistency in those Gnostic systems that both upheld the most elevated view of the divine impassibility that led to Docetism and ascribed the worst conceivable passions and crimes to the inhabitants of the Pleroma:

> They [the Valentinians] attribute the things that befall human beings to the Father of all, who, so they say, is also unknown to all. They deny that he himself made the world, lest anything small (*pusillus*) be ascribed to him. At the same time they endow him with the human affections (*affectiones*) and passions (*passiones*). If they knew the Scriptures and were taught by the truth they would know that God is not like human beings and his thoughts are not like human thoughts. The Father of all is very far from the affections and passions that are typical of humans.[85]

J. K. Mozley argued that, considered more sympathetically, the Valentinian system may be freed of the charge of inconsistency.[86] On his reading, the Valentinians reserved impassibility exclusively for the su-

[82] Iren., *haer.* 1. 4. 2; 1. 5. 1–6; Clem., *Excerpta ex Theodoto*, 45. 1–2; Hippolytus, *Ref.* 6. 29. 32. 2–6.

[83] Plotinus, *Enneads*, 2. 9.

[84] 'Gnosticism', 267. I must disagree with A. H. Armstrong's view that the impact of Greek philosophy upon Gnosticism was superficial. See his 'Gnosis and Greek Philosophy', 87–124.

[85] Iren., *haer.* 2. 13. 3 (*PG* 7: 743B–744A); cf. 2. 13. 6 (*PG* 7: 745B).

[86] *Impassibility of God*, 27–8.

preme God, the 'Father of All', whereas the rest of the deities in the Pleroma were passible. Irenaeus, as the following text illustrates, was quite aware of this line of defence and did not find it convincing:

If [as the Valentinians claim] it is impious to attribute ignorance and passions (*passionem*) to the Father of all, how can they [the Valentinians] say that he emanated a passible (*passibilem*) aeon? How can they call themselves religious, if they attribute the same impiety to the divine Sophia?

They say that the aeons emanate from the Father of all as the rays from the sun. Since all aeons come from the same source, either they all would be passible (*capaces passionis*) with the one who emanated them, or they all would remain impassible (*impassibiles*). It is impossible that some aeons so emitted would be passible, and the rest impassible. If they allow that all of the aeons are impassible, they would themselves dissolve their own argument. For how is it possible for the inferior aeon to be subject to passion, if they all are impassible? If, as some of them claim, all the aeons participated in this passion, then they would attribute passion to the Logos, who is the originator of Sophia. Since the Logos is the Nous of Propator, this would entail that he and the Father himself would be involved in passion.[87]

Irenaeus' point may be summarized as follows: if the 'Father of all' is impassible, so should have been his divine offspring; if, on the contrary, his offspring are passible, the 'Father of all' would also be subject to passion. Irenaeus' critique of the Gnostics was no different from the standard anti-anthropomorphic objection that evil intentions, passions, and actions cannot be ascribed to the supreme God. Positively, however, there was a lot more to defend. Irenaeus saw in Docetism an attack upon the very core of the apostolic teaching about Jesus and pointed out that 'according to the opinion of no one of the heretics was the Word of God made flesh'.[88] At stake in the Docetic programme was a thoroughgoing rejection of the incarnation.

As I have observed earlier, many apologists considered an open attack upon the prevailing social conventions to be the most successful defence strategy. They did not hesitate to admit, in the spirit of Tertullian's celebrated aphorism—*crucifixus est dei filius; non pudet quia pudendum est. Et mortuus est dei filius; credibile est quia ineptum est* [89]—that the divine birth, suffering, and crucifixion were unseemly, scandalous, and offensive in the eyes of the world. At the same time Tertullian and other apologists recognized that it was not enough to argue that the divine incarnation

87 Iren., *haer.* 2. 17. 6–7 (*PG* 7: 764A–B).
88 Ibid. 3. 11. 3; cf. 1. 9. 3.
89 *De carne Christi*, 5. 4.

was merely an absurdity as far as human logic was concerned. It had to be shown that the method of our salvation was worthy of God.

The Fathers had to meet the Docetic attacks on several fronts. A rival theological, cosmological, anthropological, christological, and soteriological system had to be developed. The polytheistic framework had to be dismantled. Against the pessimistic cosmology of Gnosticism, the Fathers had to insist upon the biblical vision of creation. Contrary to the Gnostics, the world was the work of a perfectly good, omnipotent, and omniscient creator, not the mistake of an evil and ignorant Demiurge. Everything in the created order was good and nothing was intrinsically worthy or unworthy of God.[90] Those material means became worthy that God chose for the sake of salvation. Hence, it was not shameful for God to participate in the process of human birth, if through that process humanity was restored to incorruption. Attacking Marcion's view of Christ Tertullian exclaimed: 'All that you regard dishonorable in my God (*dei mei penes*) is the sacrament of human salvation. God corresponded with man, so that man may learn how to act like God. God treated man as his equal, so that man could treat God as his equal. God was found to be small, so that man could become great. You [Marcion] who disdain such a God, I am not sure whether you believe that God was crucified (*deum crucifixum*).'[91] This type of argument for the God-fittingness of actions may be called teleological: given that the means are neutral and the goal is worthy, the course of actions undertaken to bring about a particular praiseworthy result is itself God-befitting.

Furthermore, to say, as the Gnostics did, that flesh was beyond redemption was to attribute weakness to God and to limit God's benevolent ability to restore the flesh to incorruptibility. Since real humanity was in need of redemption God assumed real flesh, not a phantom of the flesh. Tertullian argued against Marcion that if God despised flesh he would equally despise a phantom of the flesh.[92]

Curiously, the Fathers also advance what may be called a Cartesian argument before Descartes. Only in this case the 'God is not a deceiver argument' is not for the reality of the external world, but for the reality of particular divine actions in the incarnation.[93] Phantom birth and sham crucifixion, the Fathers were quick to point out, would be an outright

[90] Tertullian, *Adv. Marc.* 3. 10; *De carne Christi*, 5. 9.

[91] Tertullian, *Adv. Marc.* 2. 27.

[92] Ibid. 3. 10. In this essay Tertullian argues specifically against Marcion, but his point is applicable to any form of Docetism.

[93] Descartes, *Meditations*, 4.

divine deception. Since it is unfitting for God to deceive, the escapist version of the crucifixion scene could hardly be construed as a manifestation of divinity. On the contrary, the Docetic solution itself is unworthy of God.[94]

The sacrament of the Eucharist and the testimony of the martyrs provided a practical antidote against the Docetic beliefs. As Ignatius wrote, the Docetists 'abstain from the Eucharist and prayer, because they refuse to acknowledge that the Eucharist is the flesh of our Savior Jesus Christ, which suffered for our sins and which the Father by his goodness raised up'.[95] If Christ suffered in appearance only, the suffering of the martyrs became a vain suicide.[96] Some Gnostics rejected the idea of martyrdom, while others reinterpreted it as atonement for one's personal transgressions.[97] In the catholic church there was a coherence between such major practices, as the sacraments and martyrdom on the one hand and beliefs about the incarnation on the other. The Docetists, in contrast, had radically to reinterpret, modify, or eliminate these practices altogether in order to square them with their theology.

The resistance to these Docetic tendencies led to a clearer demarcation of the function of the divine impassibility. For the Docetists divine impassibility ruled out direct divine involvement in the material universe, but did not exclude the passions of the divine aeons. For the Fathers, on the contrary, divine impassibility was an apophatic qualifier of all divine emotions and did not rule out God's direct contact with creation.[98] The 'scandal' of Gnosticism lay in the contradiction between divine impassibility and far too human passions. In orthodox Christianity the scandal and the paradoxical tension lay elsewhere: in the affirmation of the incarnation of the God who infinitely surpassed everything in creation.

The church Fathers of the second and third centuries agreed that Christ suffered truly and resisted all Docetic reinterpretations of the incarnation. It remained to be spelled out more precisely just what Christ's suffering meant for God. Without abandoning divine impassibility, the Fathers at times were prepared to state the issue in boldly theopaschite terms. On other occasions they resorted to a paradoxical affirmation, implicit in the rules of faith and early christological hymns

[94] Tertullian, *Adv. Marc.* 3. 9–11.

[95] Ignatius, *Smyrn.* 6. 2, trans. Holmes, 189. Cf. Tertullian, *Adv. Marc.* 2. 27; 4. 40.

[96] Ignatius, *Smyrn.* 3; *Trall.* 10.

[97] Clem., *Strom.* 4. 12.

[98] Thomas Weinandy makes a similar point with regard to the theology of Irenaeus. See *Does God Suffer?*, 93.

that the Impassible suffered. This paradoxical affirmation was intended to emphasize the personal unity of the incarnate Son of God in the face of the Docetic division of Christ into two subjects. The permanent contribution of the apologists to the development of church teaching lies in holding tenaciously to the paradox of the incarnation. In my judgement, in the writings of the apologists we do not yet have a clear sense as to how and under what conditions suffering may be predicated of God. If there was a *consensus patrum* on the issue that Christ suffered in reality, there was as yet no tangible agreement on how to spell out the implications of the church's worship of the Crucified as God. Further light on this issue was shed in the controversies with the Patripassians and the Arians.

4

Patripassian Controversy Resolved: The Son, not God the Father, Suffered in the Incarnation

THE struggle with Docetism, surveyed in broad lines in the previous chapter, represents the first stage in the development of the church's understanding of divine (im)passibility. The central theological intention behind the Docetic reinterpretations of the gospels was to remove a divine saviour from all real involvement with the realm of matter and from participation in fully human life. For the Docetists such a reinterpretation was in part an obvious implication of divine impassibility. For the early Fathers, in contrast, divine impassibility had a quite different function. Safeguarding God's pre-eminence over everything in the created order, impassibility did not rule out God's direct intervention in the world. The early Fathers insisted that while divine impassibility functions as an apophatic qualifier of all divine emotions, it does not preclude the description of God in terms of emotionally coloured characteristics.

It was also the core affirmation of the early rules of faith and the basic intention of Christian worship to celebrate the crucified and risen Lord as divine. The debate with Docetism focused on the reality of Christ's human flesh and human experiences. The precise nature of Christ's divine status was left unclear. The question remained: what exactly was Christ's relationship to the one whom he called his heavenly Father? More specifically, how was God the Father involved in the birth, earthly ministry, suffering, and death of Christ?

These issues came to the fore in a set of controversies associated with the names of Noetus, Sabellius, Praxeas, Callistus, and their followers.[1] In the West it was common to refer to them by a derogatory umbrella term 'Patripassianism'; the corresponding Eastern term was 'Sabellianism'.[2] Our reconstruction of these early third-century debates is severely hampered by substantial gaps in the evidence. For example, the earliest reports that we have for the teaching of Sabellius come from the fourth century.[3] The trouble is not so much that we have to be satisfied exclusively with the winners' report—we quite often have to adjust our historical sensibilities to that. But rather, the state of the sources is such that it is virtually impossible to distinguish the views actually held by the Patripassians themselves from the polemical conjectures of their opponents.

Given the unsatisfactory state of the sources it is tempting to dismiss Patripassianism as having little relevance for the issue of divine (im)-passibility altogether. Thus, for example, Thomas Weinandy, who in his groundbreaking work *Does God Suffer?* treats the major christological controversies rather comprehensively, makes an exception for Patripassianism dispensing with it in a single footnote:

> It should also be noted that while patripassianism (early third century) was condemned, the real issue was not that the Modalists attributed suffering to the Father, but rather that they failed to distinguish adequately between the Father and the Son. Patripassianism was primarily a trinitarian and not a christological heresy. Because the Son was seen as merely a different temporary mode of expression of the Father, it could be said that the Father became man and so suffered. Patripassianism was therefore condemned not out of an excessive fear of ascribing suffering within the Incarnation, but out of a desire to assure that it was the Son, and not the Father, who became man and so suffered.[4]

[1] Hippolytus names Cleomenes, Epigonus, and Pope Zephyrinus among the disciples of Noetus, *Ref.* 9. 7.

[2] Ath., *De synodis*, 7 (*PG* 26: 732c); Socrates, *HE* 2. 19; *PG* 67: 229. Patripassians returned the courtesy by calling their accusers 'Ditheists'. Hippolytus, *Ref.* 9. 12; Ps.-Ath., *Ar.* 4. 10.

[3] Ps.-Ath., *Ar.* 4. 13; Epiphanius, *Haer.* 42; John Chrysostom, *De sacerdotio*, 4. 4. Epiphanius reports that Sabellius's views were not substantially different from those of Noetus. In general, 4th-c. and later reports will not be considered here, since they are predominantly dependent upon earlier written sources rather than upon actual encounters with the heretics. We may be fairly certain that the Patripassian heresy as a recognizable movement within the church died out towards the middle of the third century. See Michael Slusser, 'The Scope of Patripassianism', 169–75, 169.

[4] *Does God Suffer?*, 176. It should be noted that Weinandy gave special attention to the modern versions of Patripassianism on pp. 16–18. Along similar lines, Marcel Sarot concluded: 'the distinguishing characteristic of patripassianism is not that it denies the impassibility of God but that it refused to endorse the trinitarian distinction between the

Weinandy quite rightly pinpoints the failure 'to distinguish adequately between the Father and the Son' as the central issue in Patripassianism. However, the concern to protect strict monotheism in no way undercuts the significance of the question that came to the fore in the Patripassian controversy, namely, who precisely was the subject of the human experiences undergone by Christ? To define the debate as primarily trinitarian and not christological does not help, because it was, after all, Christ's identity, not the Father's or the Spirit's, that was at stake in this debate.

A more serious objection to the relevance of Patripassianism for the study of the divine (im)passibility may be formulated as follows: how patripassian was Patripassianism? In other words, which figures, if any, among those accused of Patripassianism in fact held the opinion that the Father suffered? A. Harnack raised the question whether the formula *Pater passus est* was ever deployed by any Patripassian, or was merely a polemical slogan of their opponents.[5]

In my judgement, Harnack's sceptical claim that no living heretic in the third century actually taught that the Father suffered goes too far. If this were so, we'd have to imagine that all third- and fourth-century anti-Patripassian theologians were valiantly fighting with windmills. There had to be at least a spark of fire to generate the smoke of debate. And there is enough evidence to conclude that at least Noetus plainly taught that the Father suffered (in contrast to Praxeas and Callistus whose positions were more carefully worded). The point of departure for all Patripassians was the problem of reconciling the church's inherited monotheism with her worship of the Crucified. According to Hippolytus, Noetus presented his case for the 'single God' (ἕνα θεόν) in the following lapidary form: 'If I acknowledge Christ to be God; He is the Father himself, if He is indeed God; and Christ suffered, being Himself God; and consequently the Father suffered, for He was the Father Himself.'[6]

This is a straightforward affirmation of the point that the Father, who is truly God, was the subject of the sufferings of Christ. Drawing upon a number of scriptural passages that speak of the one God of Israel, Noetus claimed: 'I am under necessity, since one is acknowledged, to make this One the subject of suffering (ὑπο πάθος φέρειν). For Christ

Father and the Son,' 'Patripassianism, Theopaschitism and the Suffering of God. Some Historical and Systematic Considerations', 370. Mozley treats Patripassianism fairly extensively in *Impassibility of God*, 28–52.

[5] A. Harnack, 'Monarchianismus', 329.

[6] *Contra Noetum*, 2. 3. Epiphanius' report in *Haer.* 37 has no independent value.

was God, and suffered on account of us, being Himself the Father, that He might be able also to save us. And we cannot express ourselves otherwise.'[7]

As we see, Noetus was not afraid of being somewhat repetitive in order to insist upon his central point. He conceived of the whole matter in terms of a set of simple identities: one God equals the Father equals Christ equals the One who suffered. Elsewhere Hippolytus added 'the Son' to this set of identities: 'the Father is himself Christ; he is himself the Son; he himself was born, he himself suffered' and Hippolytus added somewhat derisively, 'he himself raised himself up!'[8] In the *Refutation of all Heresies*, Hippolytus explains that Noetus meant that before his human birth God was properly called 'Father', and afterwards, 'Son'. For Noetus, the divine names 'Father' and 'Son' designated successive temporary modes of the divine existence. The distinction between the mode 'Father' and the mode 'Son' is expressed in pairs of opposite properties:

> He [the Father] is invisible, when he is not seen and visible when he is seen; unbegotten when he is not begotten, and begotten when he is born of a Virgin; impassible and immortal when he does not suffer or die, but when he surrendered himself to passion, he suffered and died. They [the Noetians] believe that the Father is called the Son according to events at different times.[9]

Noetus held that before coming to earth God was impassible, unchangeable, and immortal. During his ministry on earth God became passible, changeable, and mortal. Noetus conceived divine impassibility and passibility as temporary properties that mark out successive modes of God's existence. When Noetus repeatedly claimed that the Father suffered, he intended to stress that the one God himself was the subject of Christ's suffering. It is noteworthy that unlike some other orthodox critics, Hippolytus nowhere explicitly attacks Noetus' claim that God suffered. Hippolytus himself did not draw back from expressing the mystery of the incarnation in theopaschite terms. For example, he admitted that 'the impassible Word of God underwent suffering through the flesh'.[10]

What Hippolytus found problematic was Noetus' confusion between the Father and the Son, which resulted in identifying the subject of

[7] *Contra Noetum*, 2. 7.

[8] Ibid. 3. 2; cf. 1. 2.

[9] Hippolytus, *Ref.* 10. 27 (*PG* 16: 3439D, 3442A); cf. ibid. 9. 11 (*PG* 16: 3369).

[10] *Contra Noetum*, 15. 3.

suffering with the Father, rather than with God the Word. In response, Hippolytus appealed to selected scriptural passages that made it clear that Christ was not talking to himself when he addressed his Father, that the one addressed was distinct from the one addressing. Additionally, Hippolytus appealed to the rules of faith, which spoke of the Father and the Son as coexisting entities, not as successive temporal modes of God.[11] He pointed out that Noetus went against an influential trend in the early tradition by refusing to identify the Son with the pre-existent Logos. Hippolytus, in contrast, drew upon Logos christology in order to show that the Son was the Word of God, distinct from, yet united with God the Father. As God's Logos, the Son was active both in creation and in the ministry of the OT prophets through the centuries. These arguments have been explored in sufficient detail by historians of doctrine and need not detain us here.[12]

Two issues remained patently unclear in Hippolytus's sketchy presentation of Noetus' view. First, what role, if any, did the flesh assumed by Christ play in the suffering of the Father? Second, if according to Noetus himself the impassible Father indeed became the passible Son, it was, strictly speaking, as the Son, not as the Father, that God suffered. Both issues remained moot with Noetus (at least as presented by Hippolytus) and awaited resolution in the versions of Patripassianism developed by Praxeas and Callistus.

If one undertook to represent the views of Praxeas and Callistus in a church trial, the worst and most biased witnesses whom one could call to the stand would be Tertullian and Hippolytus respectively. At the time of writing *Adversus Praxeam*, most probably in 213, Tertullian had left the church and joined a group of North African Montanists. Praxeas, much to Tertullian's chagrin, intervened in the correspondence between the Asian Montanists and the bishop of Rome and effectively ruined the prophets' credentials before the pope. Tertullian, therefore, had more reason to scold Praxeas for having put to flight the Paraclete than for crucifying the Father.[13]

Hippolytus, too, had separated from the church of Rome and was elected an anti-pope by a small circle of adherents by the time of writing against his rival, the confessor Callistus. The central dividing issue between them was that of church discipline: Callistus, who was the

[11] Hippolytus, *Contra Noetum*, 17; cf. Tertullian, *Adv. Prax.* 2; 9; 11.

[12] See e.g. J. Quasten, *Patrology*, ii. 198–202.

[13] *Adv. Prax.* 1.

bishop of Rome at the time, relaxed the terms of acceptance of the penitents into the church.[14] Hippolytus disagreed and accused Callistus of leniency and, on second thoughts, of following the heresy of Sabellius. Canonically speaking, both Hippolytus and Tertullian had parted ways with the church, whereas Callistus and, most probably, Praxeas, were within the church's fold at the time the controversial writings against them were produced.

The reconstruction of Callistus' actual position is additionally complicated by the fact that he excommunicated Sabellius, in the hope of distancing himself from the Patripassian views of the latter. Hippolytus himself admitted that Callistus 'did not wish to assert that the Father suffered ... being careful to avoid blasphemy against the Father'.[15] Instead, Callistus claimed that τὸν πατέρα συμπεπονθέναι τῷ υἱῷ.[16] To translate this statement immediately would be to prejudge the case either for or against strict Patripassianism, i.e. the otherwise unqualified claim that the Father suffered, which Hippolytus attributed to Noetus. From Hippolytus' report two things are clear: that by using the ambiguous συμπάσχειν Callistus intended to avoid the charge of strict Patripassianism; and that, in Hippolytus' eyes this was nothing but a false pretence, an empty play of words that did not in the end succeed in avoiding the charge.

Tertullian's assessment of Praxeas' view was remarkably similar. Having charged Praxeas several times with the blasphemy of making the Father suffer, Tertullian acknowledged towards the end of his treatise that Praxeas was more careful in his wording and, strictly speaking, held that it was the Son who suffered on the cross, whereas the Father only *compassibilis est.*[17] Like Hippolytus, Tertullian thought that this way of escaping strict Patripassianism was not going to hold water and asked rhetorically: *Quid est enim compati quam cum alio pati?* What else could being compassible mean except 'to suffer with another'?[18] Unfortunately, Praxeas' response is not available to us.

The thought of both Callistus and Praxeas appeared to move along the same lines.[19] Both intended to avoid strict Patripassianism and both

[14] See Gregory Dix, *The Treatise on the Apostolic Tradition of St Hippolytus of Rome*, p. xvi.

[15] *Ref.* 9. 12. 19.

[16] Ibid. 9. 12. 18.

[17] *Adv. Prax.* 29.

[18] Ibid. 29.

[19] On these grounds some historians have conjectured that 'Praxeas' was Callistus' nickname. Praxeas is indeed a shadowy figure. It is extremely puzzling that Hippolytus

chose the verb συμπάσχειν to describe the Father's involvement in the suffering of Christ. Perhaps, we can get behind the rhetoric of their opponents if we consider the wider contours of their christology. We learn from Hippolytus that Callistus identified the divine spirit that came upon the Virgin with the Father, whereas the flesh of Christ, assumed by the spirit, he identified with the Son. This move, if Callistus indeed made it, represented a substantial departure from the christology of Noetus, who referred to the whole Christ as the Son, not to his flesh alone.

Tertullian appears to refer to a similar account of the respective roles of the Father and the Son in his presentation of Praxeas' teaching. The Monarchians, according to Tertullian, 'introduce further darkness into things manifest by attempting a distinction between the flesh, which they say is the Son, namely Jesus, and the Spirit, which they say is God or Christ. Here they are dividing things inseparable, whereas hitherto they have been attempting to identify Persons distinct.'[20] Tertullian's somewhat garbled report exposes a serious inconsistency here.[21] On the one hand, Praxeas advanced a set of simple identifications of the sort that we found in the teaching of Noetus: God equals the Father equals the Son equals the figure of the gospels, while on the other hand he claimed that the Father and the Son coexist as respectively the divine and the fleshly aspects of the one who was crucified. Should we agree with Tertullian that this was a genuine terminological confusion in Praxeas' system?

I believe there is a way to decide which of the two options represented the least distorted version of Praxeas' actual view. The statement *Pater compassus est filii* (which we are most certain Praxeas actually made) simply makes no sense if the Father and the Son were successive modes of divinity. The successionist model would not allow for the Father's acting or suffering with the Son, since, according to this model, when God

knew nothing of him. In my judgement, there are enough discrepancies in their historical portraits to treat them as two different persons.

[20] *Adv. Prax.* 27, trans. Ernest Evans, *Tertullian's Treatise Against Praxeas*, 315.

[21] Ps.-Ath., *Ar.* 4. 15, confirms that Monarchians could not agree among themselves as to the exact use of the terms 'Father' and 'Son'. This author's opinion, however, comes rather late and may not be entirely independent. Ernest Evans suggested that the inconsistency may be removed if we suppose that Tertullian mistakenly ascribes to his Praxeas the views of Theodotus the tanner, as reported by Hippolytus, *Ref.* 7. 35. 36. In my judgement, the similarity between the adoptionism of Theodotus the tanner and the view outlined in *Adv. Prax.* 27 is too superficial to make Evans's suggestion convincing. Both ideas have their roots in Gnostic speculations, as Tertullian points out. See Evans, *Tertullian's Treatise*, 316. Maurice Wiles argued in support of inconsistency in *The Spiritual Gospel*, 120.

becomes the Son he ceases to be the Father. The only remaining option is to see Praxeas' christology as fundamentally similar to that of Callistus.

Hence, it is most likely that both Callistus and Praxeas conceived of the Father and of the Son as two complementary aspects of a spirit–flesh christology. Within the framework of this christology, what could the statement *Pater compassus est filii* possibly mean? In his article 'The Christology of Callistus', R. E. Heine offers a compelling solution to this issue.[22] Heine distinguishes between two uses of the verb συμπάσχειν. He points out that within the context of a Christian theology of martyrdom the verb denoted the participation of the martyr in the suffering and death of Christ. Συμπάσχειν most frequently meant to 'die with' or 'suffer with or the same as'.[23] This was precisely the sense in which both Hippolytus and Tertullian took the verb.

Yet, the same verb and its cognate συμπάθεια long before had become technical terms in Stoicism. In Stoic cosmology, these terms described the interaction of the active principle (Logos or pneuma) with passive matter. Likewise, in the Stoic psychology συμπάσχειν denoted the interaction of the soul with the body. To illustrate this point, Heine cites the following statement from Cleanthes: 'the soul interacts (συμπάσχει) with the body when it is sick and being cut, and the body with the soul; thus when the soul feels shame and fear the body turns red and pale respectively'.[24] In this example the soul neither merely duplicates the suffering of the body, i.e. the soul is not cut when the body is cut, nor does the soul remain totally unaffected when the body suffers. But rather the soul reacts to what is going on in the body according to its own nature, and vice versa.

Heine subsequently argues that it is entirely plausible that Callistus and Praxeas used the term συμπάσχειν in the technical Stoic sense to describe the interaction of the divine pneuma (i.e. 'the Father') with the human flesh (i.e. 'the Son'). It was the human flesh that suffered on the cross, while the divine spirit neither remained unaffected nor duplicated the sufferings of the flesh. The divine spirit, in this case, was involved in

[22] 75–7.

[23] As e.g. in Rom. 8: 17; 1 Cor. 12: 26; Ignatius, *Smyrn.* 4: 2; *Polyc.* 9: 2. Very rarely was the verb used in the sense 'to sympathize with', for which a different verb, συμπαθέω, was used. See Michaelis, 'Πάσχω', *TDNT* v. 925–6, 35–6.

[24] Alexander Aphrodisiensis, *De anima*, 117. 9–11, cited in Heine, 'Christology of Callistus', 76. See also the discussion of this passage in Henry Chadwick, 'Eucharist and Christology'.

suffering through the flesh, strengthening it.[25] The plausibility of this explanation is greatly increased by the fact that it succeeds in reconciling the ambiguous *Pater compassus est filii* with Callistus' and Praxeas' adamant denials that the Father himself suffered.

If Heine's reconstruction is correct, as I believe it is, both Tertullian and Hippolytus missed a crucial insight that this version of Monarchianism possessed (despite its obviously mistaken identification of the Father with the divine spirit and of the Son with the human flesh).[26] The Monarchians may be interpreted as making a point that divinity was indeed involved in the suffering of the human flesh, and yet its involvement was unlike the suffering of the flesh itself. Divinity participated in death without dying and in suffering without being conquered by suffering. As we will see in Chapter 6, for Cyril of Alexandria two centuries later this insight, together with the analogy of the union of the soul and the body, were two of the keys that unlocked the meaning of numerous theopaschite expressions scattered in the writings of the early Fathers.

Unfortunately, this insight perished in the fire of polemic. Tertullian's own solution to the problem of the dying and suffering God was somewhat ambiguous. On the one hand, he tirelessly repeated that the suffering of Christ was a scandal for human ways of thought. Arguing against the Docetists he did not avoid expressing this fact in boldly theopaschite terms.[27] On the other hand, contending with Praxeas, Tertullian drew a sharp distinction between the two natures of the Son of God, *divinitas* and *humanitas*. Each nature, as he emphasized, had its distinct properties, 'the miracles showing the godhead, the sufferings the manhood'.[28] Christ, Tertullian explained, suffered only in his *humanitas* and remained impassible in his *divinitas*. Novatian developed the same point in the anti-Patripassian chapters of his *De trinitate*.[29] Such an explanation threatened to do away with the paradox of the incarnation because it tended to undercut the intimacy of God's involvement in the

[25] Tertullian himself came close to the same understanding of the involvement of the Spirit in the suffering of a martyr when he wrote: 'we also cannot suffer for God's sake unless the Spirit of God be in us, yet the Spirit does not suffer in us, but gives us the strength to suffer', *Adv. Prax.* 29.

[26] Cf. the comment of Pollard, 'Impassibility of God', 358: 'Tertullian refused to admit the distinction between suffering (*passio*) and sympathy (*compassio*).'

[27] Tertullian, *De carne Christi*, 5. 4.

[28] *Adv. Prax.* 27. Cf. Leo, *Tome*, 4.

[29] See esp. chap. 25. For a survey of the two-nature exegesis of the fourth gospel in the early centuries see Maurice Wiles, *The Spiritual Gospel*, 96–161.

human experience of Christ. Since the unity of Christ's person was not an issue for the Patripassians, the potential dangers of separating the activities of the two natures were not perceived as acutely as they were in the controversies with the Docetists. The issue became pressing again when Nestorius, following Theodore of Mopsuestia, pushed the distinction between the two aspects of Christ's earthly ministry to the point of virtual separation.

The upshot of the debate with Patripassianism may be summarized as follows. Noetus, as far as the available evidence permits us to reconstruct his position, did hold strict Patripassianism and taught that the Father was identical with the Son and suffered on the cross. Both Callistus and Praxeas, according to our reconstruction, eschewed this extreme position, and endorsed a view that the Father participated in the sufferings of the flesh, without being overcome by these sufferings. Their opponents, in contrast, emphasized the distinction between the Father and the Son. Consequently, they denied the claim that the Father was the subject of Christ's human experiences, most notably, suffering and crucifixion. Two propositions have now been seasoned with the fire of debates:

1. Christ suffered in reality.
2. The Father did not suffer.

These, on the surface, were fairly trivial statements. However, the theological conundrums that lurked behind them were not trivial at all. While the Docetists intended to distance the Father as completely as possible from the Son, the Monarchians probed the other extreme and claimed that two divine persons were identical. The opposite extreme, generated by the Patripassian debate, was the tendency to stress the distinction between the impassible Father and the suffering Son. As I will show in the next chapter, this tendency paved the way for the subordinationist option and was one of the sparks that lit the fire of Arianism.

5

Arianism Opposed: The Word's Divinity is Not Diminished by Involvement in Suffering

> I seek Thee early in the morning, Word of God; for in Thy tender mercy towards fallen man, without changing Thou hast emptied Thyself, and impassibly Thou hast submitted to Thy Passion. Grant me Thy peace, O Lord who lovest mankind.[1]

In its search for God-befitting accounts of divine involvement the mind of the church probed various extremes. One of these extremes was Patripassianism, which at least in its original Noetian version, tended to blur all permanent distinctions between the Father and the Son to the extent of identifying the two hypostases. It was natural that in reaction to Sabellianism the theological pendulum would swing in the opposite direction. Those who saw the inadequacy of Patripassianism tried to bring out as sharply as possible the distinctions between the Father and the Son, to the point of either separating the divine hypostases (ditheism, tritheism) or of diminishing the Son's divine status before that of the Father (subordinationism). Both extremes were explored in the fourth century, although the former remained more on a theoretical level, while the latter became a powerful movement threatening to overtake the church.

[1] *The Lenten Triodion*, trans. Mother Mary and Kallistos Ware, 593.

Subordinationism as a Solution to the Problems with Patripassianism

The fact that anti-Nicene literature[2] is full of polemical references to Sabellianism indicates that these theologians worked out their subordinationist views in conscious opposition to the Monarchian extreme.[3] Arians believed that one of the strongest sides of their position was that it successfully avoided the self-evidently heretical Sabellianism. By implication, they regarded their pro-Nicene opponents as failing to offer a serious logical alternative either to Sabellianism or to tritheism. Two cases in which more was at stake than a purely rhetorical attack upon a long-moribund heresy are especially pertinent to our study.

In the first case in point, the bishop suspected of subordinationism was none other than Dionysius of Alexandria (d. *c.*264). Intending to correct certain Sabellianizing bishops of Pentapolis, who taught that the Father himself became flesh, Dionysius wrote a letter in which he made a number of sharp distinctions between the Father and the Son. Among other things, he pointed out that 'the Son of God is a creature and made' and that the Son was as different in essence from the Father as a boat was from a ship-builder.[4]

[2] The term 'anti-Nicene' refers to early 'Arian', Homoian, Anhomoian (Neo-Arian), and Western Arian authors. Recent studies have emphasized that the designations 'Arian' and 'Anhomoian' were hostile polemical tags used by the defenders of the council of Nicaea, rather than self-designations of particular parties. See R. Hanson, *Search*, XVII; M. Simonetti, *La crisi ariana*; M. Wiles, *The Archetypal Heresy*, 26–31. The term 'Homoian' refers to those theologians who preferred to speak of the Son as being similar in essence (*homoiousios*) with the Father. The term 'Neo-Arians' or Anhomoians refers to Aetius, Eunomius, and their followers, who emphasized that the Son was dissimilar in essence (*anhomoiousios*) from the Father. The terms 'Homoian' and 'Neo-Arian' are useful, but not entirely accurate designations, introduced by modern scholars. See R. Vaggione, *Eunomius of Cyzicus and the Nicene Revolution*, 198, 204. In addition, some 4th-c. participants of the debate preferred not to express the relationship between the Father and the Son using a controversial language of essence. Their at times wavering positions are not easily classifiable.

[3] For the polemical references to Sabellianism see: Ath., *Expositio fidei*, 2; *De sententia Dionysii*, 26; *De synodis*, 16 (this one is particularly interesting since it contains the condemnation of Sabellianism in a brief exposition of the Arian creed); Gr. Nyss., *Eun.* 1. 226 (*J* i. 93); 1. 499 (*J* i. 170); Basil, *Ep.* 129. 1; Eunomius, *Liber apologeticus*, 6; Theodoret, *HE* 1. 3; R. Gryson, *Scolies Ariennes sur le Concile d'Aquilée*, 230–36; Arian anti-Sabellianism is emphasized by M. Simonetti, *Studi sull'Arianesimo*; R. D. Williams, 'The Logic of Arianism', 57, 60. Along the same lines, Michael Meslin argues that Western Arianism was characterized by overall hostility to Sabellianism, see *Les Ariens d'Occident*, 255–7.

[4] Ath., *De sententia Dionysii*, 4; *decr.* vi. 25. I do not share Luise Abramowski's doubts regarding the authenticity of quotations from Dionysius of Alexandria in *De sententia*

These expressions Dionysius would live to regret. Upon learning of this line of defence, his brother bishop, Dionysius of Rome, wrote to him and to his addressees pronouncing both the Sabellian and the subordinationist views to be heretical errors.[5] The Alexandrian pope responded with a lengthy recantation in which he retracted many of his previous statements. This did not bring an end to the story, however, for the ill-fated letter to the bishops of Pentapolis later fell into the hands of Arians. This time Athanasius valiantly stood up to defend third-century predecessor's orthodoxy. Athanasius pointed out that the distinctions that Dionysius drew between the Father and the Son apply to the Son's human nature, not to his divine nature.[6] It is highly doubtful that this apologetic move convinced the Arians. What is beyond doubt is that in this particular case the need to reprimand the living Sabellian leaders provoked some overtly subordinationist answers.

In the second case, the intention to oppose Patripassianism in its Western form led to a curious addition to local versions of the ancient Roman creed. The first article of the creed of Aquilea and (for some time in the fourth century) that of Milan ran as follows: *credo in Deo Patre omnipotenti invisibili [et] impassibili*, 'I believe in one God the Father almighty, *invisible [and] impassible*.'[7] Rufinus of Aquilea, writing in the first years of the fifth century, explained that the gloss 'invisible and impassible' was added on account of the Patripassian heresy 'which said that the Father himself was born of the Virgin and became visible, or affirmed that he suffered in the flesh'.[8] Rufinus was not aware of when exactly and under what circumstances the 'forefathers' decided to make this addition. The intention behind adding the gloss, as Rufinus understood it, was to make it clear that it was the Son, not the Father, who assumed visible and passible flesh in the incarnation.

However, in the aftermath of the battle with Arianism the gloss proved to be more problematic than Rufinus was willing to admit. In one of his catechetical sermons on the creed delivered in the late fourth century, Ambrose of Milan pointed out that the addition in question, while it had provided an antidote against Sabellianism, in his day was no longer acceptable for it played straight into the hands of the

Dionysii. See 'Dionys von Rom (d 268) und Dionys von Alexandrien (d 264/5) in den arianischen Streitigkeiten des 4ten Jahrhunderts', 240–72.

5 Ath., *decr.* vi. 26.

6 See Ath., *De sententia Dionysii*, 26.

7 Reconstruction after Rufinus, *De fide et symbolo*, 3–5; emphasis added.

8 Ibid. 5.

Arians.[9] As we will see in this chapter, one of the key Arian arguments for the subordinate status of the Son was that, unlike the immutable and impassible Father, the Son was in his very essence changeable and passible, and therefore, capable of being born and suffering on the cross.[10]

Ambrose had good reason for worrying that the explanatory words 'invisible and impassible', ascribed in this version of the creed explicitly only to the first person of the Trinity, could suggest to less theologically sophisticated Christians that the Son and the Holy Spirit were distinguished from the Father precisely by being visible and passible in their very essence, hence, inferior. Ambrose recommended omitting the gloss and sticking to the purity and simplicity of the ancient Roman creed. Again, the intention to avoid Sabellianism led straight into the subordinationist route.

The two cases discussed above point to the fact that Arianism was partly meant to provide an alternative to the Sabellian conception of the trinitarian doctrine. We should emphasize that this development was not entirely harmonious and consistent. Some third-century arguments against Sabellianism that emphasized the distinctions between the Father and the Son, were dismissed as dangerous errors in the struggle with the Arians.[11] In our story, Arianism represents the third attempt, after Docetism and Sabellianism, to dissolve the paradox of the incarnation.

Five Interpretations of Arianism

Arianism is perhaps the most studied heresy of all centuries. The contours of the debate at various stages as well as the careers of its major participants have been reconstructed, to the degree to which the available evidence allows, in painstaking detail. Scholarly re-evaluations in the last half of the twentieth century made it possible to go beyond the textbook caricature of Arius as a spiritually misguided sophist who self-consciously departed from the church's time-honoured tradition. A number of strong points of the Arian exegesis and soteriology have recently been discovered and freshly appreciated. Historians agree that

[9] Ambrose, *Explanatio symboli*, 7.

[10] See the so-called 5th Confession of Macrostich (344), which had a wide circulation in Italy. Ath., *De synodis*, 26.

[11] See Maurice Wiles, *The Making of Christian Doctrine*, 124–7; *The Spiritual Gospel*, 120.

the matters at stake in the debate were more ambiguous than the pro-Nicene reports would have us believe. Attempts have been made to pin down *the* central theological concern of the whole Arian project. To my count, five distinct interpretative trajectories have been offered in contemporary scholarly assessments of the issue.[12]

According to one interpretation, which has had both ancient and modern exponents, Arian subordinationism was an integral part of the most comprehensive vision of reality that Hellenism ever produced. The elaboration of this vision into a self-sufficient philosophical system belongs to later Platonism.[13] Since we have already had an occasion to discuss this system in the first chapter, it will be enough to add a few traits that are especially relevant for our assessment of Arianism. Fundamental to this vision is an understanding of reality as a multi-level hierarchy, with the intellectual realm at the top and the material realm at the bottom of the scale. Each lower level participates in the reality of a higher level and in a measure reflects its beauty, form, and noetic structure. The supreme God is the highest reality, completely removed from the material realm. Exhaustive knowledge (*katalepsis*) of the supreme God is not available to the lower levels of being. It is impossible for the inhabitants of the material realm to participate in the supreme God directly: their contact with the divine world is accomplished through the chain of intermediaries.

Following this vision, so runs the first interpretation, Arians strongly emphasized the transcendence of the ungenerated God (ἀγέννητος θεός). They described the Father as exclusively possessing all perfections, including the negative attributes of invisibility, immutability, and impassibility. They distinguished this deity from an inferior divine being, his Son or Logos whose origin is derived from the ungenerated God. Whether and how the Son participates in the essence of the Father was a disputed point among various exponents of Arianism. They were clear that since the Son was generated, as such he was distinct from the ungenerated God in essence. Homoians spoke of this distinction in terms of likeness of essence, while Neo-Arians stressed that the Son was unlike the Father in essence. Precisely because he was changeable

12 For an excellent survey of different interpretations offered by 19–20th-c. historians of doctrine see Rowan Williams, *Arius*, 2–25.

13 For a discussion of the Platonic elements in Arian thought see G. C. Stead, 'The Platonism of Arius', 14–31. Stead emphasizes the fact that Arius was exposed to Platonism within the church through the work of Origen and his successors, rather than through pagan channels (p. 30).

and passible, the Logos was able to communicate with the sensible world. Early Arians insisted that the Logos possessed knowledge of the Father adequate for the creation and salvation of the world, yet he did not know the Father perfectly or exhaustively.[14] His knowledge had limitations characteristic of a created and finite being.

Central to later Platonism were speculations about the origin of time and the generation of the world.[15] Arius was keenly interested in the matter, without slavishly copying any of the options proposed by the later Platonists. According to Arius, the Logos was a subordinate demiurge who was principally responsible for creating the world. On this reading, the central Arian concern was philosophical: to protect the Neoplatonist account of indirect divine involvement in the world of becoming.

Although later Platonism is regarded as a predominant, it is by no means the sole philosophical trend that has influenced Arianism. Robert Gregg captured the complexity of the issues well when he observed that 'a bewildering array of precursors have been postulated for Arian doctrine by modern scholarship: Aristotle, Plato (and Platonists like Atticus and Albinus), Philo, Origen, Lucian, Paul of Samosata, and the exegetes of the "schools" in Alexandria and Antioch'.[16] Richard Hanson's conclusion that Arius was 'eclectic in his philosophy' and that 'he was not without influence from Origen, but cannot seriously be called an Origenist'[17] strikes a fair balance.

Another interpretation, likewise championed both in antiquity and in modern times, views the Arians not as Hellenizers, but on the contrary, as 'Judaizers'.[18] On this reading, the major Arian concern was to sustain a strict monotheism coupled with a strong sense of the transcendence of

[14] Ath., *Depositio Arii*, 4; *Ar.* 1. 5. We should note that the Eunomians sharply disagreed with others on this point and stressed that the Father's essence could be known not only by the Son, but potentially by all Christians.

[15] See Williams, *Arius*, 181–98.

[16] *Early Arianism*, 79.

[17] *Search*, 98.

[18] I put the term 'Judaizers' in inverted commas, because in the atmosphere of widespread ecclesiastical anti-Judaism of the fourth century, the *ad hominem* accusation of Judaizing quite often did not refer to any specific Jewish beliefs and practices, but was used as the surest and the quickest *reductio ad heresim* argument. See Ath., *De sent. Dionysii*, 3; *decr.* i. 5; (Ps.-?)Ath., *Ar.* 3. 55. See Stead, 'Rhetorical Method', 131–2. The Athanasian authorship of the third oration has been contested by Charles Kannengiesser, 'Athanasius' So-called Third Oration against the Arians', *Studia Patristica* 26 (1993), 375–88. It is essential for my argument that both the third and the fourth orations come from the pro-Nicene circles of the 4th c.

the one God. J. H. Newman was the first among modern historians to take the patristic charge of Arian Judaizing seriously and to trace it, following patristic suggestions, to the influence of the Antiochean school of Paul of Samosata.[19] Subsequently the Antiochean roots of Arius' Judaizing were questioned by Gwatkin who pointed out that at the beginning of the fourth century Alexandria was as likely to provide exposure to Jewish thought and practice as Antioch. In 1979 Rudolf Lorenz seriously challenged all evidence for Jewish or Judaeo-Christian influences upon Arius.[20] However, Thomas Kopecek has recently shown on the basis of the *Apostolic Constitutions* that later Arianism 'emerged from and was nourished by a conservative eucharistic liturgical tradition which was pronouncedly Jewish-Christian in character'.[21]

The Arians stressed the deep divide that exists between the ungenerated God and all generated beings. Consequently, Arianism was characterized by an 'unusually intense and jealous worship of the one God'[22] that was typical of the Hellenistic synagogues of the time. The Arian Christ, according to this reading, was a unique creature, created by the will of God before all other creatures. In what sense this unique creature could also be called divine or, to use a favourite Arian designation, the 'uniquely-generated God' (μονογηνές θεός) remained a moot point, not easily explained within the 'strict monotheism' model. It must be stressed that the Arians clung tenaciously to both designations. It was the Son, not the invisible, immutable, and impassible Father, who was the subject of all the OT theophanies.[23] Being a creature, Christ was mutable, hence perfectly suitable to assume human flesh, suffer, and die. If this interpretation is correct, the concern to reconcile the church's beliefs about Christ with strict monotheism, as inherited from Judaism, was shared with equal zeal both by the Arians and by the Sabellians, although the solutions that the two parties offered were dramatically different.

The third interpretation, in distinction from the first two, places biblical exegesis at the heart of the matter. Arius is presented as a careful exegete who refused to downplay the literal force of those biblical passages that spoke of the Son's inferiority to the Father. Far from

19 J. H. Newman, *The Arians of the Fourth Century*.

20 'Arius judaizans?'.

21 'Neo-Arian Religion: the Evidence of the *Apostolic Constitutions*', 155.

22 Ibid. 160.

23 Here the Arians drew upon an earlier theme, going back to Justin's *Dialogue with Trypho*, which in itself did not have any Arian implications.

being a philosopher anxious to safeguard a particular cosmology, be it Neoplatonism or strict monotheism, Arius and his followers were first and foremost men of the Book who desired to achieve terminological clarity. Among modern scholars, Maurice Wiles's assessment of Arianism comes closest to this interpretation. According to Wiles, 'neither different philosophical allegiance nor differing evaluation of the importance of philosophical reasoning was a crucial factor in the split between Athanasius and the Arians.'[24] Wiles argues that while Arius was sensitive to the major philosophical issues of his time, no particular cosmological scheme, later Platonism included, held an exclusive claim upon his biblicism.

The Arian emphasis upon the transcendence of God remained entirely within the limits of earlier patristic scriptural interpretation. Likewise, its subordinationist christology was derived from certain NT passages in which the Son's divine status was carefully distinguished from that of the Father. First of all, Christ spoke of himself as being inferior to the Father (John 14: 28).[25] He admitted that in contrast to the Father his knowledge of the future was limited (Mark 13: 32). He remained obedient to the Father's will throughout his ministry (John 6: 38). As Eunomians were keen to observe, both imperfect knowledge and the relationship of obedience imply subordination.[26] Thus, for them the idea of subordination was not a preconceived metaphysical assumption, but the best interpretative framework in which to make sense of the biblical material. Later in this chapter we will have the opportunity to dwell upon their treatment of the NT christological statements in much greater detail.

As Wiles further points out, contrary to the claims of its orthodox opponents, Arian exegesis was far from being innovative for its time. On

24 'The Philosophy in Christianity: Arius and Athanasius', 42. Cf. id. *Archetypal Heresy*, 10–17. It would be inaccurate to say that Wiles sees literalist exegesis as the sole focal point of Arian thought. Wiles disregards neither the role of preceding patristic tradition, nor Arian awareness of various philosophical issues. Yet, for Wiles, it is literalist exegesis and a distinctive soteriological vision (discussed here as the fifth interpretation), not philosophy, that constituted the two major driving forces of Arianism. See also Charles Kannengiesser, 'Holy Scripture and Hellenistic Hermeneutics in Alexandrian Christology', 1–40. Kannengiesser sees Arius as a '"biblical theologian" standing in the Origenistic tradition of Christianized Platonism'.

25 Cf. Eunomius, *Liber apologeticus*, 10: 'But after all, there is no one so ignorant or so zealous for impiety as to say that the Son is equal to the Father! The Lord himself has expressly stated that "the Father who sent me is greater than I,"' trans. R. P. Vaggione, *Eunomius: The Extant Works*, 47.

26 Gr. Naz., *Or.* 29. 18; 30. 6, 12.

the contrary, it was in line with a respectable tradition stemming from Justin, Clement, Origen, and Dionysius of Alexandria (whose letter to the bishops of Pentapolis we have already touched upon). According to Wiles, Arian exegesis 'built in large measure upon the foundation of antimonarchian writers of the previous century'.[27] Unlike some of his Alexandrian predecessors, Arius did not make much use of allegory in his exegesis and rather sided with the party of *simpliciores* who were committed to the literal sense of the biblical text. Conservative Homoians had misgivings about the use of non-scriptural terminology in the creed.[28] Such considerations account well for the considerable space that is accorded in patristic writings to verse-by-verse rebuttals of Arian exegesis of the key christological texts.[29] This picture of Arian theology has an advantage over those earlier interpretations that viewed Arianism as a spiritually bankrupt 'mass of presumptuous theorizing'.[30] In contrast to them it offers a more sympathetic reconstruction of Arius' theological intentions.

The fourth interpretation follows the same line of trying to be fair to Arius, to the extent of becoming a kind of theological apology for Arianism. In this case, exemplarist soteriology is singled out as the theological core of the Arian position. Some twenty years ago Robert Gregg and Dennis Groh proposed such a reading.[31] These scholars disagree in principle with the first two interpretations, which focus on cosmology as the major Arian preoccupation. In contrast, they implicitly endorse the third view, namely, that Arian christology is much indebted to a traditional strand of biblical literalism. They contend that it would be difficult to explain how the debate acquired the political dimensions that it did, if the whole issue revolved primarily around highly technical details of cosmology.

Gregg and Groh drew attention to the fact that the Arians conceived of the relationship between the Father and the Son in voluntarist, as opposed to essentialist terms. The Arians insisted that the Father generated the Son out of his goodwill and love, not involuntarily out of essence.

27 Wiles, *The Spiritual Gospel*, 121.

28 Wiles, *Archetypal Heresy*, 27. See Ath., *De synodis*, 8, 28–9; 37; *Ad Afros*, 6; *decr.* v. 21; *Tomus ad Antiochenos*, 5.

29 Prov. 8: 22; Phil. 2: 5–11; Mark 10: 18; John 5: 19, 10: 36, 14: 28, 20: 17; 1 Cor. 15: 25–8; Heb. 5: 8.

30 See the critique of earlier approaches, particularly that of H. M. Gwatkin, in Maurice Wiles, 'In Defense of Arius', 339.

31 'Centrality of Soteriology in Early Arianism'; *Early Arianism—A View of Salvation.*

Gregg and Groh speculated that the Arians used the Stoic concept of εὐπάθειαι to account for the innocent emotions that the Father experienced in generating the Son.[32]

These two scholars also attribute the Arian account of Christ's moral progress (προκοπή) to the influence of Stoicism.[33] Being a model creature Christ led a life of total obedience to his creator's will. He increased in virtue throughout his spotless ministry. Foreseeing Christ's moral achievements, God adopted him as his Son and exalted him beyond every creature. By his example Christ showed the path to be followed by all believers.

This reconstruction of the central existential concern of Arianism, in part due to its somewhat sensationalist cast, has been the subject of much discussion and criticism. It may be objected that the Gregg–Groh hypothesis goes against much of the available evidence for early Arianism, which unequivocally shows that Arius was deeply interested in matters cosmological. To postulate a vital soteriological interest that overrode cosmological issues is to introduce an opposition between soteriology and cosmology that the fourth-century theologians would never have endorsed. In support of their hypothesis, Gregg and Groh emphasize repeatedly that highly speculative cosmological questions could not have brought about such a socio-political storm. But this seems anachronistic. If modern theologians are not readily excited by the question 'whether there was [time] when the Son was not'[34] and the like, this is no reason to suppose that fourth-century churchmen saw the matter in the same light. We know that hundreds of years were spent in seemingly speculative debates, on such issues as, for example, the procession of the Holy Spirit, which arguably had devastating ecclesiastical consequences. The same importance should be credited to the issue of the generation of the Son and his relation to the Father.

In addition, the case for the Stoic roots of the Arian theory of Christ's moral progress (προκοπή) rests on unsubstantiated conjectures. Nowhere in the extant sources did Arius confess his indebtedness to the Stoics. If he did, the pro-Nicenes would very likely have held it against

[32] *Early Arianism*, 94: 'The voluntarist cast of their definition of the relationship between the Father and the Son, compelled by their understanding of sonship in covenant in the biblical writings, was legitimized philosophically by means of the Stoic category of εὐπάθειαι (innocent, or worthy, affects).'

[33] 'Stoic-influenced ethical theory' is 'one of the most important keys for unlocking Arian Christology and soteriology,' see *Early Arianism*, 17.

[34] This famous Arian phrase appears, among many other places, in the anathema of the Nicene creed.

him. That Arius emphasized that the Logos was capable of moral improvement is indisputable. But nowhere do we find the Arians making such a typically Stoic claim as that Christ grew morally towards *apatheia*. Arian Christology does not betray any similarity to the Stoicizing views of Clement of Alexandria. The latter, very unlike Arius, denied all possibility of moral progress on the part of Christ. Clement's Christ was endowed with *apatheia* in the Stoic sense of immunity from the four generic *pathē* (desire, fear, grief, and pleasure) from the very beginning of his appearance on earth.[35] Arius, who emphasized the signs of human weakness in Christ, would presumably have been resolutely opposed to this form of Stoic-influenced christology. The terms that the Arians used, such as προκοπή, belonged to the common stock of moral discourse and did not necessarily indicate any Stoic influence. More specifically, there is no need to have recourse, as Gregg and Groh propose, to the technical Stoic concept of *eupatheiai* in order to describe the relation between the Father and the Son in terms of goodwill and love.

Apart from these relatively minor difficulties there are two more serious objections. The supposition that for the Arians the most precious thing was to have a redeemer who was in all respects like a human being conflicts with the much better-attested Arian contention that Christ was a unique creature who stood in a subordinate, yet exceptional relation to the Father. As we saw earlier, Arians of all convictions did not shy from referring to the Son as a God, or as a uniquely generated God. Yet, flatly contradicting this fact, Gregg and Groh stress repeatedly that 'the earthly Arian redeemer *emphatically* was not God; he was an embodied creature'.[36]

The last two words of this quotation bring us to perhaps the most serious flaw of the Gregg–Groh hypothesis, pointed out by R. P. C. Hanson. The Arian Christ was an 'embodied creature', but what sort of a creature? It is indispensable for any exemplarist soteriology that Christ be like us in all respects, that is, at least fully human. But the Arian Christ was the Logos who assumed a human body *emphatically* without a human soul.[37] It may legitimately be asked, how an agent without a human

35 *Strom.* 6. 9. Clement's rather idiosyncratic christological views appear to have had no tangible influence upon later developments.

36 *Early Arianism*, 16; emphasis in the original.

37 See Hanson's Review of *Early Arianism* in *JEH* 33 (1982), 433–4. Hanson supplies references to Epiphanius, *Ancoratus*, 35. 1–6; *Haer.* 69. 19. 7–8; Creed of Eudoxius (Hahn, *Bibliothek der Symbole*, 262); Gr. Nyss., *Refutatio confessionis Eunomii*, 15. 473 (*Eun.* II in *PG*

soul could be a perfect model for those who have a noticeably different constitution. Gregg and Groh, surprisingly, never discuss this point.[38]

While disagreeing with Gregg and Groh that the Arian soteriology was exemplarist, Hanson applauded their contention that a distinctive view of salvation was of capital importance for Arianism.[39] Following this trajectory, Hanson worked out a substantially different account of the Arian view of salvation. He emphasized the fact that Arians of all convictions continued to view the Logos as in some sense divine. The reason the Arians staunchly denied that the Logos assumed a human soul when he became flesh was because they wanted to safeguard the point that it was not a 'mere man' (ψιλὸς ἄνθρωπος), but rather a divine being who was the subject of all the human experiences of Christ, including suffering and death. On the basis of a number of theopaschite statements, drawn primarily from anonymous Arian writings, Hanson argued that 'at the heart of the Arian Gospel was a God who suffered'.[40]

He added that for the Arians, as for their opponents, God the Father was immune from suffering. This was a part of their common anti-Sabellian heritage. The principal reason for Arian subordinationism, Hanson contended, is not to be located in speculations about generated and ungenerated divinity, but in their concern to make divinity (diminished though it is) the subject of the soteriologically significant experiences of suffering and death.

This thesis, counted here as the fifth interpretation, was independently developed by Maurice Wiles in an important article on the anonymous *Homilies on the Psalms*, which Wiles then ascribed to the early Arian writer, Asterius the Sophist.[41] Wiles concluded that although the intention to protect the unity of God was not to be denied to Arians, their primary concern should be located elsewhere: 'What the Homilies

45: 473; *J* ii. 318). In addition, see Gr. Naz., *Ep.* 101; Cyril, *Ad Acacium*, 19. Nestorius, *Liber Heraclidis*, 1. 1. 5 (Nestorius' account of Arianism is otherwise distorted to fit Cyril's christology into what he considered to be a characteristically Arian view). Also important is the statement in Eunomius' *Expositio fidei*, 3: 'Born a man for the freedom and salvation of our race, yet not taking upon him "the man' made up of body and soul," trans. in Vaggione, *Eunomius*, 155, 157.

[38] Hanson, *Search*, 97–8.

[39] Ibid. 91.

[40] Ibid. 121. Cf. 26, 109: 'It was a central part of Arian theology that *God suffered*.' Emphasis in the original.

[41] M. Wiles in colloboration with R. C. Gregg, 'Asterius: A New Chapter in the History of Arianism?', 111–51. In a personal conversation at the 2001 North American Patristics Society conference, Professor Wiles shared with me that he had abandoned the hypothesis that Asterius the Sophist was the author of the anonymous homilies.

suggest is that the mainspring and primary motivation of the [Arian] movement should rather be seen in its determination to safeguard the presentation of Christ's passion and crucifixion as unequivocally the passion and crucifixion of God.'[42] The Hanson–Wiles interpretation will be thoroughly assessed later in this chapter.

In the face of these five competing interpretations of *the* leading theological concern of Arianism, it becomes expedient to ask whether Arianism ever actually had such a single overarching concern? Notwithstanding the aesthetic attraction of discovering one governing principle behind a tangled mass of controversies, I am convinced that the answer to this question is 'no'.[43] In my judgement the first three interpretations—Platonist subordinationism, strict monotheism, and biblical literalism—should be regarded as live options for reaching an illuminating account of Arianism. The objections against the exemplarist soteriology interpretation are, I believe, too damaging for it to be considered as another major point of orientation. As I hope to show later in this chapter, the Hanson–Wiles hypothesis will have to be thoroughly revised if it is to serve as the fourth major interpretation of the Arian gospel.

Broadly speaking, Arianism owes as much to philosophy as it does to the Bible, and as much to inherited Jewish monotheism as to a particular vision of salvation.[44] For the Arians a hierarchical vision of the divine realm was quite compatible with a brand of biblical literalism that saw Christ as a uniquely generated God, inferior to the High God. This ambiguity in Arianism vividly exposes the inadequacy of the Theory of Theology's Fall into Hellenistic Philosophy. To cast the debate in terms of opposition between the Bible and philosophy, as the proponents of the Theory do, is to deploy a grid that is utterly useless in mapping the Arian controversy. It is to presuppose that there is a theological vision in the Bible, free from any philosophical considerations whatsoever, to which one of the contending sides had a mysterious access. If the Theory

[42] Wiles, 'Asterius', 136.

[43] Similarly C. G. Stead in his review of *Early Arianism* in *JTS* 33 (1982), 288.

[44] A reader may wonder how Platonist subordinationism, which implies the existence of subordinate deities, squares with strict monotheism, which means that there is only one God? The term 'strict' in this context is not to be understood to mean that there are no deities at all apart from the High God, but only that there are no deities that are *equal* to the High God. It was this form of strict monotheism that was taught by Eunomius. See *Liber apologeticus*, 5, 7, 28.

fails in the case of Arianism, we should not expect it to be helpful in the assessment of the whole development of the doctrine of the incarnation.

The whole issue, as I suggested before, has to be rethought in terms of a theory of divine emotions and involvement worthy of God. Among various suggestions available in the religious milieu of late Hellenism, both the Arians and their opponents were carving out their distinct versions of such a theory. The factors that contributed to this process were multiple: theories of analogy, meaning, reference, and the limitations of religious language; understandings of the overall intent (*skopos*) of Scripture as well as meticulous exegesis of particular passages; the logic and meaning of the local baptismal creeds; the implicit theology of the sacraments of baptism and Eucharist;[45] the implications of worshipping Christ and addressing prayers to him;[46] the ascetic experience of liberation from the power of evil by means of the invocation of the name of Jesus; competing views of divine immutability and impassibility.[47] To restrict the issues at stake to two and only two parameters, the Bible and philosophy, as the proponents of the Theory of Theology's Fall into Hellenistic Philosophy tend to do, leads to serious distortions of the actual picture.

Does the Generation of the Son from the Father Entail *pathos*?

It is unquestionable that the problem of the Son's generation from the Father held a central place in many Arian speculations. It should be noted that the problem was primarily cosmological, although it had significant soteriological implications. How should the Son's generation be most appropriately conceived? What analogies, images, and metaphors were most suitable? What were the limits of those analogies? Such was the stock of common questions that occupied the minds of the Arians and their adversaries.

All contending parties faced the following dilemma: the term 'generation' applied to the relationship between the Father and the Son, in order to remain meaningful at all, had to be construed with the help of analogies either from human experience, or from other time-bound processes and categories. At the same time, in order not to become a

45 See R. Williams, 'Baptism and the Arian Controversy', 149–80.

46 Ath., *Ar.* 1. 8; 2. 42; 3. 32; Gr. Nyss., *Refutatio confessionis Eunomii*, 72 (*J* ii. 342).

47 Leaving aside marketplace *ad hominem* arguments and dismissive *reductio ad heresim* arguments that were compelling psychologically, not theologically.

distortion of the corresponding divine reality those analogies had to be kept within carefully specified limits. This delicate balance was to be achieved through the most diligent analysis of the major analogies involved. During the debate, the Arians frequently accused the orthodox of effectively draining the terms of all meaning. The orthodox, in turn, retorted that the Arians stretched analogies too far and described the divine generation too anthropomorphically.

One of the crucial points of contention between the anti-Nicenes and the pro-Nicenes was whether and in what sense the generation of the Son entails *pathos*. The term *pathos*, as used by the patristic writers of the fourth century, is any translator's nightmare, due to the embarrassing flexibility and breadth of its meaning. Hanson voiced a common frustration when he wrote: '*Pathos* as used by all fourth century theologians is an almost untranslatable word; it means anything that necessitates change or becoming or human experience.'[48] Along the same lines, William Moore observed in a footnote to his translation of Gregory of Nyssa's *Oratio catechetica magna*: 'There is no one word in English which would represent the full meaning of *pathos*. "Sufferance" sometimes comes nearest to it, but not here, where Gregory is attempting to express that which in no way whatever attached to the Savior, i.e. moral weakness, as opposed to physical infirmity.'[49] E. R. Hardy expressed a similar misgiving in his translation of the same work: 'No English term can adequately render *pathos*.'[50] In these circumstances transliteration or context-specific translations will provide viable solutions to the problem.

It would be natural to expect the anti-Nicenes to argue that the Son was inferior to the impassible Father, on the grounds that his generation was inescapably involved in *pathos*. After all, it was Arius who introduced temporal sequence into the generation of the Son and who, particularly in a market-place version of his theology, dwelt at length upon the analogy of human birth and conception in order to show that the Son's generation, in order to have any meaning at all, had to have a beginning.[51]

Yet surprisingly, several bishops who supported Arius at the council of Nicaea challenged the insertion of the *homoousios* into the Nicene creed

[48] *Search*, 101 n. 11. Jean Daniélou likewise admits that the cognate *apatheia* has infinite nuances, *Platonism et théologie mystique*, 99.

[49] NPNF v. 488 n. 5.

[50] *Christology of the Later Fathers*, 292.

[51] Ath., *Ar.* 1. 22–3.

precisely on the grounds that the generation of the Son 'out of the essence of the Father' suggested unacceptable analogies that entailed *pathos*. They explained their refusal to sign the creed in the following way: 'That is *homoousios* which is from another either by division, derivation or germination (ἢ κατὰ μερισμὸν, ἢ κατὰ ῥεῦσιν, ἢ κατὰ προβολήν); by germination, as a shoot from the roots; by derivation as children from their parents; by division, as two or three vessels of gold from a mass, and the Son is from the Father by none of these modes.'[52]

Socrates dismissed this statement as a veiled sabotage of the deposition of Arius. However, there are reasons to believe that many delegates to the council of Nicaea did not receive this objection against *homoousios* in the same unfavourable light. Eusebius reports that it took the emperor to reassure those who doubted that 'the term *homoousios* implies neither corporeal affections, nor any division (μὴ κατὰ τὰ τῶν σωμάτ ων πάθη λέγοι τὸ ὁμοούσιον, οὔτε κατά τινα ἀποτομὴν).'[53] Constantine added that since God was incorporeal and immaterial, his essence could not be thought of as being divided into parts.[54] We may recall that a similar argument from divine incorporeality and indivisibility to impassibility was made by Athenagoras in the second century.[55]

Despite the emperor's qualification, for many theologians of the age the *homoousios* continued to have distinctly materialist connotations. To address this problem, those who defended the *homoousios* took pains to stress that the Son's generation occured neither by division, nor by an effluence (ἀποῤῥοὴ), nor by an issue (προβολή) of the Father's essence, nor similar to human experiences of conception and birth.[56] At times the term *pathos* referred to all these methods of generation collectively, while at some other times it covered specifically the sphere

[52] Socrates, *HE* 1. 8 (*PG* 67: 68c), trans. A. C. Zenos, NPNF 2nd ser. ii. 10; slightly altered.

[53] Eusebius' letter quoted by Socrates, *HE* 1. 8 (*PG* 67: 72B).

[54] Ibid. 1. 8. Constantine's contribution to the debate could hardly be seen as independent. At all stages of the controversy he relied upon the expertise of his theological advisers, such as Bishop Ossius of Cordova. In his *Letter to Alexander and Arius* Constantine recommended both parties to stay away from analysing the Son's precise relationship to the Father, and hence proved himself incapable of grasping the theological problems at stake. In the eyes of the first Christian emperor the peace of the church always had priority over the precision of dogma.

[55] Athenag., *Leg.* 8. 3. Cf. Ath., *decr.* iii. 10–11; *De synodis*, 16. For an exhaustive discussion of the introduction of *homoousios* into the formula of the creed see Vaggione, *Eunomius of Cyzicus*, 53–67.

[56] Ath., *Ar.* 1. 15–16; 1. 28; *Expositio fidei*, 1; Eusebius, *Contra Marcellum*, frag. 18.

of the human physiology, emotions, and impulses accompanying sexual intercourse.

The majority of the bishops that had reservations about the use of the *homoousios* defended the impassible generation of the Son as zealously as did the orthodox. For example, the so-called 'dated creed' of 359, signed by some four hundred bishops in Sirmium, which emphasized against the Nicene creed that the Son was 'like to the Father who begot him', also stated that 'the uniquely-generated Son of God ... was begotten impassibly from God'.[57]

Thus, a version of subordinationist position moulded by the bishops at various local councils was substantially different from street Arianism, which appears to have exploited the analogy of human birth rather freely. We have already explored the negative side of this position: the critique of *homoousios*. But what did the anti-Nicenes propose constructively? A solemn anathema of the council of Sirmium (351) brings out the gist of their proposal in one terse statement: 'We anathematize those who say that the Father begot the Son unwillingly. For the Father did not beget the Son without willing it, i.e., being compelled by the necessity of his nature. The Father willed it and, having begotten the Son timelessly (ἀχρόνως) and impassibly (ἀπάθως), manifested Him.'[58] This anathema is a part of just one among numerous expositions of faith that were produced during this troubled time in order to achieve doctrinal consensus. As such it did not represent anything final. Extensive creed-making continued. Nevertheless the anathema is important because it made several points that were absolutely critical for a theory of the Son's generation alternative to the pro-Nicene view.

Instead of the language of essence, most anti-Nicene parties preferred the language of will.[59] They tried to corner the pro-Nicenes by forcing upon them a choice between two logical possibilities: either the generation was voluntary, or it was not. If it was not, then the Father acted out of compulsion, which was absurd. If it was, then the Father generated the Son by his will, not out of his essence. The Arians insisted that generation out of essence was indicative of a blind impulse, rather than of a voluntary decision. Athanasius responded that the act of essence

[57] Ath., *De synodis*, 8. Strictly speaking, this creed is not Homoian, since the bishops who signed it were quite explicit about removing an ambiguous term *ousia* from its formulation. A confession of the same flavour was produced in Seleucia in 359, *De synodis*, 29. See Hanson, *Search*, 362–71.

[58] *De synodis*, 27, anathema 25 (*PG* 26: 740B).

[59] See Vaggione, *Eunomius of Cyzicus*, 63.

was of higher order than the act of will, but it did not override God's sovereignty and freedom in any way. He emphasized that the exact nature of the Son's generation was beyond human comprehension.[60]

At some point in the sixties of the fourth century Eunomius restated the neo-Arian case against both the Homoians[61] and the pro-Nicenes in more logically rigorous terms. It is very fortunate that a reliable version of his *Liber apologeticus* has survived. Basil of Caesarea wrote a lengthy treatise in response, to which Eunomius produced a counter-attack, known as *Apologia apologiae*. The latter work is not extant, but may be partially reconstructed from Gregory of Nyssa's meticulous refutation in *Contra Eunomium*. A crucial discussion of the Son's generation occurs in book 4 of Gregory's work. Gregory presents Eunomius's central thesis in the following way:

> For, if all generation (γέννησις), as this author [Eunomius] imagines, has linked with it the condition of passion, we are hereby absolutely compelled to admit that what is foreign to passion is alien also from generation: for if these things, passion and generation, are considered as conjoined, He that has no share in the one would not have any participation in the other.[62]

According to Gregory, Eunomius claimed that every conceivable kind of generation entails *pathos*. This report should not be taken at its face value. There are reasons to believe that Gregory shifted the emphasis of Eunomius' central claim in the interests of polemic. In *Liber apologeticus* Eunomius is adamant about the fact that the divine Father's activity in generating his Son, unlike the activity of any human father in conception, was not bound with passion and the motion of the body.[63] Eunomius observed that it was rather the orthodox view that the Father imparted to the Son his essence that involved the Son's generation with *pathos* (no matter what analogies one used to describe it). We may safely assume that in *Apologia apologiae* Eunomius remained faithful to his original view as stated in *Liber apologeticus* 17. This means that, contrary to Gregory's report, Eunomius did not make a categorical

60 Ath., *Or.* 2. 33; Cf. Gr. Naz., *Or.* 29. 8; Basil, *Eun.* 2. 24.

61 See his attack upon the Homoians in *Liber apologeticus*, 18.

62 Gr. Nyss., *Eun.* 3. 2. 621 (*J* ii. 55–6), trans. Wilson, NPNF v. 12.

63 'Accordingly, it is by no means necessary, when God is called "Father", to understand this activity as having the same meaning that it does with human beings, as involving in both cases the idea of mutability and passion; the one activity is passionless (ἀπαθής), while the other involves passion (μετὰ πάθους),' *Liber apologeticus*, 17, trans. Vaggione, *Eunomius*, 55. Cf. also *Liber apologeticus*, 12, where Eunomius denies that the generation of the Son was bodily.

claim that there was no generation without *pathos*. Instead, Eunomius would be more accurately interpreted as claiming that the orthodox accounts of the Son's generation depended either upon the analogy of human conception and birth, or upon that of the division of some material, and as such involved God in *pathos*.[64] Eunomius proposed to abandon these analogies altogether, particularly that of human birth. He understood the Father's essence to be incommunicable and interpreted the generation of the Son as the first and unique instance of creation. God generates and creates effortlessly without division or motion of essence.[65] In its main lines Eunomius' argument was similar to that of the earlier Arians.

Gregory's reply revealed both extensive knowledge of the standard stock of counter-objections and his own theological ingenuity. Gregory pointed out that in order to understand what the orthodox mean by 'generation' it was not necessary to ground the discourse in physiological and sexual details associated with human conception.[66] Besides, as Basil of Caesarea had observed in his critique of the *Liber apologeticus*, if the analogy of creation were carried too far, it would bring with it an image of God who became tired and needed material in order to create. This would put the Father's impassibility at even greater risk. Hence, Eunomius' own analogy was not immune from the same criticism to which he subjected the analogy of human conception and birth. Following Basil, Gregory concluded that 'if God created without labor or matter, He surely also begot without labor or flux'.[67] The Fathers insisted that the most important point about the analogy of human birth was that humans gave birth to humans (not to birds or animals), that is, to beings of the same essence.[68] After the birth of a child the parent's human nature did not become less human and in this sense was not diminished.

64 This is precisely how Basil understood Eunomius' rather brief comments in *Liber apologeticus*, 16–17. See Basil, *Eun.* 2. 22–3. We should mention that there is a hint at this interpretation in Gr. Nyss., *Eun.* 3. 2. 628 (*J* ii. 60–1): 'I know well that it is not passion he seeks to avoid in his doctrine, for that he does not discern at all in the Divine and incorruptible nature; but to the end that the Maker of all creation may be accounted a part of creation, he builds up these arguments in order to deny the Only-begotten God, and uses his pretended caution about passion to help him in his task,' trans. Wilson, NPNF v. 155.

65 *Liber apologeticus*, 22.

66 'The mystery of theology is one thing, and the physiology of unstable human bodies is another,' *Contra Eunomium*, 4. 1.

67 Ibid. 4. 4.

68 According to Ath., *decr.* vi. 25, this point is made by Dionysius of Alexandria. Athanasius develops the same analogy in *Ar.* 1. 26.

Another image, that of light and its radiance emphasized that the Father and the Son presupposed each other, shared the same substance, existed simultaneously and were not temporally separated.[69] Gregory also drew upon the traditional analogy of the generation of thought (or the spoken word) by the mind.[70] This mental process entailed no division or separation or diminution of the mind's essence. Gregory concluded that the scriptural statement 'in the beginning was the Word' implied no *pathos* in God.

Apart from these traditional analogies, there were two themes that received distinctive development in Gregory's writings alone. First, Gregory observed that even Christ's earthly birth from Mary was without *pathos*: his conception was by the Holy Spirit and without sexual intercourse; Mary's virginity remained intact both after conception and after birth.[71]

The last analogy that Gregory brought to bear upon the issue of the Son's generation was that of the birth of every Christian in the waters of baptism.[72] This birth from above was a change from slavery to passion to freedom from passion. In this special sense baptism was an impassible birth, which was not 'of blood and of the will of the flesh' (John 1: 13) but of the Spirit. If this birth that humans could choose voluntarily was impassible, then, Gregory reasoned, surely divine generation was also free from *pathos*.

The impulse to construe the generation of the Son as closely as possible along the lines of human analogies undoubtedly came from the Arians. It was they who constantly pressed the literal meaning of these analogies from below until they made nonsense of the orthodox position. When the Eunomians claimed to know the Father in the way the Son knew him, they were, in Gregory's view, overstepping the boundaries of creaturely knowledge.[73] For Gregory, even the relevant analogies do no more than shed light upon various facets of the divine generation, which, in the end, remained unknowable and ineffable. As I emphasized in Chapter 2, the divine impassibility commonly served as an apophatic qualifier on all analogies to the divine life drawn from human experience.

[69] It is noteworthy that this image made its way into the Nicene creed, which uses the expression 'light from light'. On this image see Ath., *Ar.* 1. 20; 1. 25; 1. 27; 3. 13; *De sententia Dionysii*, 15; *decr.* v. 24; vi. 27. See also J. Pelikan, *The Light of the World*, 55–72.

[70] *Contra Eunomium* 2. 7; 4. 1. Cf. Ath., *De decr.* iii. 11; *Ar.* 1. 28; *De synodis*, 41.

[71] Gr. Nyss., *Eun.* 2. 7; 4. 4; cf. Basil, *Eun.* 2. 23.

[72] Gr. Nyss., *Eun.* 4. 4.

[73] Gr. Naz., *Or.* 29. 8.

This apophatic qualifier did not undermine the union of love between the divine hypostases, just as it did not exclude other God-befitting emotionally coloured characteristics. But it did purify theological discourse about the divine generation from all unseemly associations and provided an important apophatic correction to the use of analogy.

The Arians' Suffering God: Hanson–Wiles Interpretation Reconsidered

Turning to christology, we will give, as promised earlier in this chapter, a thorough assessment of the Hanson–Wiles interpretation of the key motif of Arian soteriology, the belief in a suffering, yet diminished God. Wiles's case rests upon a number of strikingly theopaschite statements found in an anonymous collection of *Homilies on the Psalms*.[74] These homilies, delivered sometime during the Lenten period, treated at length the events of the crucifixion. In language reminiscent of Melito of Sardis's paschal homily, the author spoke of God who was insulted when his body was struck, received blows, and was crucified;[75] of God whom humans crucified (θεὸν ἐσταύρωσαν);[76] of 'God crucified in the flesh' (θεὸς ἐν σαρκὶ ἦν ὁ σταυρούμενος);[77] of 'the crucified creator of days and the sun' (ὁ ἡμέρας καὶ ἡλίου δημιουργὸς ἐσταυρώθη);[78] and of 'the creator of Adam who having become incarnate died on a tree' (ὁ ποιητὴς τοῦ Ἀδὰμ σαρκωθεὶς ἐπὶ τῷ ξύλῳ ἀπέθανεν).[79] In the twenty-second homily the last point quoted received the following development: 'When you hear that the creator of Adam was crucified, hung, nailed in the flesh, do not for that reason call him "mere man" (ψιλὸν ἄνθρωπον) but God, who took to himself in the flesh the suffering and death of the flesh.'[80] It is entirely plausible that the psilanthropic or 'not a mere man' objection is here not directed against any identifiable heretical group, but is used for the purpose of rhetorical contrast.[81]

[74] Marcel Richard, *Asterii Sophistae Commentariorum in Psalmos*.

[75] *In Psalmum*, 22. 5; 22. 6.

[76] Ibid. 2. 4. 14–15.

[77] Ibid. 2. 6. 17–18.

[78] Ibid. 31. 2. 7.

[79] Ibid. 31. 3. 28–30.

[80] Ibid. 22. 3; cf. 8. 10; 31. 2, trans. Grillmeier, *Christ in Christian Tradition*, i. 211. See also Hanson, *Search*, 39.

[81] Grillmeier suggests that the most plausible target was Paul of Samosata, *Christ in Christian Tradition*, i. 212. Wiles, 'Asterius', 148 n. 56 thinks it could equally be the author's

More doubtful still is the authorship of these homilies. Wiles, following Marcel Richard and others, attributed the majority of the relevant homilies to the shadowy figure of Asterius the Sophist, a contemporary of Arius. The difficulties with such an attribution are numerous: (*a*) we possess only bits and pieces of works that can be securely attributed to the Arian Asterius, the so-called Athanasian and Marcellian fragments; (*b*) the fragments in question do not furnish any evidence for theopaschitism as being a distinct and controversial emphasis of the Sophist's theology; (*c*) there are reasons to believe that the Sophist did not remain fully loyal to his initial pro-Arian leanings;[82] (*d*) the theology of the homilies, due to their highly rhetorical style and expression, reveals no distinctly Arian or semi-Arian features. It is important to note that while the author spoke of Christ as being more than a 'mere man', nowhere did he deny, in a typically Arian or Apollinarian fashion, that Christ had a human soul. Recognizing these difficulties to a certain extent, both Wiles and Hanson insisted that the correlation between the theology of the surviving Asterian fragments and that of the homilies was close enough to warrant claiming them for Asterius. According to Wiles, the Asterius of the homilies could have been a wavering Arian, but he was still an Arian.

A serious challenge to the Arian authorship of the homilies in question has recently come from Wolfram Kinzig, who closely studied the theology of the fragments and concluded that it spoke quite clearly against Arian or Homoian authorship.[83] Kinzig drew attention to the fact that the author described the relation of the Son to the Father and to the Spirit in terms of *homoousios*—a point that no Arian or Homoian would have found it possible to swallow.[84] A thorough linguistic and theological analysis led Kinzig to the conclusion that the author of the homilies was a pro-Nicene theologian, a namesake of the Sophist, who composed his homilies sometime between 385 and 410.[85]

contemporary, Marcellus of Ancyra who was influenced by the Samosatene. Still, it would be safer to assume that the author did not have any particular group in mind. Cf. Cyril of Jerusalem, *Catecheses*, 13. 2, 3, 6.

[82] The Neo-Arian historian Philostorgius accused Asterius the Sophist of 'having falsified the true Arian doctrine of Lucian of Antioch', see Philostorgius, *HE* 2. 14, 15; 4. 4. Also Epiphanius, *Haer.* 76. 3. Wiles, 'Asterius', 113.

[83] *In Search of Asterius: Studies on the Authorship of the Homilies on the Psalms.*

[84] *In Psalmum*, 18. 14. 10; 31. 6. 16. Kinzig argued against Richard that the manuscript tradition was decidedly against interpolation in both instances. *In Search of Asterius*, 141–6.

[85] Kinzig, *In Search of Asterius*, 227.

Broadly speaking, the *Homilies on the Psalms* belong to a rather influential tradition of paschal sermons, traceable to Melito of Sardis,[86] Apollinaris of Hierapolis (second half of the second century),[87] Hippolytus of Rome (170–236),[88] Pseudo-Hippolytus (late second century ?),[89] Ephrem the Syrian (306–73),[90] and Cyril of Jerusalem (315–86).[91] There is nothing distinctly Arian about the theopaschite expressions found in the anonymous *Homilies on the Psalms*; paschal sermons by authors of unquestioned orthodoxy use such expressions with great freedom.

On the strength of these considerations, it is no longer possible to accept the *Homilies on the Psalms* as evidence coming from a certainly Arian source. In contrast to Wiles, Hanson's case for the theopaschite emphasis of the Arian soteriology by no means rests upon the Homilies alone. An uncompromisingly Arian *Expositio fidei*, which is commonly dated to the middle of the fourth century and attributed to Eudoxius (300–70), bishop of Antioch and later bishop of Germanicia, contains this explanation of the incarnation:

> He became flesh, not man, for he did not take a human soul, but he became flesh, in order that he might be called for men 'God with us' by means of his flesh as by means of a veil. There were not two natures, because he was not a complete man, but he was God in the flesh instead of a soul: the whole was a single composite nature; he was passible by the Incarnation for if only soul and body suffered he could not have saved the world. Let them answer then how this passible and mortal person could be consubstantial with God who is beyond these things: suffering and death.[92]

Hanson claimed that 'the heart of Arianism' was to be found in the words of this credal exposition. 'The Arians'—he commented—'want to have a God who can suffer, but they cannot attribute suffering to the

[86] *Peri Pascha.* Critical edition: S. G. Hall, *On Pascha and Fragments.*

[87] A fragment of his paschal sermon is preserved in *Chronicon Paschale*, Corpus Scriptorum Historiae Byzantinae 16, i. 13–14.

[88] Hippolytus, *Contra Noetum*, 18.

[89] The name 'pseudo-Hippolytus' refers to the author of the sermon Εἰς τὸ ἅγιον πάσχα, published first among the spurious works of John Chrysostom. R. Cantalamessa (*L'omelia 'In s. Pascha' dello pseudo-Ippolito di Roma*, 452–60) placed Εἰς τὸ ἅγιον πάσχα in the theological context of the late 2nd-c. Asia Minor.

[90] *De crucifixione*, II; III; IV. P. Nautin, 'Trois homélies dans la tradition d'Origène', in SC 36 (Paris: Éditions du Cerf, 1953).

[91] *Catechesis*, 13.

[92] Hahn, *Symbole*, s. 191, pp. 261–2, trans. Hanson, *Search*, 112. The same passage is quoted again in a different translation on p. 628.

High God, and this is what (with some reason) they believed the Homoousian doctrine would entail.'[93]

Another piece of evidence, critical for Hanson's case, is supplied by three passages from the *Opus Imperfectum in Matthaeum*,[94] a mid-fifth century work by an unknown Latin cleric who most probably lived in Constantinople.[95] The treatise exhibits a type of subordinationism that is quite recognizably Arian, reflects Pelagian influences, and comes down to us in a badly interpolated form.[96] In several places in this unfinished commentary the author inveighs against unnamed heretics who claim that a 'mere man' (*homo purus*) was crucified.[97] In one passage, after two polemical cadenzas, one directed at the Sabellians, the other at the pro-Nicenes, the author proceeds to say:

When you hear them saying: 'A mere man was crucified, body and soul, in which there was no divinity, not God in the body alone (*Quando vides eos dicentes, purum hominem crucifixum et anima, et corpore, non deum in corpore solum, in quo nulla esset divinitas*)' —know that they fill up the measure of their Fathers, the Jews. For they too believe that a mere man was crucified, saying to the apostle: 'You have filled Jerusalem with your teaching and you are determined to bring this man's blood on us.' If a mere man (*homo purus*) suffered, I give up, for [in this case] we were saved by the death of man, not of God.[98]

Later in the commentary the author reiterates his charge against the unnamed *heretici* who 'deceive themselves when they say that a mere man was crucified'. 'Why' —he asks rhetorically' — are the Jews declared the murderers of the Son of God, if a mere man (*homo purus*), not the Son of God, was crucified?'[99] The identity of the anonymous *heretici* is by no means obvious in these cases. Hanson believes that the attack is in both

[93] Hanson, *Search*, 112.

[94] *Opus Imperfectum*, 46. 33 (see below); 49. 30 (see below), and 51. 47 (*PG* 56: 928): 'God placed human salvation above his own impassibility' (*sui ipsius impassibilitati praeposuit salutem humanam*). The latter statement, which Hanson quotes several times as evidence of Arian theopaschitism, actually suggests something quite un-Arian, i.e. that the divine Logos was impassible (which point the Arians staunchly denied) and was in a position to give up his impassibility for the sake of human salvation.

[95] On the question of authorship see Frederic W. Schlatter, 'The Author of the *Opus Imperfectum in Matthaeum*', 368. On Constantinopolitan provenance see P. Nautin, 'L'*Opus Imperfectum in Matthaeum* et les Ariens de Constantinople', 381–408.

[96] Frederic W. Schlatter, 'The Pelagianism of the *Opus Imperfectum in Matthaeum*', 267–85; Joseph van Banning, 'The Critical Edition of the *Opus Imperfectum in Matthaeum*', 382–7.

[97] *Opus Imperfectum*' 11 (*PG* 56: 853); 41. 2 (*PG* 56: 859).

[98] Ibid. 46. 33 (*PG* 56: 889).

[99] Ibid. 49. 30 (*PG* 56: 919). Cf. Iren., *haer.* 3. 12. 6; Melito, *Peri Pascha*, 86. 631; 93. 692.

cases directed against the pro-Nicenes. It seems that this attribution is somewhat anachronistic. Given the mid-fifth century dating of the *Opus Imperfectum,* this particular group of *heretici* could more plausibly be the Nestorians, not the party loyal to Cyril of Alexandria. Indeed, the accusation of teaching that a mere man suffered was made against Theodore of Mopsuestia and was repeatedly levelled against Nestorius by John Cassian, Cyril of Alexandria, and Proclus of Constantinople.[100] It is important to note that both Theodore and Nestorius indignantly dismissed the charge as a completely unfounded accusation, which had force only against those who denied Christ's divinity.[101]

For Hanson the contention that the subject of Christ's soteriologically significant experiences of suffering and death was not a 'mere man', but God in a body, was 'almost the hall-mark of the Arian doctrine concerning the Incarnation'.[102] There is no question that the Arians indeed made the psilanthropic objection. The real issue, however, is what exactly did they make *of it* when they used it in the interests of polemic against the adherents of Nicaea?

This issue is by no means self-evident, especially if we recall that the Arians were not the only ones to make use of the psilanthropic argument. Hanson himself concedes that Apollinaris made a similar claim. In fact, Apollinaris composed a whole litany of syllogisms to show that Christ was both more than human and not fully human:

Every man is a part of the world and no part of the world takes away the sin of the world, under which he also lies. But Christ does take away the sin of the world; therefore Christ is not a man.

Every man is under death and no one who is under death destroys death. But Christ destroys death; therefore Christ is not a man.

[100] John Cassian, *De incarnatione*, 6. 14, 16, 22; Cyril, *Ep.* 7; *Adversus Nestorii blasphemias*, 3. 1. 60; *Contra Nestorium*, 3. 2 (*ACO* 1. 1. 6. 58, 60); *Explicatio duodecim capitum*, 31; *Ad augustas*, 7; Proclus, *Sermo*, 1. 7–8.

[101] Theodore, *De incarnatione*, frag. From Bk. 6: ' "But", they [the unnamed opponents] say, "by asserting that Christ is mere man, we [the Orientals] deserve to be called man-worshippers". Now this is an open lie, if indeed this is what they wish to say. For no one has ever heard us say this. And I do not believe that even they can undertake to lie so openly: not because they do not knowingly resort to falsehood, but because they see how easily they can be refuted... For we consider that it is the height of madness to deny divinity to the Only-begotten.' Cf. Theodore, *On the Nicene Creed*, trans. Migana, 90; Nestorius, *Liber Heraclidis*, 1. 1. 53; Socrates, *HE* 7. 32. 6, 8. Also cf. Nestorius' statement quoted by Cyril, *Contra Nestorium*, 2. 10 (*ACO* 1. 1. 6. 47).

[102] *Search*, 40. Cf. p. 110. In addition, see his discussion of the rejection of *psilos anthropos* in the Pseudo-Ignatian letters on pp. 115–16. On the psilanthropic argument, see also Wiles, *Archetypal Heresy*, 39–40; Grillmeier, *Christ in Christian Tradition*, i. 306.

Every man is of the earth. But Christ is not of the earth, but of heaven; therefore Christ is not a man.

No man has glory before the ages. But Christ does; therefore Christ is not a man.

He who saves from sin is above sin; and Christ saves from sin. But no man is above sin; therefore Christ is not a man.[103]

Later in the same work Apollinaris declares: 'If Christ were only man (μόνον ἄνθρωπος), he would not save the world . . . If Christ were only man (μόνον ἄνθρωπος) he would not make the dead alive.'[104] On the surface Apollinaris' claim was substantially the same as that made by Eudoxius, the author of the *Opus Imperfectum*, and other Arian polemicists. Yet, the conclusion that Apollinaris draws was quite different. Let us recall that Apollinaris was as ardent a defender of the full divinity of Christ as was Athanasius. On this score, at least, Apollinaris clashed with the Arians in the most fundamental way.[105] Furthermore, in his clearest theological moments Apollinaris taught that the fully divine Logos took the place of a human mind in Christ and admitted that Christ possessed a human body complete with a soul. Therefore, in Apollinaris' hands, the claim that the one who suffered was more than a 'mere man' was given a rather different spin.

We must emphasize that Apollinaris was not the only one among the non-Arian authors to make use of the psilanthropic objection. Cyril of Jerusalem reiterated it three times in one of his Lenten sermons, to make sure that the catechumens had grasped the significance of this point:

And wonder not that the whole world was ransomed; for it was no mere man (ἄνθρωπος ψιλὸς), but the only-begotten Son of God, who died on its behalf.

For it was not a mere man (ψιλὸς ἄνθρωπος) who died for us, as I said before, but the Son of God, God made man.

For it was no common man (Οὐ γὰρ ἦν ἄνθρωπος εὐτελὴς ὁ πάσχων, ἀλλὰ θεὸς ἐνανθρωπήσας) who suffered, but God in man's nature, striving for the prize of his patience.[106]

Here again we find a kind of argument similar to the one that we have already encountered in the Arian and Apollinarian writings: if salvation

103 Apollinaris, *Anacephalaiosis*, 2–4, 7, 9, trans. W. S. Babcock, 18–19.

104 Ibid. 19, 20.

105 On Apollinaris, see Norris, *Manhood in Christ*, 79–122.

106 *Catecheses*, 13. 2, 3, 6.

was to have a universal effect, it had to be more than a mere man, namely God in human nature, who suffered and died. Although Cyril's loyalty to the Nicene *homoousios* is somewhat questionable, contemporary scholarship is clear that he cannot be classified as either strictly or moderately Arian, and that his leanings from the beginning were broadly orthodox.[107] Unlike Arius and Apollinaris, Cyril did not think of Christ's humanity as somehow incomplete or defective. The *Homilies on the Psalms*, discussed above, furnish additional evidence for the use of the psilanthropic argument by an author who was neither Arian, nor unquestionably pro-Nicene.

Therefore, the claim that the Crucified was more than a 'mere man' was not peculiar to Arianism alone (*pace* Hanson), but provided a way for all parties involved to sharpen the problem of God's involvement in the human experiences of Christ.[108] The Arians concluded that Christ was a semi-divine creature who assumed a human body, devoid of human soul; the Apollinarians inferred that the Saviour was a fully divine Logos who took the place of the human mind when he assumed human nature; and the orthodox affirmed that the fully divine Logos assumed human nature, complete with human mind and soul.

As to the use of the theopaschite expressions, it must be stressed that the orthodox deployed them with reference to Christ's crucifixion as freely as did the Arians. For example, Athanasius in his *Epistula ad Epictetum*, rose up against the error of those who denied that the Crucified was God.[109]

Similarly, Gregory of Nazianzus could exclaim in his second paschal sermon: 'We needed an Incarnate God, a God put to death, that we might live.'[110] In the same sermon Gregory spoke of 'God

[107] See Hanson, *Search*, 412. Although Hanson considered Cyril's theology at length in his book, surprisingly, he completely ignored the psilanthropic statements.

[108] The psilanthropic argument became a rhetorical commonplace in later orthodox tradition. See e.g. Maximus Confessor repeating a Cyrillian theologumenon in *Ambigua*, 113b (*PG* 91. 1056A–B): 'If I may say so, he [Christ] suffered divinely, because he suffered voluntarily, for he was not a mere man (μὴ ψιλὸς ἄνθρωπος). He wrought miracles humanly, through the flesh, for he was not a bare divinity.'

[109] Ath., *Ep. ad Epictetum*, 59. 10.

[110] Gr. Naz., *Or.* 45. 28. See Gregory Telepneff, 'Theopaschite Language in the Soteriology of Saint Gregory the Theologian', 403–16. The language of Eusebius of Emesa (300–59) was equally bold: '*Deus ab hominibus condemnatus est. Deus pro nobis mortuus est,*' frag. 5. 72. Discussed in Grillmeier, *Christ in Christian Tradition*, 305. Cf. frag. 8. 73.

crucified'.[111] This sermon, along with the anonymous *Homilies on the Psalms*, stood in a venerable tradition of paschal homiletic literature, later reflected in the hymnody of the Byzantine *Lenten Triodion*. In this hymnographic tradition, theopaschite statements were a commonplace poetic device that vividly captured the drama of human ingratitude, the depth of Christ's humiliation, and the tragedy of crucifixion.[112]

In the course of this study I have repeatedly stressed that theopaschite statements in themselves do not resolve any theological conundrums. On the contrary, they stand in need of further explication. It is misleading to claim that 'The Arians saw that the New Testament demanded a suffering God, as their opponents failed to see. They were convinced that only a God whose divinity was somehow reduced must suffer. Hence the radical Arian doctrine of Christ, but hence also the Arian readiness to speak of God as suffering. We can see here the attraction of Arian doctrine. But we can also see the high price which it had to pay in order to attain its ends.'[113] To argue, as Hanson and Wiles do, that the Arians, in contrast to pro-Nicenes, believed in a passible God is to misread the evidence. Indeed, if we were to take the theopaschite statements on both sides at their face value, the orthodox could also be understood as proclaiming God's suffering, crucifixion, and death.

Instead, we must look below the surface of such statements and ask what place they occupied in the overall theological programme of a particular party. What precisely were they meant to convey? What were the respective roles of the Logos and the flesh in the incarnation? As Wiles and Hanson insist, the disagreement between the Arians and the pro-Nicenes consisted to a great degree in the fundamental differences between two equally legitimate hermeneutical tracks.[114]

The Arians applied all passages describing the earthly experiences of Christ directly to the Logos, emphasizing those that most evidently suggested human weakness. Unlike the orthodox writers, they were reluctant to differentiate between those actions and properties of Christ that were properly divine, like the working of miracles, foreknowledge, and freedom to give and take life, and those properties and experiences that were properly human, like the need for physical sustenance and the fear of death. The main purpose of this emphasis, Hanson contends, was primarily soteriological: the Logos, according to the Arians, directly

[111] Gr. Naz., *Or.* 45. 29. Cf. Apollinaris, frag. 62, 95.

[112] *Triodion Kataniktion*, 360, 392–4, 409.

[113] Hanson, *Search*, 41.

[114] Wiles, *Spiritual Gospel*, 116, 121–8; *Archetypal Heresy*, 10–17; Hanson, *Search*, 848.

partook of all experiences of his body, e.g. when the body of Christ suffered, the Logos that indwelt the body suffered too.[115] In Hanson's opinion, the orthodox writers of the fourth century, in the end, failed to sustain this vital soteriological point of the gospels.

The Orthodox Responses to the Arians

In what follows I would like to call into question the two leading ideas of Hanson's interpretation (the first one also shared by Wiles): (1) that the Arian insistence upon the passibility of the Logos had predominantly a soteriological, as opposed to a subordinationist concern as its focus, and (2) that the orthodox account of the incarnation failed, comparatively speaking, to involve the fully divine Logos in the human experiences of Christ.

With regard to the first point, I believe that Hanson has misplaced the focus of the primary Arian concern. For all of its attraction to modern theological sensibilities, this interpretation of Arianism is based upon considerable stretching of the available evidence. Our sources unanimously claim that both Arius and Eunomius appealed to the human experiences of Christ in order to find a proof for the Logos' passibility and dissimilarity from the impassible Father, not for soteriological reasons. Gregory of Nyssa stated the case quite clearly: 'If, according to their statement, the Godhead of the Son suffers, while that of the Father is preserved in absolute impassibility, then the impassible nature is essentially different from that which admits passion.'[116] Gregory's point is fully consistent with Eudoxius' rhetorical question, directed at the pro-Nicenes: 'How could this passible and mortal person be consubstantial with God who is beyond these things: suffering and death?'[117] Eudoxius' major concern here is to protect the impassibility of the High God from being compromised by the incarnation in any way.

We find the same emphasis in Arius. Dwelling upon the subject of Christ's full divinity in his letter to Constantine, Arius exclaimed: 'No! I do not wish God to be involved with the suffering of insults!'[118] Briefly

[115] Hanson, *Search*, 103: 'The Arians dislike dividing Christ's words and acts into those relevant to his human nature and those to his divine nature. It was the God in Christ who died; he was that sort of vulnerable God.'

[116] Gr. Nyss., *Eun.* 3. 4. 712 (*J* ii. 135), trans. Wilson, NPNF 2nd ser. v. 182.

[117] Hahn, *Symbole*, s. 191, pp. 261–2.

[118] H. G. Opitz, *Urkunden zur Geschichte des arianischen Streites*, III no. 29, p. 73, trans. Hanson, *Search*, 9.

touching upon this fragment, Hanson hesitantly remarks that it is 'not inconsistent (as we shall see) with the doctrine of early and later followers of his [Arius'] theological tradition on the same subject.'[119] How Hanson envisioned reconciling this point with his main claim that 'at the heart of the Arian gospel was a God who suffered' is rather difficult to see. The Arians, in the Hanson–Wiles reconstruction, attempt to sit on two chairs at the same time: protecting the impassibility of the High God and his complete immunity from involvement in the messy affairs of human history, and insisting with even greater energy upon the soteriological significance of the divine suffering of the uniquely generated God.

This interpretation, for all of its ingenuity and sophistication, is highly implausible. First of all, the soteriological worth of the claim that an inferior, created deity suffered through defective humanity is highly questionable. It is true that the Arians accused their opponents of claiming that a 'mere man' suffered. As we saw earlier, the force of this accusation is considerably weakened by the fact that both Arians, Apollinarians, and writers of unquestionable orthodoxy used similar arguments and reached widely different conclusions. When all scores with the pro-Nicenes were settled, all that the Arians could respond to their own charge was that a unique creature suffered, a created creator died, a saviour who had to be resurrected was crucified. If the Arians indeed were so fond of the psilanthropic argument, they themselves supplied a rather anticlimactic and soteriologically unconvincing conclusion. I must agree with P. R. Foster's observation:

> Despite the obvious and welcome gain in our understanding of Arianism which has been achieved in recent years, the concept of Christ as a reduced divinity whose suffering enables the impassibility of the supreme God to remain intact looks as unsatisfactory as ever. It is not even clear, on Hanson's account, just why the suffering of the reduced divinity results in our salvation: his final claim, that the suffering of Christ was 'in order to redeem man' hangs in the air, without any supporting explanation.[120]

It is much more plausible that the Arians, both in cosmology and in christology, consistently pushed forward a quite different central issue: the passible Son was inferior in essence to the impassible Father in that he was (*a*) generated, and (*b*) subject to suffering.[121] Nobody has ex-

[119] Hanson, *Search*, 10.

[120] 'Divine Passibility and the Early Christian Doctrine of God', 44.

[121] My interpretation is in agreement with G. D. Dragas, *St. Athanasius Contra Apollinarem*, 252: 'It is crystal clear that the point of dispute between Athanasius and his Arian

pressed this point of the Arian controversy more clearly than Gregory of Nyssa:

Both sides believe in the economy of the passion. We hold that the God who was manifested by the cross should be honored in the same way in which the Father is honored. For them [the Eunomians] the passion is a hindrance to glorifying the only-begotten God equally with the Father who begot him . . . For it is clear that the reason why he [Eunomius] sets the Father above the Son, and exalts him with supreme honor is that in the Father is not seen the shame of the Cross. He insists that the nature of the Son is inferior because the reproach of the Cross is referred to the Son alone, and does not touch the Father . . . 'If'—he [Eunomius] says—'he [Basil of Caesarea] can show that the God who is over all, who is the unapproachable Light, was incarnate, or could be incarnate, came under authority, obeyed commands, came under the law of man, bore the Cross, then let him say that the Light is equal to the Light.' Who is then ashamed of the Cross? He who, even after the passion, worships the Son equally with the Father, or he who even before the passion insults the Son, not only by ranking him with the creation, but by maintaining that he is of passible (τῆς ἐμπαθοῦς) nature, on the ground that he could not have come to experience his sufferings had he not had a nature capable of suffering? . . . So far are we from entertaining any low idea concerning the Only-begotten God, that if anything belonging to our lowly nature was assumed in His dispensation of love for man, we believe that even this was transformed to what is divine and incorruptible; but Eunomius makes the suffering of the Cross to be a sign of divergence (παραλλαγῆς) in essence, in the sense of inferiority, considering, I know not how, the surpassing act of power, by which he was able to perform this, to be an evidence of weakness . . .

He who by reason of his unspeakable and unapproachable greatness is not comprehensible by any, save by Himself and by the Father and the Holy Spirit, He, I say, was able even to descend to community with our weakness. But they adduce this proof of the Son's alienation (ἀλλοτριότητος) in nature from the Father . . . arguing on the ground that the Father's nature remained pure in impassibility (καθαρῶς ἐν ἀπαθειᾳ), and did not admit communion with passion . . . [122]

According to Gregory, the distinctive concern of Arianism was not to affirm a God who suffered in Christ, but above all else, to secure the claim that the High God suffered neither in Christ, nor apart from

opponents against whom he writes this treatise, is not the nature of suffering and death, but whether the fact of suffering and death implies that Christ is not who He has been claimed to have been, namely, Son and Logos of God and God.' Cf. Simonetti, *La crisi Ariana*, 469.

[122] Gr. Nyss., *Eun.* 3. 3. 691–6 (*J* ii. 118–20), trans. Wilson, NPNF, 2nd ser. v. 176–7; altered.

Christ. Gregory's reading agrees with another pro-Nicene theologian who reports that Arians drove their point home by asking the following rhetorical questions: 'How do you [the Nicene party] dare to say that the one having a body is the proper Word of the Father's essence, so that he endured such a thing as this [the cross]' and 'How is he able to be Logos or God who slept as a man, wept, and had to learn by inquiry?'[123] To ascribe suffering to the High God was nothing short of a blasphemy. For the Arians the divine impassibility meant that the High God could not reveal himself, could not be involved in human history, could not become incarnate and, therefore, could not subject himself to the *pathos* of human existence. Only a passible creature could do all that.

For the orthodox the function of the divine impassibility was quite different. For them the divine impassibility, along with other negative characteristics of God, did not preclude divine care or God's direct involvement in history. With this issue we move to the second guiding idea of Hanson's interpretation, namely, that the orthodox insistence upon the impassibility of Christ's divinity precluded direct divine involvement in Christ's passion. According to Hanson, in the orthodox account of the incarnation, Christ's humanity effectively shielded his divinity from participating directly in human experiences.[124] This line of interpretation is considerably discredited by the fact (which Hanson himself emphasized) that Athanasius came to appreciate the soteriological importance of Christ's human soul and hence Christ's complete humanity fairly late in his battle with Arianism, perhaps as late as 362.[125] During the early days of the controversy, the Arian claim that Logos had replaced human soul in Christ in order to experience suffering more directly could not have acquired the prominence that it later came to have in the Apollinarian controversy.

In addition, Hanson's interpretation is based upon a questionable presupposition that God's most intimate involvement in human suffering entails complete divine identification with humanity's misfortunes. The Arians claimed that when Christ's body shed tears, the passible Logos literally shed tears; when Christ's body was crucified, the Logos was likewise nailed to the cross, and so on. According to Hanson, there was nothing in the orthodox account of the incarnation that could match the profundity of this Arian insight.

123 (Ps.-?)Ath, *Ar.* 3. 27. Cf. ibid. 3. 55; *Ep.* 10. 9, trans. Bright, 182.
124 Hanson, *Search*, 41. Cf. Grillmeier, *Christ in Christian Tradition*, i. 304–5.
125 See Hanson, *Search*, 452.

It is true that for the pro-Nicenes the Logos did not become an exact copy of his passible human nature. At the same time, as one of Athanasius' supporters pointed out, 'when the flesh suffered, the Logos was not outside of it (ἐκτὸς), which is why the suffering is said to be his'.[126] As we will see in the next chapter, Cyril of Alexandria made the concept of appropriation (ἰδιοποιήσις) of the flesh by the Logos central to his defence of the unity of Christ's person in the economy of salvation. In the incarnation God put human nature to God-befitting use, sanctified it, and made it life-giving.[127]

The question must be pressed again, what exactly, on the orthodox view, was the impassible Logos doing when his flesh was subject to *pathos*? Among other things, they emphasized that in all the actions and experiences of the Logos the human and divine natures were inseparable. The Logos may be said to suffer in the flesh, hunger in the flesh, grow tired in the flesh, advance in the flesh, and the like.[128] The Logos' indwelling of the human nature in Christ was quite different from his presence in the martyrs and prophets. Athanasius stressed that the Logos could be said to help the prophets and strengthen the martyrs, but he could not be said to suffer personally in them. The latter claim could be made exclusively about his activity in Christ.[129]

According to pro-Nicene theologians, human nature was an instrument through which the Logos both experienced the sufferings and wrought his miracles.[130] Wiles, in contrast to Hanson, paid full justice to this point of Athanasius' two-nature exegesis when he observed:

> He [Athanasius] is, however, extremely careful in his use of it [two-nature exegesis] to insist that it must not be understood to imply two distinct sets of actions or experiences. Every act is the act of the one divine Lord, acting sometimes in his purely divine capacity, sometimes in accordance with his adopted human status. In fact the two cannot possibly be rigidly separated in practice when even such an exalted utterance as 'I and my Father are one' has to be uttered with a human tongue.[131]

While the impassibility of the Logos served as an identifier of his full divinity, this attribute did not imply that the Logos remained inactive and withdrawn from Christ's human experiences. Because of his

126 (Ps-?)Ath., *Ar.* 3. 32 (*PG* 26: 389c). Cf. *decr.* iii. 14.

127 Ath., *Inc.* 17.

128 (Ps-?)Ath., *Ar.* 3. 53.

129 Ibid. 30–31; *Tomus ad Antiochenos*, 7; *Ep. ad Epictetum*, 59. 2, 11.

130 Ath., *Inc.* 8–9.

131 Wiles, *The Spiritual Gospel*, 117. Wiles refers to Ath., *Ep. ad Serap.* 4. 14. Cf. (Ps-?) Ath., *Ar.* 3. 35.

impassibility the Logos enabled the human nature to undergo freely what were otherwise involuntary human experiences. The Logos, as Athanasius put it, 'permitted his body to weep and hunger',[132] and 'let his own body suffer'.[133] The Logos temporarily suspended his power, allowing human nature to endure these experiences in a real way. The presence of the Logos secured Christ's freedom and control over these otherwise uncontrollable human experiences: 'For man dies—Athanasius explained—not by his own power, but by necessity of nature and against his will; but the Lord, being himself immortal, but having a mortal flesh, had power as God, to become separate from the body and to take it again, when He would.'[134] In this way the Logos destroyed the *pathē* of the flesh, including sin and death. He restored human nature to incorruption, immortality, and impassibility. He set human nature free from *pathē* and healed it.[135] He destroyed death by death.[136]

Thus, we can hardly agree with Hanson's second point that in the orthodox account of the incarnation Christ's complete human nature shielded his divinity from all direct involvement in human life. On the contrary, the pro-Nicenes felt this problem even more intensely than did the Arians. The pro-Nicenes claimed that the Logos was involved in human sufferings without being overwhelmed by them and without copying the sufferings of his flesh. In the long run, it was the Arians who explained away the paradox and the scandal of the incarnation by claiming that a unique creature suffered and by extricating the High God from all involvement in human history. The orthodox sustained the vital tension of the creed, just as they upheld the scandalous message of the cross. In the last chapter we will see how the church's loyalty to the incarnational vision of the Nicene creed was tested with new force in the struggle with Nestorianism.

132 (Ps-?)Ath., *Ar.* 3. 55.

133 Ibid. 3. 55; 3. 58.

134 Ibid. 3. 57.

135 Ibid. 3. 34. Cf. Cyril, *In Ioannem*, 11. 12 (Pusey, 15).

136 Ibid. 3. 57. Cf. *Ep. ad Epictetum*, 59. 6.

6

Nestorianism Countered: Cyril's Theology of the Divine Kenosis

> Today He who hung the earth upon the waters is hung upon the Cross.
>
> He who is King of the angels is arrayed in a crown of thorns.
>
> He who wraps the heaven in clouds is wrapped in the purple of mockery.
>
> He who in Jordan set Adam free receives blows upon His face.
>
> The Bridegroom of the Church is transfixed with nails.[1]

THE debate with the Arians further narrowed the range of options acceptable in the church's articulation of the doctrine of the incarnation. By now the Docetic, the Patripassian, and the Arian responses to the message of the cross were ruled out as inadequate solutions. It has become non-negotiable that (1) the Son was of the same essence with the Father; (2) that the Father did not become incarnate and did not suffer; (3) and that the Son's birth, suffering, and death in the incarnation were real and did not diminish his divine status. As is to be expected, these three propositions taken together sharpened the issue of the divine involvement in the human experiences of Christ to an unprecedented degree. In the exposition that follows I will show that the Nestorian controversy and Cyril's christology in particular made a decisive breakthrough in furthering the church's understanding of the mystery of incarnation.

[1] *The Lenten Triodion*, 587.

Inadequate Modern Approaches to the Nestorian Controversy

The subtlety of the theological questions involved in the Nestorian controversy has made its interpretation a highly controversial issue among historians of doctrine. While it would be premature to trace any patterns of scholarly consensus, it would be worthwhile to distance the present study from the three influential approaches that I consider to be blind alleys of investigation.

One such an approach is to regard the theological issues at stake in the debate as a pile of sophisms masking the 'real' political power struggle of the archiepiscopal sees.[2] This approach is usually wedded to a Gibbonian caricature of Cyril as a tyrannical Egyptian pharaoh, utterly devious in the killing of Hypatia, unscrupulous in bribing the Theodosian court, and equally dishonest in handling the affairs of the church. There is an attraction of historical symmetry here: Theophilus, Cyril's uncle and predecessor in the Alexandrian see was a monster; Dioscorus, Cyril's secretary and successor was a monster; and so should Cyril fittingly be a monster. Cyril, we must remember, never admitted his uncle's grievous error in driving John Chrysostom into exile.[3] In his less than gentlemanly confrontation with Nestorius Cyril further embittered the far from perfect relations between the archiepiscopal sees of Alexandria and Constantinople.

However, the recent groundbreaking study by John McGuckin shows this historical picture to be a distortion of the evidence.[4] McGuckin emphasizes that Cyril made numerous attempts to achieve reconciliation with the alienated parties and showed himself to be more sensitive to the virtues of the opposition than did Nestorius.[5] The murder of Hypatia,

[2] This position is advocated e.g. by Hans von Campenhausen, *The Fathers of the Greek Church*, 145–55. See also Eduard Schwartz, *Cyrill und der Mönch Viktor*.

[3] Cyril refused to include John Chrysostom in the diptychs of the church of Alexandria, see *Ep*. 75–6. On the Synod of Oak see *Ep*. 33. 4.

[4] McGuckin, *Christological Controversy*. Francis Young offers a perceptive and nuanced treatment of Cyril's blunders and accomplishments in *From Nicaea to Chalcedon*, 240–6. Henry Chadwick criticizes political reductionism in his 'Eucharist and Christlogy', 145–64.

[5] McGuckin, *Christological Controversy*, 227–9. This is particularly clear in Cyril's repeated rapprochements with the Antiochenes after the council of Ephesus. Cyril was quite prepared to go beyond the slogan-like accusations. For example, he conceded that the terminology of the two natures was quite admissible, as long as the union of God the Word with our nature was sufficiently clearly affirmed. See *Ad Eulogium*, *Ad Celestinum*, 2, *Ad Acacium* (of Beroea), 1–11. Ezra Gebremedhin, in contrast, sees Cyril as a 'crusader of his own theological emphases', not a 'bridge-builder'. See his *Life-Giving Blessing*, 18–19.

which has acquired in many history books the significance of Cleopatra's nose, viewed against the record of street violence in fifth-century Alexandria, shows the young bishop's inexperience in handling riotous groups of people rather than his deviousness. Likewise, scholars with modern Western sensibilities only betray a lack of historical sensitivity when they see shameless bribery in transactions that in the minds of Cyril's contemporaries were regarded (and are to this day regarded in the East) as a rather mundane exchange of favours between dignitaries.[6]

Instead of reducing the debate to merely political interests, we should rather see in Cyril's character an ambiguous and ultimately unanalysable interplay of love of power and sincere desire to guard the teaching of the church from what he believed were dangerous distortions. Nestorius likewise was an ambitious man, full of honourable intentions.[7]

A second blind alley of inquiry consists in the attempt to fit the theological debate between Cyril and Nestorius into the framework of differences between the theological schools of Alexandria and Antioch.[8] In this well-known scheme, the teaching of the Alexandrian school is characterized by the dominance of Platonism and allegorical interpretation and a greater emphasis upon the divinity of Christ to the neglect of his humanity. In contrast, the school of Antioch cultivated the philosophy of Aristotle and was committed to the literal sense of the Scripture. The result was an emphasis upon the full humanity of Christ and the circumstances of his earthly life.

This interpretation, despite its enduring influence upon introductory textbooks in church history,[9] is unsatisfactory for a number of reasons. One objection would be that the term 'school' here functions as a vague designation of four different entities: a catechetical school in Alexandria, a monastic school of scriptural exegesis near Antioch, a geographically restricted theological tradition, and a party loyal to a particular theologian. The problem of theological continuity arises in the case of at least the first three of these entities. The catechetical school of Alexandria had

[6] Cyril, *Ep.* 96.

[7] For a sympathetic and sensitive portrait of Nestorius' intentions see F. Loofs, *Nestorius and His Place in the History of Christian Doctrine*, 19.

[8] This view found its main advocate in Adolf Harnack. For later endorsements of the two-schools hypothesis see Charles Raven, *Apollinarianism*, 54. R. V. Sellers, *Two Ancient Christologies*, operated under the basic assumption of two schools and came to the conclusion that the differences between them were political, not theological. R. Norris offered a systematic rebuttal of the two-schools hypothesis in his *Manhood and Christ*, 250–2. See also his 'Chalcedon Revisited', 141.

[9] See Justo L. Gonzáles, *The Story of Christianity*, i. 252.

an ambiguous relationship to Origenism and suffered a major disruption during the Arian crisis. Athanasius' distinct articulation of the doctrine of incarnation stands in sharp contrast to Origen's subordinationist tendencies and the master's characteristically liberal use of *allegoresis*.

As far as the *asketerion* near Antioch is concerned, precious little can be securely reconstructed about its founder, Diodore of Tarsus, as well as about the early years of the school's operation.[10] We know that it produced two colossal figures—John Chrysostom and Theodore the Interpreter. It is noteworthy that John's christology bears none of the characteristic features of his intimate friend, the later bishop of Mopsuestia. In the light of this fact, the extent to which Theodore's two-subjects christology can be traced to Diodore of Tarsus must not be exaggerated.[11] There is no question, however, that Theodore's distinctive two-subject christology had considerable support in Antioch and, more generally, in the East.

To the degree to which the council of Ephesus had for some time caused a rift between those loyal to Theodore's and those loyal to Cyril's interpretation of Nicaea, one could quite legitimately speak of two parties, the Orientals and the Cyrillians. But 'the two-schools hypothesis' goes far beyond a fairly modest observation that the quarrelling hierarchs relied upon the theological support groups in making their distinct claims. The hypothesis purports to explain the principal christological differences in terms of divergent philosophical influences and conflicting exegetical methods, associating them with specific geographical locations.

As far as the philosophical influences are concerned, it is today almost universally recognized that a pure Aristotelianism was not a live option in late antiquity.[12] In the light of this fact, the Antiochean school's indebtedness to the Peripatetics to the exclusion of and in distinction from late Platonism is a pure fiction. In a study of Theodore's biblical exegesis, published in 1961, Rowan Greer attempted to demonstrate that the bishop of Mopsuestia was a 'biblicist', whose theology was

[10] See Palladius, *Dialogus*, 9; Sozomen, *HE* 8. 2; Socrates, *HE* 6. 3.

[11] Grillmeier, *Christ in Christian Tradition*, i. 352–60. Cf. Cyril, *Ep*. 45. 2 (*ACO* 1. 1. 6. 151). It is worth noting that a generation before Theodore, Apollinaris wrote against a group of theologians who were making a sharp distinction between the two subjects in Christ. Gregory Nazianzus found it necessary to defend his christology which emphasized full humanity against Apollinarian accusation of preaching 'two sons', see *Ep*. 102. K. M. Spoerl and others have suggested that the target of Apollinaris' attack was Marcellus of Ancyra. See K. M. Spoerl, 'Apollinarian Christology and the Anti-Marcellan Tradition'.

[12] Norris, *Manhood and Christ*, 4.

dominated by the imagery of the Bible rather than by the alien metaphysical assumptions of philosophers. Greer then argued that Nestorius had betrayed his teacher and, together with Cyril, had fallen prey to the damaging influence of later Platonism.[13] Greer's approach agrees in principle with the Theory of Theology's Fall into Hellenistic Philosophy, which measures the failures of patristic theology by the extent of its captivity to the thought-forms of Hellenism. It is ironic that Greer reached a material conclusion that is diametrically opposed to that endorsed by the Fall into Hellenistic Philosophy theorists: Theodore, who was a staunch defender of the absolute and uncompromised divine impassibility turned out, in Greer's view, to be a biblical theologian who opposed the philosophizing 'theopaschite' Cyril!

It is, as the reader may recall, one of the main purposes of this study to dislodge the Theory of Theology's Fall into Hellenistic Philosophy. In this chapter I will argue that divergent philosophical influences, even if those could be established, would not account for the principal differences in Theodore's and Cyril's christology. The same holds true for the alleged differences in the methods of scriptural exegesis. It should be observed that Cyril was rather economical in his use of allegory in his voluminous biblical commentaries.[14] At the same time, far from being a strict literalist, Theodore was a great master of typology.[15] More important still is the fact that Cyril's interpretation of the key christological texts debated with Nestorius was entirely free from allegorizing. On the contrary, it was Cyril, not Nestorius, who pressed the literal meaning of the kenotic passage of Phil. 2: 5–11 to its logical limits and made this passage central for understanding of what was at stake in the divine incarnation.

To conclude, all that remains from the interpretative framework of the 'two-schools hypothesis' is the fairly trivial observation that Cyril quite consciously built upon the foundation of the Nicene theology in its Athanasian form, whereas Nestorius saw himself as the follower and disciple of Theodore.[16]

In contrast to approaches that seek to explain the debate in terms of external factors, be it philosophy or politics, the third approach zeroes

[13] Rowan A. Greer, *Theodore of Mopsuestia*, 45, 152.

[14] On Cyril's exegesis see A. Kerrigan, *St. Cyril of Alexandria.*

[15] For discussion of typology in Theodore's exegesis see ibid. 76–9, 93–8, 107–11. See also Frances Young, *Biblical Exegesis and the Formation of Christian Culture.*

[16] Alois Grillmeier's influential version of the two-schools theory deserves to be considered briefly here. According to Grillmeier, the school of Alexandria taught a Logos-sarx christology, while the Antiochenes favoured the Logos-anthropos model.

on a single theological question. The fundamental presupposition of this approach is that the precise nature of the union between divinity and humanity in Christ was at the heart of the Nestorian controversy. A set of technical distinctions is then developed between prosopic, hypostatic, natural, essential, moral, voluntarist, conjunctive, and other types of union.[17] While this approach is not entirely misleading, in the long run it is not very illuminating, since the use-patterns of the key terms involved were in fact very fluid in the first half of the fifth century. The fact that Cyril often used the terms *physis, hypostasis*, and *prosopon* interchangeably makes any explanation based upon sharp distinctions between these terms anachronistic. We must find a more adequate way of reckoning with Cyril's insistence that the union (ἕνωσις) of Christ's person was ultimately mysterious, ineffable, and unique, for which no one model was adequate. Abstract adjectives, such as the terms 'prosopic' or 'natural', tend to obscure the matter due to the fact that the disputing parties used them in mutually exclusive ways. The study of Cyril's thought has been hindered by overemphasis upon isolated formulae, such as 'one nature of God the Word incarnate', and by almost exclusive concentration upon a few technical terms.[18] Metaphors, images, and models of the union must not be neglected as alternative ways of conceiving that which ultimately defies all expression and rational conceptualization.[19]

In the case of Cyril's theology this classification is artificial and even misleading, since it fails to account for the fact that Cyril defended Christ's full humanity and, as we will see in this chapter, went beyond Athanasius in allotting a more substantial function to Christ's human soul in his vision of salvation. For a searching criticism of Grillmeier's theory see McGuckin, *Christological Controversy*, 206–7. Cf. also R. Norris, 'Christological Models in Cyril of Alexandria', 255–68. For a comprehensive survey of modern interpretations see S. McKinion, *Words, Imagery, and the Mystery of Christ*, 149–59.

[17] See J. F. Bethune-Baker, *Nestorius and his Teaching*; Vaselin Kesich, 'Hypostatic and Prosopic Union in the Exegesis of Christ's Temptation'; Paul Galtier, '*Unio secundum hypostasim* chez Saint Cyrille'. This approach, it should be noted, has now fallen into disrepute; in its defence see M. Anastos, 'Nestorius was Orthodox', 117–40. Anastos argued that, at the end of the day, the difference between Cyril and Nestorius was purely verbal. For a penetrating critique of Anastos's position see Weinandy, *Does God Suffer?*, 178–80.

[18] M. Jugie described the monophysite controversy as 'moins une hérésie qu'un schisme, moins une controverse de doctrine, qu'une querelle de mots', in 'La Primauté romaine d'après les premiers théologiens monophysites', 181. See also John Romanides, 'St Cyril's "One Physis or Hypostasis of God the Logos Incarnate" and Chalcedon', 82–107.

[19] This is the major argument of S. A. McKinion's *Words, Imagery and the Mystery of Christ.*

Instead of the above-mentioned views, I propose a different framework and a new starting point. I will argue that Theodore and Nestorius were dominantly theists who, above all else, sought to protect absolute divine impassibility from being compromised by any involvement in the turbulent affairs of human life. It is in the light of this central concern that they developed their two-subjects account of the incarnation.[20] For Cyril, in contrast, the starting point was the voluntary self-emptying of a single divine subject who accepted the limitations of human life.

The Similarity between the Function of Divine Impassibility in Arianism and Nestorianism

Despite fundamental differences in their christologies, there is a peculiar affinity between the Arian and Nestorian conceptualizations of the divine transcendence. For Arius, the High God remained completely untouched by the incarnation. God's involvement in any *pathos* or process in creation would put the divine impassibility and immutability at risk. Arius believed that it was impossible for the High God both to be associated with human suffering and to preserve his divinity uncompromised and undiminished. Similarly, God's work in creation could not be accomplished directly. God always works through suitable intermediaries. The infinite gap between the High God and creation has not been bridged in the incarnation and could not be overcome in principle.

We find the same basic impulse to protect absolute divine impassibility in Theodore and Nestorius. In his *Commentary on the Nicene Creed* Theodore takes considerable pains to show how great is the difference between created and uncreated, temporary and eternal, corruptible and incorruptible. Theodore asked rhetorically: 'What possible resemblance and relation can exist between two beings so widely separated from each other?' and answered that the gulf found between them was unbridgeable.[21]

[20] J. J. O'Keefe proposes a similar framework in 'Impassible Suffering? Divine Passion and Fifth Century Christology', 57. Cf. also Mozley, *Impassibility of God*, 88.

[21] Theodore of Mopsuestia, *A Commentary on the Nicene Creed*, 45. For a discussion of this characteristic feature of Theodore's theology, see R. Norris, 'The Problem of Human Identity in Patristic Christological Speculation', 157; F. A. Sullivan, *The Christology of Theodore of Mopsuestia*, and Greer, *Theodore of Mopsuestia*, 37. Greer interprets Theodore's position as authentically biblical and criticizes Cyril and Nestorius (*sic*!) for falling prey to the 'Platonist' blending of the distinction between human and divine natures. As I mentioned before, this is yet another instance of the Theory of Theology's Fall into Hellenistic Philosophy at work. Its inadequacy will be re-emphasized in this chapter.

One might ask, what precisely is peculiar or new about Theodore's insistence upon the radical unlikeness between the creator and creation? After all, the whole preceding patristic tradition would appear to make the same point. A sense of deep awe before the transcendence and mystery of God characterizes not only Nestorian piety, but also the worship of the Arians and the orthodox.

What sets Theodore apart from the preceding tradition is a peculiar way in which he took this classical patristic distinction to its logical extreme. For Theodore, the divine action in the incarnation did not bring God qualitatively closer to creation.[22] The difference is merely quantitative: the man Jesus was 'the first to be deemed worthy of the indwelling of the Spirit in a degree surpassing the rest of mankind.'[23] Theodore admitted that the man who was assumed was more than an ordinary human being, in the sense that he was endowed with greater spiritual gifts and excelled others in virtue.

The conjunction (συνάφεια) of divine and human subjects in Christ had to be conceived along the lines consistent with the ontological division between the creator and created. It is absolutely necessary, Nestorius insisted, first 'to praise the distinction of natures'[24] when approaching the subject of the incarnation. It is this distinction that prevents any attempts to ascribe divine actions and human sufferings to a single subject. Instead, the man assumed and the God who did the assuming must be clearly distinguished:

> The Godhead was separated from the one who was suffering in the trial of death, because it was impossible for Him to taste the trial of death if (the Godhead) were not cautiously remote from him [the man assumed]...God Himself was not tried with the trial of death but He was near to him [the man assumed] and doing to him the things that were congruous to His nature as the Maker who is the cause of everything, i.e. He brought him [the man assumed] to perfection through sufferings and made him for ever immortal, impassible, incorruptible, and immutable for the salvation of the multitudes who would be receiving communion with him.[25]

[22] Theodore, *De symbolo*, 7.

[23] Theodore, *De incarnatione*, frag. from Bk. 7. See the discussion of various modes of indwelling in Greer, *Theodore of Mopsuestia*, 57.

[24] Nestorius, *Ad Cyrillum*, II. 6. Cf. Cyril, *Quod unus*, 457E. All references to *Quod unus* are given to the critical edition in G. M. de Durand, *Cyrille d'Alexandrie*.

[25] Theodore, *De symbolo*, 8, trans. Mingana, *Commentary of Theodore*, 87. Cf. Cyril, *Ad Succensum*, i. 3.

According to Theodore, there was a one-way communication between the two subjects. Divinity could communicate its properties to the changeable humanity. However, it was impossible for the divinity to participate in any way in the properties of humanity. Christ's divine nature remained impenetrable to and totally unaffected by the experiences of the incarnation. The Nestorian tradition followed the starting point of Theodore's theology and consistently emphasized a rigid demarcation of the corresponding properties and actions of the two subjects in Christ. There is a striking passage in a later Nestorian confession of faith, which it is worth quoting here:

> We believe in one divine nature, everlasting, without beginning, living and quickening all, powerful, creating all powers, wise, imparting all wisdom, simple spirit, infinite, incomprehensible, not compounded and without parts, incorporeal, both invisible and immutable, impassible and immortal; nor is it possible, whether by itself, or by another, or with another, that suffering and change should enter in unto it . . . and because the Father is impassible and unchangeable, so also is the Son and the Spirit confessed with him (to be) as he is without suffering and change . . .
>
> For the (divine) substance cannot fall under the necessity of change and suffering, because if the godhead underwent change, there would no longer be a revelation but a corruption of godhead, and if again the manhood departed from its nature, there would no longer be salvation, but an extinction of the manhood.[26]

This early seventh-century creed, directed against the Severian *theopaschitai*, clearly rules out any possibility of the divine nature sharing in the suffering of the human nature. The Nestorians could not allow the thought that God could act in a way that might impinge upon his impassibility; that he could genuinely participate in the human experiences to the point of suffering, without ceasing to be what he is. To admit this would be to abrogate the fundamental division between creator and creation. This train of thought would lead, so Nestorius argued, to a confusion of the corresponding properties of the two subjects and would ultimately jeopardize the integrity of Christ's divinity.[27] To claim, as Apollinaris and (on some occasions) Cyril did, that Christ's divinity and humanity formed a single *physis* was paramount to

26 Babai the Great (?), 'The Creed of the Bishops of Persia delivered to Kosroes in the year 612', trans. Luise Abramowski and Alan E. Goodman, *A Nestorian Collection of Christological Texts*, ii. 88–9, 91.

27 'The properties of God the Word they set at naught and make them human', *Liber Heraclidis*, 1. 2. 136, trans. Driver, 93.

obliterating the fundamental distinction between the properties of the two subjects.[28]

As we see, the divine impassibility functioned in Nestorian theology in a way similar to its role in Arianism. For both parties, despite their profound christological differences, the divine impassibility precluded God's direct involvement in everything related to the created order, especially the experiences that indicated human weakness. Such an intimate involvement would be unworthy of God and destructive for creation. We should emphasize that such an understanding did not stem from philosophy, but from the patristic distinction between the creator and created, which was articulated in a conscious opposition to Stoic monistic materialism, Platonist emanationism, various forms of metaphysical dualism, and any other cosmological proposal available in the Hellenistic market of ideas. The central preoccupation of Nestorian piety and theology was to purify theological discourse of any suggestion of divine suffering.[29]

Theopatheia as Cyril's Gravest Doctrinal Error, According to the Orientals

In the light of this overriding concern to protect the absolute divine impassibility, it is not surprising that the major charge that Nestorius levelled against Cyril was precisely that of θεοπάθεια. Nestorius started his first serious theological counter-attack against Cyril by retorting that Cyril had misinterpreted the second article of the creed when he applied all the human experiences of Christ, including his suffering and death, directly to God the Word. Nestorius wrote:

> You [Cyril] thought that they [the Fathers] had said that the Word, who is coeternal with the Father, is able to suffer. Look closely, if you please, at the precise meaning of their words, and you will find that the inspired chorus of the Fathers has not said that the consubstantial divinity is able to suffer, nor that divinity, coeternal with the Father, was begotten, nor that divinity rose from the dead when raising his destroyed temple.[30]

[28] Theodore of Mopsuestia, *De incarnatione*, frag. from Bk. 2.

[29] 'Do you allot the suffering to human being alone, fending it off from God the Word to avoid God's being declared passible? This is the point of their pedantic, muddle-headed fictions,' Cyril, *De symbolo*, 31, trans. Wickham, *Cyril*, 131. Cf. Hallman, 'Seed of Fire', 371.

[30] Nestorius, *Ad Cyrillum*, II. 3. See the discussion of this passage in Wickham, *Cyril*, p. xxxvi.

Later in his life, already in exile, Nestorius adamantly held to the same line of argument:

> They [the Cyrillians] take everything which is in his nature and attribute them naturally to God the Word: the human fear and the betrayal, the interrogation, the answer, the smiting upon the cheeks, [follows a lengthy list of other experiences in Nestorius's eyes unworthy of God] . . . Surely it is an awful and dreadful thing to conceive this and to tell men what and what sort of thoughts they have concerning the Son, that he is both made and created and that he has been changed from impassible to passible and from immortal to mortal and from unchangeable to changeable.[31]

It was precisely the allegation that Cyril did away with the divine impassibility that became a battle cry of the Oriental party, which supported Nestorius. While Cyril's second and third letters to Nestorius received the majority approval from the bishops who came to Ephesus in 431, many shared reservations about Cyril's notorious twelve anathemas appended to the third letter.[32] The pamphlet war under the banner of anti-theopaschitism began shortly before the council of Ephesus.[33] Among the Oriental bishops, Andrew of Samosata and Theodoret of Cyrus voiced their disagreement. In their opinion Cyril had a lot of explaining to do. John of Antioch received the chapters as an open affront against his own position. A rival assembly of the forty-three bishops, which John held upon his late arrival to Ephesus, deposed Cyril demanding that he repudiated the twelve anathemas.

While Cyril and Nestorius were both held under house-arrest in Ephesus, Emperor Theodosius II requested that two delegations, representing the two hierarchs, would defend their cases before him in Constantinople. According to the report of the Oriental party, when

[31] *Liber Heraclidis*, 1.2, trans. Driver, 92–3.

[32] The question whether the anathemas adequately reflected the opinion of the church at large was debated for the next hundred years to be finally resolved at the fifth ecumenical council, which canonized them. We should note that Cyril's chapters undoubtedly had enthusiastic supporters at the council of Ephesus, such as Acacius of Melitene and Proclus, future bishop of Constantinople. On the history of the twelve chapters see Russell, *Cyril*, 175–6. Joseph Mahé, 'Les Anathématismes de Saint Cyrille d'Alexandrie et les Éveques Orientaux du Patriarchat d'Antioche'; H.-M. Diepen, 'Les Douze Anathématismes au Concile d'Éphèse et jusqu'en 519'; J. McGuckin, 'The "Theopaschite Confession"', 243.

[33] Cyril, *Ep.* 10. 2; *Ad Eulogium.* Cyril wrote three explanatory apologies: *Apologia xii capitulorum contra Orientales* (*ACO* 1. 1. 7. 33–65) in response to Andrew, *Apologia xii capitulorum contra Theodoretum* (*ACO* 1. 1. 6. 107–46) before 431, and a more balanced *Explicatio duodecim capitum* after the council of Ephesus.

Theodosius II heard Bishop Acacius, the spokesman of the Cyrillian party, saying that the Godhead was passible, the emperor was so scandalized that he theatrically tore apart his cloak on account of such blasphemies.[34] Nevertheless, the winds of popular dissatisfaction with Nestorius were too strong in the capital for the emperor to be governed by considerations of theological propriety alone. As a result of negotiations, Cyril was reinstalled in his see in Alexandria, whereas Nestorius was deposed and escorted to his former monastery in Antioch. Writing from his monastic exile years later, Nestorius would represent the Oriental party as heroic confessors of the divine impassibility, who courageously confronted Theodosius II with the following ultimatum: 'Even if the Emperor treats us with violence, we shall not be persuaded to admit a suffering God.'[35]

Nestorius shared the common concern of the whole patristic tradition for a language that would most appropriately describe divine action in the world. He believed that the only pattern of involvement worthy of God was one that did not in any way override the divine perfections of impassibility and immutability. The central preoccupation of Nestorian piety and theology was to purify theological discourse of any suggestion of divine suffering.[36] Nestorius considered popular 'God in the womb—God in the tomb' christology to be a piece of barbaric impiety. Cyril once sarcastically remarked that, 'Out of his excessive piety he [Nestorius] blushes at the degree of the self-emptying and cannot bear to see the Son who is co-eternal with God the Father, the one who in every possible respect is of the same form as he who begot him and equal to him, descend to such a humble level.'[37]

For Nestorius, it was above all else unworthy of God to suffer and die as a mere mortal. Time and again Nestorius returned to his favourite charge of *theopatheia* in his *Liber Heraclidis*.[38] Towards the end of his life he wrote a treatise with the revealing title *Adversus Theopaschitas*, only meagre fragments of which have survived. Overall, Nestorius' criticism remained without substantial development from the beginning to the

[34] *Ep. ad eos qui Ephesi* in *ACO* 1. 1. 7. 77.

[35] Nestorius, *Liber Heraclidis*, 2. 1, trans. Driver, 284.

[36] 'Do you allot the suffering to human being alone, fending it off from God the Word to avoid God's being declared passible? This is the point of their pedantic, muddle-headed fictions.' Cyril, *De symbolo*, 31, trans. L. R. Wickham, *Cyril*, 131. Cf. Hallman, 'Seed of Fire', 371.

[37] Cyril, *Contra Nestorium*, 4. 5 (*ACO* 1. 1. 6. 85).

[38] Nestorius, *Liber Heraclidis*, 1. 1. 49; 1. 2. 7; 1. 3.

end of the controversy inasmuch as he never took back his allegation that Cyril preached a suffering God.[39]

In his more theologically perceptive moments Nestorius admitted that Cyril was not just bluntly asserting that God in his own nature was endowed with anthropomorphic features, such as suffering and mortality. Nestorius conceded that, at least in word, Cyril admitted that the divine nature was impassible.[40] What profoundly puzzled Nestorius was the fact that Cyril could in the same breath claim that God the Word was the subject of all the human experiences of the incarnation. 'For the one you first proclaimed as impassible and not needing a second generation, you subsequently introduce (how I know not) as passible and newly created.'[41] In Nestorius' opinion, Cyril's controversial dictum that 'the Word suffered impassibly' (ἀπαθῶς ἔπαθεν) was a desperate attempt to cover up the Alexandrian's real intention to forgo the divine impassibility altogether.

Nestorius also insisted that any admission of the Son's involvement in suffering logically led to the conclusion that the Son was not of the same essence with the impassible Father, or somehow abandoned his impassible nature in the incarnation. Nestorius was especially keen to prove that because of the claim that the Word suffered in the flesh Cyril's proposal had a family relationship to Arianism.[42] More to the point was the suspicion of the Oriental theologians that Cyril's ideas were dangerously approaching those of Apollinaris. Cyril complained in *Ad Eulogium* that 'all the Orientals reckon us as following the opinions of Apollinaris in thinking that there occurred the mixture or merger (such are the terms they have employed, implying that God the Word changed into the nature of the flesh and the flesh was turned into the nature of deity)'.[43]

[39] As Cyril complains in *Ad Succensum*, II. 4 (*ACO* 1. 1. 6. 161).

[40] 'Those who pass for orthodox [i.e. the Cyrillians] . . . attribute unto him [Christ] in word a nature unchangeable, impassible and without needs, and they ascribe unto him all sufferings and every need of the body and make over all the things of the soul and the intelligence to God the Word in virtue of an hypostatic union,' *Liber Heraclidis*, 1. 2, trans. Driver, 93–4.

[41] *Ad Cyrillum*, II. 6, trans. McGuckin, *Christological Controversy*, 366.

[42] 'And they [the Cyrillians] make indeed use of the name of orthodox, but in fact they are Arians,' *Liber Heraclidis*, 1. 2, trans. Driver, 94. As Henry Chadwick pointed out, for Nestorius 'to accept even a relative or qualified impassibility such as Cyril seemed to propose meant Arianism', 'Eucharist and Christology', 158.

[43] Cf. Cyril, *Ad Acacium*, 20. Cf. also Nestorius, Frag. 306, Driver, 391: 'Those Theopaschites hold true the religion of Apollinaris.'

Paul Galtier has demonstrated a detailed correspondence between Cyril's twelve anathemas and certain writings of the Apollinarian circle, which Cyril unsuspectingly took as perfectly orthodox.[44] Cyril, of course, was quite aware of the fact that Apollinaris was condemned by the Second Ecumenical Council. The whole issue was complicated by the fact that some Apollinarian writings continued to circulate under the authoritative name of Athanasius of Alexandria. Later Cyril took great pains to distance himself from Apollinaris's heretical claim that the Logos in Christ supplanted the mind or the rational soul.[45] Nestorius was not convinced, however. He continued to insist that by predicating human experiences directly of the divine Word Cyril fell into at least one of the three errors: a crude pagan anthropopathism, Arianism, or Apollinarianism.[46]

In addition to the *reductio ad heresim* argument, Nestorius claimed that Cyril's formula 'the Word suffered impassibly' or 'the impassible suffered' was a blatant contradiction at best and theological double-talk at worst. 'The same', Nestorius was quick to point out, 'could not be by nature impassible and passible.'[47] Cyril should quit speaking in riddles, saying one thing and implying another. If Mary did not give birth to God the Word before all ages, why call her Theotokos? If divine nature did not suffer, why make God the subject of the suffering in the

44 P. Galtier, 'Saint Cyrille et Apollinaire', 584–609. See also F. Young, *From Nicaea*, 259–63.

45 This is most clearly brought out in *In Ioannem*, 8 (*PG* 74: 89D) where Cyril explains the function of Christ's rational soul and cites Nazianzus' famous anti-Apollinarian maxim: 'That which has not been assumed, has not been saved.' Cf. also *Ad Succensum*, I. 5; *Scholia*, 25. Cyril also quoted the standard gospel proof-texts where Christ's soul is mentioned explicitly.

46 'To attribute to his divinity the properties of the united flesh, I mean birth, suffering, and death, is, my brother [Cyril], the act of a mind truly led astray like the pagans or diseased like the minds of that mad Apollinaris, Arius, and the other heresies, but rather more grievously than they,' Nestorius, *Ad Cyrillum*, II. 7, trans. McEnerney, *St. Cyril of Alexandria*, 47. Cyril indignantly dismissed these charges in *Ad Acacium* (of Beroea), 7.

47 *Liber Heraclidis*, 1. 3, trans. Driver, 97. Cf. *Liber Heraclidis*, 1. 2, trans. Driver, 94: 'And, like those who change him from his nature [i.e. the Arians], at one time they [the Cyrillians] call him now impassible and immortal and unchangeable, and afterwards they prohibit him from being then called immortal and impassible and unchangeable, being angry against any one who repeatedly calls God the Word impassible [i.e. the Nestorians].' Cf. also Theodoret, *Eranistes*, 218, 303–4: 'Who in their senses would ever stand for such foolish riddles? No one has ever heard of an impassible passion or an immortal mortality. The impassible has never undergone passion, and what has undergone passion could not possibly be impassible.' For discussion of this passage see J. O'Keefe, 'Impassible Suffering', 57; Greer, *Theodore of Mopsuestia*, 36–7. Cyril takes this critique on in *Quod unus*, 766B, 775E–776C.

flesh? If God is immortal, why speak of him as dying in his mortal body? If the claim that God was born of a woman, suffered, and died has no literal force, why continue to use such provocative expressions? Such was the set of problems with which Nestorius challenged Cyril.

Nestorius believed that a sharp distinction between the properties of the two natures was an effective and simple solution to all the ambiguities and contradictions that Cyril's christology presented. Cyril, in Nestorius' judgement, had overall failed to sustain this distinction clearly and consistently. Cyril was at times vague, at other times clearly inconsistent and ultimately blaspheming the Godhead of the Son. It was because Cyril blurred the distinction between the two centres of action that he was a theopaschite, despite all his protestations to the contrary. Such was Nestorius' judgement upon Cyril, and it was this interpretation that characterized the attitudes towards Cyril in the Nestorian church centuries later.

We must ask in turn, was Nestorius on target in his analysis of Cyril? In what sense precisely was Cyril a theopaschite? How did the basic kenotic inspiration of Cyril's theology influence the mind of the church in subsequent generations? Cyril's own writings offer no easy answers to these questions.

We would do Cyril a great disservice if we measured his theological achievement by the degree to which he distanced himself from the allegedly philosophical axiom of the divine impassibility. To interpret Cyril in this way is to impose a dichotomy between the biblical God who suffers and the philosophical deity who does not—a misleading framework, which I have been calling in this study the Theory of Theology's Fall into Hellenistic Philosophy.[48] Cyril did not see the choice between divine impassibility and passibility as an either/or matter; nor did he view the abandonment of divine impassibility as a liberation of the gospel from the shackles of Greek philosophy.[49]

[48] Hallman presupposes this framework both in *The Descent of God* and in his later article 'The Seed of Fire'. See also Jerry D. McCoy, 'Philosophical Influences on the Doctrine of the Incarnation in Athanasius and Cyril of Alexandria', 362–91.

[49] J. J. O'Keefe frames this question as an either/or issue in his article 'Kenosis or Impassibility: Cyril of Alexandria and Theodoret of Cyrus on the Problem of Divine Pathos', 358–65. O'Keefe concludes that Cyril was more biblical and less philosophical, while Theodoret was more philosophical and less biblical in their respective views on the issue of divine *pathos* (p. 365). While I agree with the point that the protection of divine impassibility was an overriding concern of Nestorianism, I do not find the supposed opposition between the Bible and Greek philosophy to be a helpful key to interpreting Nestorius' concern.

To remind the reader, the attribution of human emotions and experiences to God is regarded by the biblical authors themselves as a problem of anthropomorphism, not necessarily as an advantage over non-anthropomorphic descriptions of God. Cyril was keenly aware of the problem of anthropomorphism and returned to it frequently in his writings.[50] He understood that to affirm without qualifications that the divine nature was passible was to open a Pandora's box of theological problems.

As we saw earlier, divine impassibility had its proper function in the framework of patristic negative theology and was not intended to rule out all emotionally coloured characteristics of God or God's involvement in creation. For Cyril, both qualified divine impassibility and qualified divine passibility were necessary for a sound theology of incarnation. The affirmation of impassibility was a way of protecting the truth that the one who became incarnate was truly God. Admitting a qualified passibility secured the point that God truly submitted himself to the conditions of the incarnation. For Nestorius impassibility functioned in a radically different way: it ruled out any possibility of divine involvement in human suffering as utterly unworthy of God.

In Cyril's view, the key Nestorian concern for the distinction of the two natures was a relatively trivial point, one that did not deserve to be emphasized repeatedly.[51] Following Athanasius, Cyril proposed a different starting point for understanding the incarnation. For him, the words of Phil. 2: 5–11 provided a point of entry into the meaning of the christological article of the creed.[52] Already in an early treatise, written shortly after the outbreak of the Nestorian controversy in 428, Cyril observed: 'the discussion of the kenosis (ὁ περὶ τῆς κενώσεως λόγος) must precede other topics'.[53] In his third letter to Nestorius, Cyril inserted the explanatory words 'emptying himself' in the middle of his brief restatement of the second article of the creed: 'And we declare that the only-begotten Word of God . . . came down for our salvation, emptying himself, he it is who was incarnate and made man, that is to say,

[50] *In Is.* 50. 1. (*PG* 70: 1084A); *De solutione dogmatum*, Pusey, 550. *Contra Julianum* (*PG* 76: 713C).

[51] Cyril, as we noted earlier, deemed the terminology of the two natures quite acceptable, as long as it did not undermine the oneness of Christ, see *Ad Eulogium.*

[52] Cyril, *De symbolo*, 13; cf. Origen, *Princ.* 1. Praef. 4 ; (Ps.-?)Ath., *Ar.* 3.29; The centrality of Phil. 2: 5–11 in Cyril's theology has been noted by several scholars. See P. Henry, 'Kénose', v. 92; Young, *From Nicaea*, 260; O'Keefe, 'Impassible Suffering', 46–9. A fuller list of Cyril's favourite scriptural loci includes: 2 Cor. 8: 9, Heb. 2: 14–17, and John 1: 14.

[53] *Ad Augustas*, 4 (*ACO* 1. 1. 5. 28).

took flesh of the holy Virgin, making it his own (ἰδίαν αὐτὴν ποιησάμενος) from the womb.'[54] Cyril remained faithful to his rule in his later writings: any interpretation of the incarnation had to do justice to Phil. 2: 5–11.[55]

God the Word Incarnate as the Subject of Kenosis

Two problems loom large in Cyril's numerous expositions of the kenotic hymn: who was the subject of the emptying and what did the emptying consist of?[56] Theodore made a sharp distinction between 'the one who is in the form of God' and 'the one who is in the form of a slave'.[57] Nestorius, following Theodore, held that the subject of the emptying was 'the form of a slave', a passible man indwelt by the Word.[58] It was a God-bearing man who became worthy of adoration and worship along with God who assumed him.[59] It was a God-bearing man who became poor, suffered, was emptied out of his human life, and died. The Nestorians believed that any involvement of the Word in the emptying would violate his impassibility.

Cyril disagreed in principle with such an interpretation. The intention of Cyril's whole theology was to stress that something unique and absolutely unparalleled happened in the incarnation. Cyril believed that, by speaking of Christ as merely a God-bearing man, Theodore and Nestorius missed the very nerve centre of the gospel.[60] Following Theodore, Nestorius taught that God's indwelling of the man Jesus was only quantitatively different from his indwelling of the prophets and the saints of the past. God chose to dwell in the saints by his good pleasure (κατ' εὐδοκίαν) on the grounds that they were worthy of his nearness. Jesus excelled all other human beings in virtue and moral insight, and for that reason was worthy of God's indwelling to the highest degree.[61]

Following Athanasius, Cyril objected that the difference between God's presence in Christ and in deified human beings was not merely a matter of degree of grace. Cyril argued that it was the implication of the Nestorian teaching that 'Christ surpassed the holy prophets who came

[54] *Ad Nestorium*, III. 3, trans. Wickham, *Cyril*, 17.

[55] Kenosis is the major theme of Cyril's christological dialogue *Quod unus*. Cf. also *Scholia*, 12.

[56] *Ad augustas*, 18 (*ACO* 1. 1. 5. 35).

[57] Theodore, *De symbolo*, 6.

[58] Nestorius, *Ad Cyrillum*, II. 6; Theodoret, *Eranistes*, III.

[59] Theodore, *De symbolo*, 7; Cyril, *Quod unus*, 727C–730B.

[60] *Ad Nestorium*, III. 4; anathem. 5.

[61] Theodore, *De incarnatione*, Bk. 7.

before him only in terms of the amount of grace and its duration, and this was what constituted his pre-eminence.'[62] For Cyril such an understanding of the union of natures in Christ did not do justice to the full force of John 1: 14: 'He [the Evangelist] does not say that the Word came into flesh; he says he became flesh in order to exclude any idea of a relative indwelling, as in the case of the prophets and the other saints.'[63] The difference between Christ and the saints was qualitative, and for that reason all christological statements required a grammatical subject that would make this fact clear: 'It was not the case that initially an ordinary man (ἄνθρωπος κοινὸς) was born of the holy Virgin and then the Word simply settled on him (καταπεφοίτηκεν ἐπ' αὐτὸν)—no, what is said is that he underwent fleshly birth united from the very womb, making the birth of his flesh his very own.'[64] Cyril insisted that it was not a man indwelt by God, but God the Word incarnate who was the subject of all statements about Christ. In his letter to the monks of Egypt Cyril asked: 'Well, my friends, would the fact that the Word of God only dwelt in a man be enough to connote his self-emptying?'[65] If there was no qualitative difference between God's sanctification of the saints and God's participation in the life of Christ, one would have to conclude that God, in all three persons, emptied himself in the souls of all those whom he indwelt. Besides, if the God-bearing man Jesus was worthy of worship, so should be all ordinary believers, in whom the Spirit of God dwells. Thus, Cyril met the accusation of *theopatheia* with the countercharge of *athrōpolatria*.[66] In addition, a God-bearing man christology would also lead to a controversial conclusion that not only the body of Christ, but also the bodies of all those indwelt by the Spirit were life-giving.[67]

Ascribing the emptying exclusively to the human subject also led to the following problem, which Cyril pointed out repeatedly: human nature is already empty and powerless, and, therefore, incapable of

[62] *Quod unus*, 751B–C, trans. McGuckin, *On the Unity of Christ*, 98. Cf. Ath., *Ep.* 61.2.

[63] *In Ioannem*, 1. 9. 95E, trans. Russell, *Cyril*, 106. Cf. *Contra Nestorium*, 2. 4. 41; 3. 2 (*ACO* 1. 1. 6. 60); 4. 3 (*ACO* 1. 1. 6. 83); *Explicatio duodecim capitum*, 16–22 (*ACO* 1. 1. 5. 21); *Scholia*, 2, 17–19, 23, 25, 35; *Ad monachos*, 14, 19–21; *Quod unus*, 717A, 741D–E, 750C–D.

[64] *Ad Nestorium*, II. 4, trans. Wickham, *Cyril*, 7.

[65] *Ad monachos*, 14, trans. McGuckin, *Christological Controversy*, 253. Cf. *Quod unus*, 734E, 750C.

[66] Cyril advanced these arguments in *Scholia*, 18, 24; *Quod unus*, 771B; 732E; *Contra Nestorium*, 4. 6 (*ACO* 1. 1. 6. 89)

[67] *Scholia*, 24.

further emptying out. Drawing upon 2 Cor. 8: 9, Cyril observed that since humanity was 'utterly poor' in the eyes of God, it could not possibly 'become poor'. Poverty and emptiness are humanity's natural condition; they cannot in principle become its voluntary goals in the incarnation. One cannot give up what one does not possess. Cyril expressed this thought most powerfully in his *Commentary on the Gospel of Luke*, written after the council of Ephesus:

Enquire, therefore, Who He was that was first in the likeness of God the Father, and could be regarded as on an equality with Him, but took the form of a slave, and became then a man, and besides this made Himself poor. Was it He of the seed of David, as they [the Nestorians] argue, Whom they specially regard separately and by himself as the other Son, distinct from the Word of God the Father? If so, let them show that He ever was on an equality with the Father. Let them show how He assumed the form of a slave. Or what shall we say was that form of a slave? And how did He empty Himself? For what is poorer than human nature? He, therefore, Who is the exact image of God the Father, the likeness, and visible expression of His person, Who shines resplendent in equality unto Him, Who by right of nature is free, and the yoke of Whose kingdom is put upon all creation—He it is Who took the form of a slave, that is, became a man, and made Himself poor by consenting to endure these human things, sin only excepted.[68]

Only the one in whom the fullness of God dwelt could become empty, only the one who was rich was in a position to give up his riches for the sake of others. The emptying of a *mere* human being was not an emptying at all.[69] In his *Explicatio duodecim capitum* written under house-arrest in Ephesus in the late summer of 431, Cyril underlined that the notorious twelfth anathema was written specifically against those who were 'saying that an ordinary man (ἀνθρώπος κοινὸς) endured the cross for our sake'.[70]

As we have already noted in the previous chapter, Theodore and Nestorius quite legitimately objected that they had never claimed that Christ was a mere man. In fact, the Oriental Christians of Theodore's

68 Cyril, *In Lucam*, 11, trans. Smith, 80. Cf. *Ad monachos*, 13.

69 'If it was simply and solely a man born of a woman [which is what Nestorius implied by calling Mary "man-bearer"], then how did he possess such fullness so as to be understood as "emptied out"? Or in what lofty state was he formerly positioned that he could be said to have "humbled himself"? Or how was he made in the likeness of men if he was already that beforehand by nature? . . . Or how could he be said to have been "emptied out" if he was assuming the fullness of the deity?' *Scholia*, 12, trans. McGuckin, *Christological Controversy*, 305. Cf. *Quod unus*, 730B, 777A–B.

70 *Explicatio duodecim capitum*, 31. Cf. *Quod unus*, 763B, 766C.

time suffered a good deal from the Arians for holding unflinchingly to the confession of Nicaea.[71] This is a measure of just how far they were from the heresy of anyone who taught that Christ was not fully God. On these grounds Cyril's version of the psilanthropic objection could be quite easily dismissed—a fact that Cyril and his supporters in their belligerent moments had a hard time recognizing.[72]

In the vicinity of the psilanthropic objection was buried another problem that Nestorius would never be able to get away with. As we have repeatedly stressed in this chapter, in their attempt to protect the divine impassibility, Theodore and Nestorius introduced a sharp demarcation between the two subjects of Christ's experiences and actions. They wanted to make sure that Christ's human experiences were not ascribed to the divine nature in any way. Inevitably, this move made a human individual *alone* the subject of the emptying.[73] In Cyril's opinion, the Nestorians went too far in their seemingly pious effort to protect God's dignity: 'They fail to bear in mind God's plan and make mischievous attempts to shift the suffering to the man on his own, in foolish pursuit of false piety. Their aim is that the Word of God should not be acknowledged as the Savior who gave his own blood for us but instead that Jesus, viewed as a distinct individual man, should be credited with that.'[74]

Nestorius attempted to defend himself by proposing to Cyril the following false dilemma: either the human or the divine subject suffered. The denial of the former led to the acceptance of the latter. But to claim that God suffered in his divinity was, for Nestorius, both a blasphemy and an absurdity. In order to make this idea apparent, Nestorius used the following linguistic trick: he substituted 'God' as the grammatical subject of all those sentences in Scripture that spoke of Christ's human experi-

[71] Theodore mentions that his church suffered under a local Arian persecution. See *De incarnatione*, 6.

[72] See below p. 125. Cf. also Theodoret, *Eranistes*, III. 221. This point is also noted by Greer, *Theodore of Mopsuestia*, 43.

[73] 'And this is the Word whom he [Nestorius] has just presented to us as a God-bearing man, seeing that he who suffers is a separate subject, and he who is life-giving is another,' Cyril, *Contra Nestorium*, 3. 2 (*ACO* 1. 1. 6. 58, 60), trans. Russell, *Cyril*, 164. Cf. *Contra Nestorium*, Prooem 2 (*ACO* 1. 1. 6. 33); 2. 10 (*ACO* 1. 1. 6. 47).

[74] *Ad Succensum*, 4, trans. Wickham, *Cyril*, 91. Cf. *Explicatio duodecim capitum*, 13–14: 'Why would he [the Word] empty himself out if the limitations of the manhood made him ashamed? Or if he was going to shun human characteristics who was it that compelled him by force or necessity to become as we are? For this reason we apply all the sayings in the Gospels, the human ones as well as those befitting God, to one prosopon,' trans. McGuckin, *Christological Controversy*, 287.

ences. Among Nestorius' favourite paraphrases were the words of the angel to Joseph before the flight to Egypt: 'Rise, take up *God* and his mother'[75] (Matt. 2: 13) and the words of Christ before his arrest: 'Why do you seek to kill me, a *God* who has told you the truth?'[76] Touching upon the subject of the Eucharist, Nestorius stressed that Christ did not say 'He who eats my Godhead (θεότητα) and drinks my Godhead', but 'He who eats my flesh and drinks my blood abides in me and I in him.'[77] To substitute 'God' for the human subject in any of these sentences would be a piece of vulgar theologizing unworthy of God. As Nestorius saw it, *theopatheia* was the necessary implication of Cyril's attack upon his own two-subjects christology.

Cyril retorted that he nowhere said that 'bare divinity' suffered or died. God did not suffer 'nakedly' (γύμνως), that is, outside the limitations of his self-emptying.[78] If man did not suffer alone, neither did God suffer on his own. Cyril was determined to resist any attempt at dividing the gospel sayings into those passages pertaining to the divinity and those speaking about the humanity of Christ.[79] Instead of speaking of the two subjects, leading two loosely connected lives, Cyril preferred to speak of the single subject, one divine Word, and to refer to him as existing in two distinct states: apart from the incarnation and within the framework of the incarnation.[80] As follows from Cyril's letter to John of Antioch, Cyril's later endorsement of the Formula of Reunion, which spoke of the two natures, did not mean that Cyril conceded the Nestorian division of the gospel sayings under the political pressure from the Oriental party. In his interpretation of the formula Cyril retained his central concern for the unity of the person of Christ.[81] Outside the incarnation, the Word was characterized by all the divine perfections and negative attributes. In that state clear-cut distinctions between the creator and creation

75 Nestorius, *Quaternion*, 21, trans. McGuckin, *Christological Controversy*, 370.

76 John 8: 40. Cyril, *Contra Nestorium*, 2. 10 (*ACO* 1. 1. 6. 47), trans. Russell, *Cyril*, 157.

77 Nestorius, *Quaternion*, 4 (*ACO* 1. 1. 2. 51), trans. McGuckin, *Christological Controversy*, 376. Cf. *Contra Nestorium*, 4. 7 (*ACO* 1. 1. 6. 90).

78 'God the Word became an example for us in the days of his flesh, but not nakedly (οὐ γυμνὸς ὢν) or outside the limits of self-emptying (τῶν τῆς κενώσεως ἀμέτοχος μέτρων),' *Quod unus*, 754E. McGuckin, *On the Unity of Christ*, 103. Cf.: '[The Word] is not given on behalf of us *nakedly* (οὐ γυμνὸν), as it were, or as yet without flesh, but rather when he became flesh,' *Quod unus*, 764B, ibid. 114. Cf. also *Quod unus*, 758B, 773A; *Ad augustas*, 31 (*ACO* 1. 1. 5. 50): 'Christ is neither a mere man (ψιλὸς ἄνθρωπος), nor the fleshless Logos'. Cf. *Ad augustas*, 11 (*ACO* 1. 1. 5. 31).

79 See esp. *Ad Nestorium*, III, fourth anathema.

80 The distinction is made explicitly in *Quod unus*, 727C–D, 728B–C.

81 See McGuckin, *Christological Controversy*, 345 n. 4.

obtained and anthropomorphic descriptions of divine action were not to be construed literally: God could be said to act *like* a man, but he could not be said to *become* human in order to act in this way.

Within the confines of the incarnation, the language of the negative attributes still obtained, since the Word had not abandoned his divine status. At the same time, something new happened in the incarnation, so new and unparalleled that it became possible to predicate human experiences of God the Word, not considered 'nakedly', but within the framework of the incarnation. While God in his omniscience 'knew our frame', in the incarnation he became a participant in our weaknesses and in this sense it is possible to speak of an utterly unique divine acceptance of human limitations:

Even if it is appropriate for him [the divine Logos] to know that which belongs to humans, he has not yet been called to gain experience of our weaknesses. But when he enclosed himself in our flesh he was 'tempted in every respect'. We obviously do not mean that he had been ignorant before, but rather that to the God-befitting knowledge that he already possessed was added the knowledge gained through temptation. He did not become compassionate (συμπαθὴς) because of being tempted. Why? Because he was and is merciful by nature as God.[82]

In this passage Cyril speaks of God's gaining experiential knowledge of human misery that was known to him before in a less direct, non-experiential, although no less perfect way. This is why, in the incarnation it became entirely legitimate, even necessary, to make the divine Word the grammatical subject of the passages that Nestorius used to prove his point. Thus, according to Cyril, the statements 'God wept' or 'God was crucified' were theologically legitimate, as long as it was added that the subject was God-in-the-flesh, and not God outside the framework of the incarnation.[83]

Cyril believed that a way of coming to terms with the newness of the incarnation was to resort to language fraught with paradoxes:

We see in Christ the strange and rare paradox (ἄηθες τε και ξένον παράδοξον) of Lordship in servant's form and divine glory in human abasement.[84] He who was above all creation was in our human condition; the invisible one was made visible in the flesh; he who is from the heavens and from on high was in the likeness of earthly things; the immaterial one could be touched; he who is

[82] *Ad augustas*, 29 (*ACO* 1. 1. 5. 47).
[83] This point is especially well brought out by McGuckin, *Christological Controversy*, 191.
[84] *Quod unus*, 753B–C, trans. McGuckin, *On the Unity of Christ*, 101.

free in his own nature came in the form of a slave; he who blesses all creation became accursed; he who is all righteousness was numbered among the transgressors; life itself came in the appearance of death.[85]

He Who as God is all perfect, submits to bodily growth; the Incorporeal has limbs that advance to the ripeness of manhood; He is filled with wisdom Who is Himself all wisdom. And what say we to this? Behold by these things Him Who was in the form of the Father made like unto us; the Rich in poverty; the High in humiliation; Him said to receive, Whose is the fullness as God. So thoroughly did God the Word empty Himself![86]

Nestorius objected that to have recourse to paradoxical language of this kind meant only to beg the question. To repeat the objection already mentioned, how could one and the same person both suffer and not suffer?[87] Nestorius argued that what Cyril called a paradox was in fact a lamentable contradiction for which the two-subjects christology had a cure.

Cyril, predictably, disagreed. In the passages quoted he pointed out that the same paradoxical logic applies to all the other negative predicates that secured Christ's unmistakably divine identity—invisibility, incorporeality, incorruptibility, immutability, and the like—and were also put in creative tension with Christ's human characteristics. Cyril was committed to preserving 'the strange and rare paradox' of the Lord's coming in servant's form, the coming that was quite unlike any other divine manifestation through human agents. The paradoxical language made it crystal clear that in Christ we do not find two distinct agents—God and a saint—but one divine Word incarnate.[88] Even pressed with the charge of *theopatheia*, Cyril never gave up insisting that the paradox of the impassible who accepted the conditions of *pathos* was ultimately irreducible.[89] This is what it means to say that God did not simply act *like* a man, but *became* one.

We come now to the question: what was the point of securing one undivided subject of the emptying? What did the self-emptying of the one divine Word precisely consist of? Both Cyril and Nestorius agreed that the self-emptying was not to be seen as a corruption or degradation

[85] *Quod unus*, 723E, trans. ibid. 61. Cf. *Explicatio duodecim capitum*, 11.

[86] Cyril, *In Lucam*, 5, trans. Smith, 63. Cf. *In Lucam* 1. 1; *Ad augustas*, 31 (*ACO* 1. 1. 5. 51); *De symbolo*, 29; Proclus of Constantinople, *Tomus ad Armenios* (435).

[87] *Quod unus*, 766B.

[88] *Ad Nestorium*, III. 8, anathem. 2 and 3.

[89] On this point see Wickham, *Cyril*, p. xxxiii; Donald G. Dawe, *Jesus: The Death and Resurrection of God*, 92; Bauckham, 'Only the Suffering God Can Help', 8.

of divinity. The Word remained what he was, namely God, and did not abandon his divine status.[90]

The question, then, has to be pressed with a new force, what was it that happened in the emptying? If there was any change at all, how should this change be described? Nestorius, following Theodore, explained that the emptying consisted in the conjunction (συνάφεια) of humanity with the divine Word. Cyril responded that conjunction was something that 'any other man could have with God, being bonded to him as it were in terms of virtue and holiness'.[91] If conjunction was no more than an external appending of human nature to the divine, in what sense was it emptying? What was the Word emptied of? Theodore was adamant that in so far as one could speak of emptying or change, these experiences could be ascribed only to the man assumed, not to God who did the assuming.[92]

Cyril responded that the emptying did not consist in merely appending humanity to a divinity that remained unaffected. The incarnation for Cyril meant God's 'descent to the limits of humanity' and his allowing of 'the limitations (μέτροι) of the manhood to have dominion over himself (ἐφ' ἑαυτῷ τὸ κρατεῖν)'.[93] Thus, the Word's submission to the limitations of human existence entailed a temporary restraint of divine power and other perfections.

As Cyril stressed on many occasions, the Word remained impassible in his own nature throughout the incarnation. The proponents of the Theory of Theology's Fall into Hellenistic Philosophy isolate this claim in Cyril's writings and argue that at the end of the day Cyril abandoned his radically theopaschite claims and made the same concessions to the philosophical axiom of divine impassibility as did his Nestorian opponents. On this reading, Nestorius was a thoroughgoing philosophical impassibilist, whereas Cyril was an inconsistent and hesitating theopaschite. Were it not for his inadequate philosophical framework, Cyril would have seen the light and joined the circles of those who advocate unrestricted divine suffering today.[94]

[90] 'When we say that he [the Word] was "emptied out" it has no derogatory reference to the Word's own nature nor, as might be thought, was he changed or made inferior in any respect,' *Scholia*, 5, trans. McGuckin, *Christological Controversy*, 298. Cf. *Ad monachos*, 23.

[91] *Quod unus*, 733B, trans. McGuckin, *On the Unity of Christ*, 74.

[92] Theodore of Mopsuestia, *Catechetical Homilies*, 6. 6; 8. 7.

[93] *Quod unus*, 760C, trans. McGuckin, *On the Unity of Christ*, 110. Cf. *Ad augustas*, 44 (*ACO* 1. 1. 5. 58–9).

[94] J. D. McCoy proposes process metaphysics as a more suitable philosophical framework for understanding the divine passibility. Cyril, on McCoy's reading, was captivated by the static metaphysical scheme of later Platonism. See his 'Philosophical

Such a reading of the evidence, as I have repeatedly stressed in the course of this study, puts patristic theologians into quite artificial boxes of 'biblicists' and 'philosophers', 'theopaschites' and 'impassibilists'. As I pointed out earlier, the Nestorian 'impassibilism' represented a particular type of piety that was inspired by the scriptural vision of the ontological distinction between the creator and creation. Likewise, Cyril's refusal to dissolve the paradox of the incarnation was not philosophy-driven, but was motivated by the desire to articulate a distinctly Christian account of the divine involvement. Indeed, to claim that 'bare divinity' suffers or that God suffers outside the framework of the incarnation (as many contemporary theopaschites tend to do) is to incur the following two major problems. First, it would mean that the anthropomorphic descriptions applied to God literally, that God had a constitution that would enable him to feel human emotions and suffering prior to the incarnation.[95] Second, the presupposition that the divine nature could itself suffer renders the assumption of humanity superfluous. If God could suffer as humans do without assuming humanity, the incarnation would be unnecessary.[96]

When Cyril said that the Word suffered impassibly, he did not intend to say that God remained unaffected and uninvolved in the human experiences of Christ. On the contrary, it was Cyril's clear intention to repudiate any such view. Rather, Cyril intended to say that it was an unmistakably divine subject who submitted himself to the limitations of the incarnation and accepted all the consequences associated with this condition. It is not accidental that the apophatic claim that the divine nature is impassible always appears in Cyril's writings in tandem with the affirmation that God suffered in the flesh.

Cyril's awareness of the subtlety of the theological balance that he attempted to maintain came out most clearly in the exchange of letters

Influences on the Doctrine of the Incarnation in Athanasius and Cyril of Alexandria', 362–91. Cf. Hallman, *Descent of God*, 125–45.

[95] Cyril spells this problem out most clearly in his letter to an admirer of Nestorius: 'The council [of Ephesus] did not in any way say that the Word itself, begotten of God by nature, died or was pierced in the side by a spear. For what sort of side, pray, tell, does that which is incorporeal have? Or how could life die? But the council said that, because the Word was united to flesh, when his flesh was suffering he appropriated the suffering to himself since his own body was suffering,' *Ep.* 10. 1 (*ACO* 1. 1. 1. 110–12). Cyril also takes up the whole subject of anthropomorphism in his *Adversus Anthropomorphitas*. For a valuable discussion of this work, which places it in the context of modern passibilism, see E. P. Meijering, 'Some Reflections on Cyril of Alexandria's Rejection of Anthropomorphism', 297–301.

[96] *Ad Succensum*, II. 2.

with the bishops of the opposition which took place after the council of Ephesus. In one of such letters, written to Acacius of Beroea, who on behalf of the Oriental party demanded that Cyril retract all his writings on christology, Cyril was determined to sustain a theological tension between the divine transcendence and the divine involvement in suffering:

I [Cyril] certainly do not say that any confusion or blending, or mixture took place, as some people maintain, because I know that the Word of God is by nature changeless and unalterable, and in his proper nature is altogether incapable of any suffering. That which is divine is impassible and does not admit even the 'shadow of a change' (James 1: 17) of suffering. On the contrary it is established with unshakeable stability in the realities of its own goodness. I maintain, *however*, that it was the Only Begotten Son of God, the One Christ and Lord, who suffered in the flesh for our sake, in accordance with the scriptures, particularly with that saying of the blessed Peter (1Pet. 4: 1).[97]

In this passage Cyril carefully distanced himself from a typically Apollinarian error of confusing and mixing the two natures. We should also note Cyril's conscious reliance upon the NT in affirming both qualified impassibility and qualified passibility. In the following passage Cyril explained his position to Succensus of Diocaesarea, who shared the reservations of the Orientals:

Your Perfection [Succensus] expounds the rationale of our Savior's passion very correctly and wisely, when you insist that the Only-begotten Son of God did not personally experience bodily sufferings in his own nature, as he is seen to be and is God, but suffered in his earthly nature. *Both points*, indeed, must be maintained of the one true Son: the absence of divine suffering and the attribution to him of human suffering because his flesh did suffer. These people [the Orientals], though, imagine that we are hereby introducing what they call *theopatheia*; they fail to bear in mind God's plan and make mischievous attempts to shift the suffering to the man on his own in foolish pursuit of a false piety.[98]

Cyril has very skilfully carved out his vision of the incarnation between the Scylla of God's suffering in his own nature outside the economy of the incarnation and the Charybdis of the man's suffering on his own. Cyril differentiated between unqualified and qualified divine passibility. Divine passibility without qualifications entailed that God was anthropomorphic and subject to human weaknesses. Qualified divine passibility, in contrast, allowed for the possibility of the tran-

[97] *Ad Acacium*, (of Beroea), 7; emphasis added.
[98] *Ad Succensum*, II. 4, trans. Wickham, *Cyril*, 91; emphasis added.

scendent God's suffering in and through human nature. Cyril pointed out that the charge of *theopatheia* strictly speaking applied only to the unqualified divine impassibility, not to the qualified one.

In the passage quoted below Cyril spelled out most clearly that divine impassibility functioned as an indicator of the divine transcendence and irreducible divinity. Divine impassibility was not meant to rule out the Word's suffering in human nature:

> God's Word is, of course, undoubtedly impassible in his own nature and nobody is so mad as to imagine the all-transcending (ὑπὲρ πάντα) nature capable of suffering (δύνασθαι πάθους); *but* by very reason of the fact that he has become man, making flesh from the Holy Virgin his own, we adhere to the principles of the divine plan and maintain that he who as God transcends suffering (τὸν ἐπέκεινα τοῦ παθεῖν ὡς θεόν), suffered humanly in his flesh (τῇ ἰδίᾳ παθεῖν ἀνθρωπίνως).[99]

The examples of such 'tandem statements' could easily be multiplied.[100] Cyril's intention is clear: he wants to uphold both God's irreducible divinity and God's involvement in the human experiences of the incarnation. Although God did not suffer in the divine nature, he did suffer in his human nature. The flesh became an instrument that enabled the Word to suffer humanly.[101]

Nestorius objected that Cyril's claim that God suffered in another nature was an evasion of the problem, not a resolution of it. The divine impassibility for Nestorius was unconditional and absolute: that which could not suffer in its own nature, could not possibly suffer in any other nature.[102] To meet this criticism, Cyril developed the Athanasian idea of God's appropriation of human characteristics and drew from a variety of traditional analogies that shed light upon the divine participation in the suffering of the flesh.

Cyril's Contribution to the Doctrine of Appropriation

If there was one central idea that conveyed for Cyril the depth of divine self-emptying, it was that God made human life his very

99 *De symbolo*, 24, trans. Wickham, *Cyril*, 123; emphasis added.

100 *Ad Nestorium*, II. 5; *Scholia*, 5, 13, 26; *Explicatio duodecim capitum*, 31. *Ad Acacium* (of Beroea), 7; *Ad monachos*, 23–4; *Ep*. 39. 9 (*ACO* 1. 1. 4. 17).

101 *Scholia*, 25.

102 *Liber Heraclidis*, 2. 1. 295. Cyril, *Scholia*, 33. Theodoret provides a rather convoluted argument in support of Nestorius' claim in *Eranistes*, III. 221–4.

own (ἴδια).[103] Kenosis, for Cyril, was ἰδιοποίησις and οἰκείωσις, God's appropriation of human characteristics. Without God's compassionate submission to the limitations of human existence, such as thirst, hunger, fatigue, ignorance, fear, and death, Christ's self-emptying would be only a word.[104]

Cyril, of course, did not introduce the idea of appropriation into patristic theology. Athanasius, as we remember, had recourse to this idea in the context of the Arian crisis.[105] Cyril held in special esteem Athanasius' *Epistula ad Epictetum*, which contained the doctrine of appropriation in its most developed form. Cyril relied upon the letter as an authoritative statement of faith and on several occasions lamented the Nestorian corruption of its copies, which apparently enjoyed a wide circulation.[106] For Cyril the theory of appropriation became 'the key to the holy Fathers' thinking'.[107] The appropriation of the flesh meant that in the incarnation God acted and suffered in and through the flesh, and did nothing apart from the flesh.

Cyril stressed repeatedly that the 'flesh' denoted the whole human nature, complete with the rational soul.[108] In so doing, he was not merely paying lip-service to the theological objections of those who suspected him of Apollinarian sympathies.[109] Christ's human soul was as soteriologically significant for Cyril as it was for the Cappadocian Fathers, especially for Gregory of Nazianzus.[110] Cyril underlined that without the human soul the divine Word would be incapable of experiencing such human emotions as fear, sorrow, and grief. To ascribe these emotions directly to the 'naked divinity' would be crude anthropomorphism, it would be to charge God with powerlessness and cowardice.[111] At the

[103] See McGuckin, *Christological Controversy*, 201–7. For an exhaustive treatment of Cyril's doctrine of appropriation see D. A. Keating, 'The Appropriation of Divine Life in Cyril of Alexandria'.

[104] *Ad augustas*, 8 (*ACO* 1. 1. 5. 29–30); 15 (*ACO* 1. 1. 5. 33); *Ad monachos*, 18.

[105] See above, pp. 133–4.

[106] *Ad Acacium Melitenum*, 21; *Ad Succensum*, I. 11; *Ep*. 39. 11.

[107] Cyril, *Ad Nestorium*, II. 7.

[108] *Quod unus*, 718D; *Ad Nestorium*, III. 8; *Answers to Tiberius*, 7; *De symbolo*, 14; *Ad Succensum*, II. 2; *Contra Nestorium*, II. Prooem (*ACO* 1. 1. 6. 33); *Scholia*, 25.

[109] For criticism of Grillmeier's claim that Cyril neglected the soteriological function of the soul of Christ see L. Welch, 'Logos-Sarx?', 271–92; J. McGuckin, *Christological Controversy*, 206–7. For a comprehensive survey of this issue see S. McKinion, *Words*, 149–59.

[110] Gr. Naz., *Ep*. 101. 7.

[111] As we discussed in Chap. 2, Cyril admitted that God on his own was capable of experiencing God-befitting emotions, such as anger and joy.

same time, a mindless and soulless body was equally incapable of feeling these emotions: 'A soulless and mindless body would not feel grief any more than it would conceive any kind of sadness, or would be seized with fear of future events. It is the rational soul that is considered to experience such things by examining with the mind what has happened and inferring what will come to pass.'[112] In order to participate fully in the human condition God assumed a complete human constitution, a body endowed with a rational soul.

Like Gregory of Nyssa before him, Cyril distinguished natural and innocent *pathē*, such as fear, grief, hunger, and weariness, from the sinful ones.[113] In making this distinction, Cyril parted ways with the moral teaching of the Stoics, for whom all *pathē*, most especially fear and grief, were diseases of the soul. Cyril explained that during his earthly ministry the Word permitted his own flesh to experience natural passions and at the same time prevented it from experiencing the sinful ones.

Cyril describes the peculiar actions of the Word in a variety of ways. We read that the Word consented to subjecting his flesh to the natural *pathē*. The Word held natural *pathē* in check and, for example, did not allow grief and sorrow to become overwhelming. God also strengthened the flesh in the time of trial. He taught the flesh how to withstand the assault of temptations. Most importantly, the presence of the Word in Christ changed the experiences that mere human beings undergo out of necessity, due to their bodily and psychological constitution, into voluntary actions.[114]

Cyril spoke of Christ's passion being voluntary in three distinct but interrelated ways: (1) Christ could avoid suffering, if he so chose; (2) Christ was not ignorant of his passion: on the contrary, he foreknew the final outcome of his ministry, including the circumstances and the time of his death; (3) Christ chose to suffer out of compassion for the human race. Christ was not compelled to suffer, he did not suffer in ignorance or without a purpose.[115] At the same time, his suffering and anguish were real and included a measure of human deliberation and hesitation, as is seen from his prayer in Gethsemane. Here again Cyril intends to uphold a delicate balance between two equally significant truths: the

[112] *Ad augustas*, 44 (*ACO* 1. 1. 5. 58).

[113] *In Ioannem*, 8 (*PG* 74:703E): 'Now fear and timidity, being natural emotions in us, are not to be classified among sins,' trans. Russell, *Cyril*, 120. Cf. *Scholia*, 35.

[114] *In Lucam*, Serm. 12 on Luke 4: 2.

[115] *In Ioannem*, 8 (PG 74: 705 B–C); 4. 1 (331A–E); 11. 9 (970B); *In Lucam*, Serm. 12 on Luke 4: 28; *Scholia*, 25.

suffering of the Word in the flesh was truly human (not only in appearance) and was not merely human.

The result of the Word's voluntary suffering was that 'the flesh was taught to feel things beyond its own nature'.[116] What was the character of this transformation? For Cyril, the Word's appropriation of a human soul capable of feeling emotions had wide-ranging soteriological consequences:

> For unless He [Christ] had been afraid (μὴ ἐδειλίασεν), human nature could not have become free from cowardice (τοῦ δειλιᾶν); unless He had experienced grief (ἐλυπήθη) there would never have been any deliverance from grief; unless He had been troubled and alarmed, no escape from these feelings could have been found. And with regard to every human experience (ἀνθρωπίνως γεγονότων), you will find exactly the corresponding thing in Christ. The passions of his flesh (σαρκὸς πάθη) were aroused, not that they might have the upper hand as they do in us, but in order that when aroused they might be thoroughly subdued by the power of the Word dwelling in the flesh, the nature thus undergoing a change for the better.[117]

Far from being a covert Apollinarian, Cyril should be credited with developing the Athanasian appropriation theory in a direction that made Christ's human soul as soteriologically significant as his body: 'Just as every characteristic of his own body is made his own (οἰκειοῦται), so too are the characteristics of his soul.'[118] The soul stood in need of healing, as did the body. Correspondingly, when Christ gave up his spirit to the Father, he made it possible for our souls to follow his soul, instead of being sent down to hell.[119]

Elaborating the theory of appropriation, Cyril draws upon the major motifs of Irenaeus' conception of recapitulation. The divine Word became man in order to reconstitute (ἀναστοίχειν) in himself all aspects of human existence, from life to death, sin only excepted.[120] In Christ human nature achieved its highest fulfilment by becoming the flesh of the Word.

116 *In Ioannem*, 7, trans. Randell, 122.

117 *In Ioannem*, 8 (*PG* 74: 92D), trans. Randell, 154 with minor changes. Cf. (Ps.-?)Ath., *Ar.* 3. 57. The transformative nature of the Logos' appropriation of human emotions is emphasized by Wiles, *The Spiritual Gospel*, 146–57. I, however, disagree with Wiles's contention that Cyril viewed the role of the soul as entirely passive. See Wiles, 'The Nature of the Early Debate about Christ's Human Soul', 150.

118 *Ad Augustas*, 44 (*ACO* 1. 1. 5. 58).

119 Ibid. (*ACO* 1. 1. 5. 59).

120 *Quod unus*, 724C.

Having become incarnate, the Word did not perform any actions apart from or outside his flesh. Commenting on the healing of the paralytic in Luke, Cyril emphasized that Christ cured the sick by touching them with his hand, although he was perfectly capable of curing them by word, or even by mere inclination of his will. In Cyril's view, Christ chose this particular method of healing in order to show us that the divine Word does nothing without his body. In this inseparable union the flesh of the Word became life-giving.[121]

This ability of the Word's flesh to communicate eternal life had for Cyril vital practical implications and was immediately related to his understanding of the sacraments of the Eucharist and baptism. Nestorius contended that it would be improper to think of the Godhead as being broken into several parts and then distributed to the faithful in the form of bread and wine. He asked quite bluntly: 'What do we eat? The Godhead, or the flesh?'[122] If these were the only two alternatives, Cyril would admit that the consecrated elements were not transformed into the 'naked divinity'. At the same time, they did not stand for the body and blood of the man assumed, considered apart from the divine Word. In Cyril's view, the first option was plainly absurd, since the divine nature was incorporeal and therefore could not be broken in parts; while the second option was inadequate, for a merely human body could not be life-giving on its own merits: 'When we eat, we are not consuming the Godhead—perish the awful thought—but the Word's own flesh, which has been made life-giving because it is the flesh of him who lives because of the Father.'[123] It should be noted that the same dialectical turn—the Eucharistic particles represent neither bare divinity, nor mere humanity—was made by Apollinaris fifty years before Cyril in a context of the debate with unidentified theologians whose line of thought was remarkably similar to that of Nestorius.[124] It is to Cyril, however, that we owe a creative development of this and other Apollinarian insights.

121 *In Lucam*, Serm. 12 on Luke 4: 31; Serm. 36 on Luke 7: 11–18. Cyril made the same point with regard to the miraculous resuscitation of Jairus' daughter in *In Lucam*, Serm. 46 on Luke 8: 49–56.

122 *Contra Nestorium*, 4. 4 (*ACO* 1. 1. 6. 84).

123 Ibid. 4. 5 (*ACO* 1. 1. 6. 85), trans. Russell, *Cyril*, 169. Cf. *Ad Nestorium*, III. 7; anathem. 11; *Explicatio duodecim capitum*, 28 (*ACO* 1. 1. 5. 24); *Quod unus*, 776C–777E; *Ep.* 11A. 5; *Ad Augustas*, 45 (*ACO* 1. 1. 5. 59); *De symbolo*, 28. For discussion of this point, see Chadwick, 'Eucharist and Christology', 153–7; Ezra Gebremedhin, *Life-Giving Blessing*.

124 On this issue see an important article by Kelley McCarthy Spoerl, 'The Liturgical Argument in Apollinaris', 142–4.

Just as in the days of his earthly ministry the Word incarnate healed by touch, so too in the Eucharist the faithful touched with their lips and partook of the body and blood that God the Word made his own.[125] Cyril deliberately used concretely physical language: Christ hides the seeds of immortality in us by inserting his own flesh into our bodies. Cyril encouraged frequent communion, stressing that everlasting life was physically communicated to believers who approached the sacrament in reverence and repentance.[126]

The theory of appropriation could be applied with equal force to the sacrament of baptism. When the question was raised, into whose death were the catechumens baptized, Nestorius, predictably, answered that it was improper and absurd to speak of the death of the Godhead. Cyril retorted that Nestorius' solution was equally inadequate: the death of a mere man, even united in a conjunction of honour with the Godhead, was unable to procure salvation. It was necessary that God suffered and died in human nature in order to conquer death by death and restore immortality and incorruptibility. This did not mean that the 'naked divinity' died, but that by appropriating flesh, God made human death his own.[127] The main contours of this argument were already present in the corpus of Apollinarian writings to which Cyril had access.[128]

In order to explain this rather obscure point more clearly, Cyril had recourse to the analogy of the death and birth of a human being. In the case of the death of an individual, comprising body and immortal soul, we do not say: 'Peter's body died.' We say instead: 'Peter died,' understanding that Peter's soul does not cease to exist when it is separated from his body. This manner of expression emphasizes the fact that Peter is a single subject of both bodily and psychic experiences. Likewise, we may quite properly speak of God the Word being crucified and dying in

125 Chadwick, 'Eucharist and Christology', 155–7.

126 *In Ioannem*, 3. 6 (324D–325A). A similar argument has been deployed by Apollinaris. Joseph Hogan, 'Our Bodily Union with Christ', 10–15.

127 *Quod unus*, 773D–E: 'As I have said, he made his very own a body capable of tasting death and capable of coming back to life again, so that he himself might remain impassible and yet be said to suffer in his own flesh (σαρκὶ τῇ ἰδίᾳ λέγοιτο παθεῖν),' trans. McGuckin, *On the Unity of Christ*, 127. Cf. *Ad monachos*, 23: 'How can Life be said to die? It is because Life suffered death in its very own body that it might be revealed as life when it brought the body back to life again,' trans. ibid. 259. Cf. also *Ad Augustas*, 7, 9, 41 (*ACO* 1. 1. 5. 29, 30, 56–7); *Ad monachos*, 25; *Explicatio duodecim capitum*, 23 (*ACO* 1. 1. 5. 23); *De symbolo*, 28; Nestorius, *Quaternion*, 16.

128 Apollinaris, *Ad Dionysium*, 6; *De fide et incarnatione*, 5. 196. 26–197. 15. See Spoerl, 'Liturgical Argument', 140–1.

the flesh (with the understanding that the Word did not cease to exist with the death of his flesh), instead of attributing suffering and death to the man alone.[129]

Similarly, when someone is born we do not say: 'Peter's mother gave birth to Peter's body' but instead say 'Peter was born.' We understand that Peter's mother supplied his embryonic body, whereas God ineffably introduced the life-giving spirit into Peter's growing embryo. However, it would be as pedantic and awkward to say 'Peter's body died' as to say 'Peter's mother gave birth to Peter's body and not to his soul.' When we refer to the whole individual we stress the fact that we are dealing with a single agent, not with two separate agents loosely conjoined to each other. On these grounds the use of the title Theotokos is fully justified, since Mary gave birth to one undivided incarnate Lord, not to a separate human being.[130]

The Soul–Body Model and the Doctrine of Appropriation

Patristic application of the analogy of the soul–body union to the relationship between the divine Word and the flesh has deservedly received much attention in scholarship.[131] The scholarly discussion has tended to focus on the question of to what degree a particular Father is indebted to this or that school of philosophy in his deliberations on this matter. In my judgement, it has not been sufficiently emphasized that the Hellenistic philosophers themselves had not reached any

129 Cyril, *Ep.* 6. 1; *Quod unus*, 764D–E: 'The Word was alive even when his holy flesh was tasting death, so that when death was beaten and corruption trodden underfoot the power of the resurrection might come upon the whole human race,' trans. McGuckin, *On the Unity of Christ*, 115.

130 *Ad monachos*, 12. It is most likely that Apollinaris, *De fide et incarnatione*, 5. 196. 22, was first to introduce the Marian argument in the context of the debate about the unity of Christ's person. See Spoerl, 'Liturgical Argument', 138–9.

131 For the most comprehensive treatment of this issue see R. Norris, *Manhood and Christ*, 21–78. Also Wiles, 'The Nature of the Early Debate about Christ's Human Soul'. Immediately pertinent to the study of Cyril are the following works: Chadwick, 'Eucharist and Christology'; McKinion, *Words, Imagery, and the Mystery of Christ*, 69–75; G. Joussard, 'Impassibilité du Logos et impassibilité de l'âme humaine chez saint Cyrille d'Alexandrie', 209–24; 'Un Problème d'anthropologie et de christologie chez saint Cyrille d'Alexandrie', 361–78; McGuckin, *Christological Controversy*, 198–201. Weinandy, *Does God Suffer?*, 182–90, rightly stresses multiple problems with the soul–body model and shows how Cyril dealt with these problems successfully.

tangible consensus on the nature of the soul–body union. (Let it be noted that modern thinkers too have not yet made a decisive breakthrough: the mind–body problem still remains one of the essentially contested issues of our time.)

As I mentioned in the first chapter, there was a major disagreement between the Academy and the Stoa on this matter. Plotinus taught that since the soul was an incorporeal substance, it could not be acted upon by the body (οὐδὲν ἀσώματον συμπάσχει σώματι) and in this sense was impassible.[132] Understood in this way, impassibility was a purely negative characteristic, ruling out the soul's ability to engage in interaction with material entities. A pivotal question was whether the soul was in any way affected, once it was united to the body? Plotinus was prepared to concede that the soul had an impassible awareness (γνῶσις ἀπαθής) of the experiences of the body, but not that the soul in itself could be affected. In contrast, Plotinus' own teacher, Ammonius Saccas, spoke of the soul as sharing in the sufferings of the body.[133] Thus, on this issue the Academy was itself a divided house.

The Stoics disagreed with Plotinus on both metaphysical and ethical grounds. They argued from the standpoint of materialist monism that the soul was a rare material substance diffused in the body. As such, the soul could suffer with (συμπάσχειν) the body. As we discussed in Chapter 4, the Stoics meant by συμπάσχειν that the soul could both be affected by the experiences of the body and in turn cause changes in the body (say, cause redness or shivering). The Stoics believed that there was a two way interaction between the body and the soul.

Let us also recall that according to Stoic ethics, *apatheia* was attained in the philosophic life by mastering and eradicating the passions. If *apatheia*, as Plotinus claimed, indeed was a natural property of the soul, then it would make no sense to speak of attaining in struggle with the passions something that the soul already possessed by virtue of being incorporeal.

Given such a wide discrepancy of philosophical proposals, it is far from clear how Cyril could accept 'the assumptions of the best religious philosophy current at the time'.[134] The debate between Cyril and Nestorius cannot be neatly classified along the lines of the philosophical

[132] Plotinus, *Enneads*, 4. 4. 18–19. Discussed in Chadwick, 'Eucharist and Christology', 161.

[133] In Nemesius, *De natura homini*, 3 (*PG* 40: 596B). Discussed in Chadwick, 'Eucharist and Christology', 162.

[134] Francis Young makes this claim in 'A Reconsideration of Alexandrian Christology', 112.

options available in late antiquity. Cyril's references to the soul–body union analogy on many occasions remain unclear and tantalizingly underdeveloped. For example, discussing the question whether the term 'union' may apply to the combination of two things of different nature in *Quod unus sit Christus*, Cyril vaguely refers to the 'considered opinion of the experts (σοφοῖς) in such matters'.[135] It is unclear from this reference just whom among the *sophoi* Cyril had in mind.

In addition, the explanatory power of the soul–body union analogy is greatly weakened by the fact that Cyril and Nestorius developed it in radically different directions. There are many reasons to suspect that this analogy did not guide their christological deliberations. The situation, as I read it, was rather quite the opposite: it was their christological views that determined their application of the soul–body union analogy.

Cyril cautiously admitted on a number of occasions that the precise nature of the soul–body union was ineffable and that in this respect it was similar to the equally ineffable union of the Word with the flesh. He also warned about the obvious disanalogy: the Word united itself to the flesh which itself consisted of Christ's body and soul. Hence, the union of the Word with the soul of Christ could not be construed along the lines of soul–body union. It was crucial for Cyril that the distinction between the soul and the body could be drawn only conceptually and that in reality one could speak only of a single undivided subject. In Cyril's judgement, the soul–body analogy adequately conveyed the closeness and inseparability of the union of the Word with the flesh.[136] Cyril stressed that the soul did not act apart from the body.

The last point was a departure from the Platonist position, which allowed for some independence of mental acts from the body. The question of whether the soul was capable of feeling emotions apart from the body was a matter of contention. Some Platonists conceded that the soul was capable of feeling emotions on its own.[137] Cyril, on the contrary, held that the soul was not capable of experiencing any emotions or sensations without the body. It is in this narrow sense that the soul for Cyril was impassible.[138] Just as the soul suffered by means of the

135 *Quod unus*, 733B.

136 *Ad Nestorium*, III. 4; *Ad Eulogium*; *Quod unus*, 736B–C; *Explicatio duodecim capitum*, 14; *Scholia*, 25; *Ad Succensum*, II. 5.

137 See Chap. 1.

138 Georges Joussard argued that Cyril borrowed his doctrine of the impassibility of the soul entirely from the Platonists and held that the soul was not involved in the sufferings of the body. Herman Diepen challenged Joussard's conclusion and suggested

body and could not experience bodily suffering in itself, so the Word suffered by means of the flesh and in the flesh. On this analogy, the soul did not suffer bodily suffering in its own nature, but was capable of experiencing suffering in the nature of the body. Likewise, the Word who was in his own nature impassible, because he was incorporeal, suffered in the nature of the flesh.[139] The Word 'intimately accepted in himself the sufferings of the body, while in his own nature he suffered nothing.'[140]

At this juncture Nestorius raised two serious questions. First, he pointed out that the natural union between the soul and the body did not leave the soul with any essential freedom of action with regard to the sufferings of the body. For example, when the body was hurt, the soul, although it was not in bodily pain, could be said to grieve and to suffer with the body. The soul's suffering was an involuntary reaction to the external disturbance. In many cases the soul had no control over its reactions to bodily pain.[141] This was, Nestorius argued, radically different from the conjunction of the Logos with the man assumed, in which conjunction the Logos always retained his sovereign divine freedom and control over the passions of the body.[142]

that for Cyril the soul was not directly subject to bodily suffering, although by means of the body the soul could be said to be affected by passions. For an illuminating discussion of this issue see Lawrence J. Welch, *Christology and Eucharist in the Early Thought of Cyril of Alexandria*, 26–8.

139 *Scholia*, 33: 'It is because the suffering belongs to the economy, with God the Word reckoning those things that pertain to the flesh as his very own because of the ineffable union, and yet remaining outside suffering in so far as pertains to his own nature, since God is impassible. This is not exceptional, when we see that even the soul of man, although it remains outside suffering when the body suffers, in so far as pertains to its own nature, nonetheless is still reckoned to be involved in the suffering in so far as that which suffers is its very own body. Even though the soul is immaterial and simple, nevertheless that which suffers is not alien to it,' trans. McGuckin, *Christological Controversy*, 327. Cf. *Ad Succensum*, II. 2; *Ep.* 10. 3. Cf. also Theodoret, *Eranistes*, III. 221: 'But the reason why he [God the Word] took flesh was that the impassible might undergo the passion by means of the passible (ἵνα διὰ τοῦ παθητοῦ τὸ ἀπαθὲς ὑπομείνῃ τὸ πάθος),' trans. B. Jackson, NPNF, 2nd ser., iii. 217.

140 *Scholia*, 34 trans. McGuckin, *Christological Controversy*, 329.

141 The latter point was far from being self-evident: the Stoics followed the Platonists in emphasizing that the soul was capable of cultivating a strong psychological sense of detachment from the world and from physical suffering.

142 *Liber Heraclidis*, 1. 1. 13; 1. 2. 127–9; 1. 2. 136. Cyril did not have much to say by way of an answer, except for the fact that the soul–body union was not intended to be applied literally to the Logos–sarx union. It was at this point that the analogy broke down. On this issue see R. Greer, 'The Image of God and the Prosopic Union in Nestorius' *Bazaar of*

Nestorius' ultimate objection was that by the time Cyril was through with the qualifications he put on *theopatheia*, there was nothing left of substance that would distinguish Cyril's position from his own. Nestorius affirmed the impassibility of the divine nature, and so did Cyril. Nestorius insisted that human nature suffered, and so did Cyril. The only difference was that Cyril stated these two truths in a less coherent manner. So, what was the point of arguing over petty differences of expression?[143]

Cyril responded that the difference was indeed profound. While Nestorius maintained unqualified divine impassibility, which undermined the union of Christ's person, Cyril held to a substantially modified view of the divine impassibility. For Cyril, divine impassibility meant that the Word remained unconquered by suffering and death and that he was unable to experience suffering in his 'naked divinity', but only in and through the flesh. The presence of the Word transformed Christ's human sufferings, while preserving their tragic reality. The Word was in a qualified sense passible to the degree to which he made the sufferings of humanity his very own. In appropriating the experiences of humanity the Word directed them towards the salvific end and rendered them life-giving.

Ultimately, Nestorius had dissolved the paradox of the incarnation, while Cyril carefully preserved it, by keeping the unity of Christ at the core of his theological claims. Nestorius' view of the incarnation, when all was said and done, accounted only for the exaltation of man, a mere joining of a human being to God, and left no room for the self-emptying of the divine Word. Nestorius saw in Cyril's theory of appropriation a piece of sloppy theologizing that ultimately led to a confusion and mixture of the two subjects in Christ. Cyril objected that in order to remain faithful to the Nicene creed, one had to insist upon the centrality of the divine self-emptying in the incarnation. It was God's kenosis that secured humanity's theosis.

Heracleides', 56; also his *Theodore of Mopsuestia*, 38–9; H. E. W. Turner, 'Nestorius Reconsidered', 306–21.

143 *Scholia*, 35.

Conclusion

THERE is a remarkable logical elegance to the gradual development of the doctrine of the incarnation in the patristic period. We will be in a better position to appreciate the intellectual beauty of this development if we free our historical sensibilities from the main presuppositions of the Theory of Theology's Fall into Hellenistic Philosophy. As I have shown in the present study, with respect to the patristic theology of God's involvement in suffering this interpretative angle is especially misleading. Contrary to a widespread misconception, there was nothing in the Hellenistic world amounting to a universally endorsed 'axiom of divine impassibility'. The pagan schools of philosophy advanced several conflicting accounts of divine nature, emotions, and involvement in the world. At the same time, the biblical picture of God is far from unrestrictedly passibilist. The tension between the divine transcendence and the divine participation in history is constitutive of the biblical canon. Patristic theology did not face a choice between the apathetic deity of the philosophers and the suffering God of the Bible, because these views of God represent questionable scholarly constructs, rather than the actual theological options available to the theologians of late antiquity. The mind of the church carved out an account of the incarnation that was distinct from anything that Hellenistic thought had to offer.

I have argued in this book that the church's rejection of the major christological heresies followed a series of dialectical turns, all taken to safeguard an account of divine involvement worthy of God. 'Dialectical' is not an empty word in this description: the mind of the church rejected, step by step, the three inadequate strategies that aimed at eliminating the tension between Christ's divine status and the human experiences of his earthly ministry, most poignantly expressed in a paradoxical statement: 'the Impassible suffered'.

The vital tension of the incarnation can be dissolved in three main ways (which have had numerous variations throughout Christian history). One can either (1) deny the reality of Christ's human experiences; (2) give up Christ's divine status; or (3) claim that divine actions and human experiences have different subjects. The Docetists chose the first solution, the Arians took the second, and the Nestorians accepted the third one.

The Docetists, Arians, and Nestorians—substantial metaphysical and theological differences between them notwithstanding—agreed that divine impassibility ruled out the divine subject's direct involvement in human history and suffering. In my terminology, the Docetists, Arians, and Nestorians endorsed unqualified and unrestricted divine impassibility. They held that such experiences were unworthy of God and could not be predicated to God without undermining the integrity of the divine nature.

In contrast, the orthodox theologians regarded qualified divine impassibility as being compatible with certain God-befitting emotions and with the incarnate Word's suffering in and through human nature. For the orthodox divine impassibility functioned as an apophatic qualifier of all divine emotions and as the marker of the unmistakably divine identity. Thus, the concern to protect the paradox of the impassible God suffering in the flesh became the driving theological force of the debates in question.

The Docetists, as the reader may recall, embraced a popular critique of Christianity which saw in crucifixion an offence against pagan piety. Apart from being bad manners, it was metaphysically impossible for the supreme deity to be directly involved in the evil realm of matter. For the Docetists, divine impassibility ruled out any possibility of God's involvement in human pain and suffering. On these grounds, the Docetic groups contended that Christ's human experiences were putative and did not in any way involve his divinity. The church staunchly opposed this move and insisted that the reality of Christ's suffering was both historically undeniable and soteriologically significant. The apostolic tradition, church's sacramental practices and the death of the martyrs cumulatively testified to the reality and centrality of the crucifixion for the faith. While the logic of the church's worship suggested that Christ was in some important sense divine, the exact nature of Christ's divine status awaited more precise articulation in the fourth century.

The second stage of this dialectical development is represented by the Arian attempt at dissolving the paradox of the incarnation. The Arian strategy, from at least one angle, was exactly the opposite from that of the Docetists. It was the brutal and unseemly reality of Christ's earthly sufferings that made it impossible for the Arians to hold that the suffering Christ equalled in his divinity the High God. Reacting against the Patripassian position, the Arians drew a sharp distinction between the impassible High God and the passible Logos. In the Arian scheme, the Logos had to be both more than a mere man, in order for his suffering to have universal soteriological significance attested by the gospels and less than the High God, in order to be capable of change and suffering. After a prolonged struggle, the conciliar mind of the church came to the uncompromising recognition that in Christ it was God the creator who entered his creation to redeem it, and that the logic of our salvation required Christ's undiminished divinity. This newly achieved precision sharpened the tension between Christ's divine identity, marked by impassibility, and his human experiences to a degree never encountered before. It was inevitable that the question, how precisely was God involved in the human suffering of Christ? would be raised with a new force. While the pro-Nicene authors provided partial clues to this problem, this issue received more systematic attention in the Nestorian controversy.

The Nestorian answer to this question was to distinguish between two subjects in the story of the gospels: the man assumed by the Logos and the Logos indwelling the man. Nestorius contended that it was not befitting the impassible Logos to be in any way associated with change and suffering. Therefore, all human experiences of the incarnation had to be referred to the man assumed, not to the divine Logos.

Responding to the Nestorian charge of *theopatheia*, Cyril of Alexandria brought to a fitting conclusion centuries of patristic deliberation. Cyril recognized that the predication of suffering to the divine nature alone would render the assumption of humanity superfluous, whereas the opposite extreme, the attribution of suffering to the human nature alone would jeopardize divine involvement. Nestorius, as we know, embraced the second option, while many modern defenders of divine suffering tend to settle for the first one. For example, Jürgen Moltmann, Eberhard Jüngel, and Richard Bauckham see the crucifixion as the decisive revelation of Jesus' divine identity.[1] But if this were the case, if divine identity was somehow defined by the event of crucifixion in

[1] Moltmann, *Crucified God*, 282; E. Jüngel, *God as the Mystery of the World*, 373; R. Bauckham, *God Crucified*, 79.

such a way as to suggest that it was God's very nature to suffer in human fashion, then the assumption of the flesh would become quite unnecessary. For in this case the flesh would merely duplicate in its imperfect way the suffering that the Word had already undergone in his own nature. It is crucial, therefore, to differentiate between that which the Word undergoes in his own nature and the experiences that can only be attributed to the Word by virtue of his appropriation of the human nature.

It was precisely this differentiation that Cyril of Alexandria was concerned to sustain in his response to Nestorius. Cyril made the self-emptying of the Word, which consisted in the Word's voluntary acceptance of the limitations of the incarnation and restraint of divine power, the starting point of all of his deliberations on the incarnation. The Word made human experiences his very own by transforming them from within: that which was violent, involuntary, tragically purposeless, and fatal for an ordinary human being was made voluntary, soteriologically purposeful, and life-giving in the ministry of the Word. The Word who is above suffering in his own nature suffered by appropriating human nature and obtained victory over suffering. The celebration of this paradox in the creeds and hymns is the crowning achievement of a distinctly Christian account of divine involvement, an account for which no school of philosophy may take credit. It was Cyril who, to a degree unsurpassed by other patristic theologians, realized that in this paradox lay the very nerve centre of the gospel.

APPENDIX

Additional Evidence for the Prevalence of the Theory of Theology's Fall into Hellenistic Philosophy

I pointed out in the introduction that the issue of the divine impassibility in patristic theology was most often treated within the framework of what I had called 'the Theory of Theology's Fall into Hellenistic Philosophy'. To remind the reader, I have identified five main points of this theory:

1. divine impassibility is an attribute of God in Greek and Hellenistic philosophy;
2. divine impassibility was adopted by the early Fathers uncritically from the philosophers;
3. divine impassibility does not leave room for any sound account of divine emotions and divine involvement in history, as attested in the Bible;
4. divine impassibility is incompatible with the revelation of the suffering God in Jesus Christ;
5. the latter fact was recognized by a minority group of theologians who affirmed that God is passible, going against the majority opinion.

Since the Theory itself has been discussed in the Introduction and Chapter 1, it will be sufficient to cite here only the most articulate proponents of this influential trend in modern scholarship.

The contrast between the mutable and passible God of 'biblical religion' and the immutable and impassible God of Greek philosophy has been drawn sharply in many studies. A groundbreaking work in this arena is A. J. Hetchel's *The Prophets*. Less known is T. Boman's *Hebrew Thought Compared with Greek*. In addition to the opinions of W. Temple, T. E. Pollard, and J. M. Hallman quoted in the Introduction, consider, for example, the following general statement made by R. S. Franks back in 1917: 'The Biblical idea of God is religious, not philosophical, and as such is, especially in the Old Testament, frankly anthropomorphic. Hence God is represented as both mutable and passible.' For the Greek philosophers, on the contrary, 'one of the chief features of this idea [of

God] was the conception of the divine immutability and impassibility', 'Passibility and Impassibility', ix. 658.

The following words of Francis House echo the same position in a credal form: '[W]e confess and proclaim that the nature of God is totally self-giving sacrificial love. Here we have the biblical criterion by which the truth of all philosophical-theological speculation about God must be tested. By this criterion much that has been taught and assumed under the heading of "Divine Impassibility" must be recognized as only a presupposition taken over from non-Christian philosophy. It should be eliminated from our thinking as being incompatible with God's self-revelation in Christ,' 'The Barrier of Impassibility', 414.

Cf.: 'The notion that the Godhead must be described as impassible, with the corollary that Christ suffered only in his human nature and not in his Godhead, seemed to the Greek fathers to be implicit in the very definition of God. On this point they were deriving their definition of changeless perfection and utter serenity of deity from Greek philosophical theology rather than from the revelation of the God and Father of our Lord Jesus Christ... This Greek way of defining the perfection of God was utterly inadequate to become the philosophical base for Christian theism, but that is what became established as "orthodox" early in patristic development. It was like trying to mix oil with water,' W. J. Wolf, *No Cross, No Crown*, 196.

Cf.: 'And yet after all we may perhaps be justified in trying to find some fuller meaning than this in the idea that in Christ God has actually suffered. We need not be debarred from doing so by the extreme aversion of the patristic and scholastic theologians to think of divinity as "passible"; for it must be confessed that this aversion of theirs, which the Church took over from Greek thought rather than from Christ or St. Paul, is hard to reconcile with the essential Christian conception of God as a loving Father. The Christian God is not the pure Intelligence—cold, passionless, and loveless, "Himself unmoved, all motion's source"—that He was to Aristotle,' H. Rashdall, *Idea of Atonement*, 452.

Cf.: 'To the Greek mind, the fundamental attribute of God was immutability and the complete absence of any form of human passion. From this derived the Christian doctrine of the impassibility of God: the doctrine that, God being perfect, nothing can affect the divine nature,' O. T. Owen, 'Does God Suffer', 177.

Cf.: 'The experience of the pathos of God in the Old Testament is the presupposition for the understanding of the history of his "passion" in the New Testament... Such an historical understanding of God cannot easily be reconciled with the affirmation that God is "unchangeable", that God is "immutable". The acceptance of the apathetic God into classical Christology led to insoluble theological difficulties. Qualities such as pity, compassion and love appear incompatible with absolute "immutability". Impassibility and immutability belong to the order of being which has nothing to do with the order of becoming, with our world. According to Aristotle, God the First Mover causes change without itself being changed, without having potentiality. The First Mover rules the world from the outside and has no interaction with the world of humanity. As *actus purus* God is pure causality and cannot be the object of suffering.' Lucien J. Richard, *A Kenotic Christology*, 249–50.

Cf.: 'Since Plato and Aristotle the metaphysical and ethical perfection of God has been described as *apatheia* ... The *apathetic theology* of antiquity was accepted as a preparation for the trinitarian theology of the love of God and of men,' Moltmann, *The Crucified God*, 267, 70. It should be noted that Moltmann's position is not easily classifiable, since he rightly recognizes that *apatheia* for the Greek authors denoted God's freedom and self-sufficiency, rather than apathy and indifference.

In his study of divine anger E. F. Micka drew a sharp distinction between the Greek philosophers who held that anger was inappropriate for the divine nature and the Bible, which ascribed this emotion to God. In his view, 'The Apologists of the second century, though they had a knowledge of the then current philosophical ideas, seem not to have been much affected by this opposition between the Scriptures and pagan philosophy. They calmly accepted the notion of divine impassibility.' The discussion of passages from Aristides, Athenagoras, and Justin follows. See Micka, *The Problem of Divine Anger*, 17.

Philo is often credited with contaminating Christian theology with Greek ideas. Consider, for example, the following uncompromising dictum of H. Kraft: 'His [Philo's] speculations no longer bear any relation to the Hebrew way of thinking, as this is found in the Old Testament ... For it was Philo who taught the Church to read back into the Old Testament its own Christian philosophy, which in reality was a late form of the philosophy of Plato,' *Early Christian Thinkers*, 14.

Cf.: 'The problem is, where did Anselm, Aquinas, and all the rest get the criterion by which they decide that the Scriptures are speaking literally when they deny change in God and merely figuratively or metaphorically when they attribute change, complexity and real compassion to God? The criterion certainly did not come from Scripture itself, for Biblical writers wrote just as confidently and as unselfconsciously about the changing experiences and decisions of God as he interacted with the world of his creating as they did of his unchanging goodness and righteousness. The truth of the matter is that the criterion was derived from Greek ideas of perfection which were superimposed upon the interpretation of Biblical religion first by Philo, the Jewish theologian of Alexandria in the first century A. D. who created the conceptually unstable supernaturalistic theology by fusing (or confusing) Greek with Hebraic notions of divine perfection, then by many early Church Fathers such as Justin, Clement of Alexandria, Origen, Ambrose, etc. who uncritically accepted Philo's position. By the time of Augustine Philo's belief in the utter unchangeability of God had been crystallized into infallible, unquestioned dogma,' R. B. Edwards, 'The Pagan Dogma of the Absolute Unchangeableness of God', 308.

A. G. Nnamani (*The Paradox of a Suffering God*) interprets Christianity's Hellenization as a process of inculturation, 'the apparently unfinished cultural integration between Semitic and Hellenistic traditions' (p. 56). In line with the Fall Theory, Nnamani maintains that there is an irreconcilable contradiction between the Greek apathetic God and the Hebrew God who is passible: 'We have examined the axiom of divine impassibility in the light of the Hellenistic and Semitic conceptions of God and noted that it stems from the concept of apatheia in the ancient Greek philosophy ... On the contrary, apatheia in the sense explained above is totally absent in the biblical and Semitic conception of God' (p. 57). He subsequently argues that the Fathers had to harmonize those two positions primarily for cultural reasons. Thus, Nnamani dissolves the paradox that he had set himself to defend. One is left wondering as to why such a paradoxical dynamic is so vital for the Christian tradition at large, if the affirmation of divine impassibility depends, as it does for Nnamani, only upon the Greek cultural context. In his assessment of patristic theology Nnamani does not depart substantially from the Fall Theory.

In addition, C. P. E. Burns, C. C. Cain, J. Galot, C. G. Hoaas, E. Jacob, K. Kitamori, H. M. Hughes, J. Y. Lee, G. MacGregor, H. Pinnock, H. Rashdall, D. Soelle, and D. L. Wheeler for different reasons share the main assumptions of the Fall Theory. See their works in the bibliography. It should be noted that most proponents of the passibilist position, for example, W. Temple, M. Jarrett-Kerr, J. Moltmann, and R. Bauckham, admit to different degrees that there are some elements of truth in patristic understanding of the divine impassibility. Despite these important voices of caution, the Theory of Theology's Fall into Hellenistic Philosophy remains a widely assumed interpretative framework for the issue of the divine impassibility. In this book I have attempted to debunk the Fall Theory once and for ever.

BIBLIOGRAPHY

Ancient Authors

ABELARD, PIERRE, *Historia calamitatum*, trans. B. Radice, *The Letters of Abelard and Heloise* (London: Penguin Books, 1974).

ABRAMOWSKI, LUISE, and ALAN E. GOODMAN (eds.), *A Nestorian Collection of Christological Texts*, 2 vols. (Cambridge: Cambridge University Press, 1972).

AESCHYLUS, *Agamemnon*, ed. J. D. Denniston (Oxford: Clarendon, 1957).

AMBROSE OF MILAN, *The Sacrament of the Incarnation of Our Lord*, trans. R. J. Deferrari, FC 44 (1963).

ARISTOTLE, *Poetics*, in S. H. Butcher (trans.), *Aristotle's Theory of Poetry and Fine Art with a Critical Text and Translation of the Poetics* (London: Macmillan, 1911).

CICERO, *De Natura Deorum*, trans. H. M. Poteat (Chicago: University of Chicago Press, 1950).

ATHANASIUS OF ALEXANDRIA, *Apologia contra Arianos, PG* 25: 247–410.

—— *Athanasius' Werke*, ed. H. G. Opitz (Berlin: Walter de Gruyter, 1935 ff.), ii, iii.

—— *Contra Gentes* and *De Incarnatione*, ed. E. W. Thompson (Oxford: Clarendon, 1971).

—— *Epistula ad Epictetum episcopum Corinthi*, ed. G. Ludwig (Jena, 1911).

—— *Orationes contra Arianos, PG* 12: 12–468.

ATHENAGORAS, *Legatio*, ed. W. R. Schoedel (Oxford: Clarendon Press, 1972).

AUGUSTINE, *Confessions*, trans. H. Chadwick (Oxford: Oxford University Press, 1998).

BASORE, JOHN W. (trans.), *Seneca: Moral Essays*, 3 vols. (Cambridge, Mass.: Harvard University Press, 1958), i. 106–355.

CLEMENT OF ALEXANDRIA, *Stromateis*, ed. J. Ferguson, FC 85 (1991).

CYRIL OF ALEXANDRIA, *Commentary on the Gospel According to S. John*, i. *S. John i–viii*, trans. P. E. Pusey (Oxford: J. Parker, 1874).

—— *Commentary on the Gospel According to S. John*, ii. *S. John* IX–XXI, trans. R. Randell (London: Walter Smith, 1885).

—— *Commentary on the Gospel of Saint Luke*, trans. R. Payne Smith (New York: Studion, 1983).

—— *Deux dialogues christologiques*, ed. and trans. G. M. de Durand, SC 97 (1964).

—— *Letters*, trans. J. I. McEnerney, FC 76–7 (1985).

—— *Lettres Festales*, trans. L. Arragon *et al.* SC 372 (1991).

—— *On the Unity of Christ*, trans. J. A. McGuckin (Crestwood: St Vladimir's Seminary Press, 1995).

—— *Quod unus sit Christus*, in G. M. de Durand, *Cyrille d'Alexandrie: Deux dialogues christologiques*, SC 97 (Paris: Les Éditions du Cerf, 1964).

—— *Select Letters*, ed. L. R. Wickham (Oxford: Clarendon, 1983).

—— *Dialogues sur la Trinité*, ed. and trans. G. M. de Durand, SC 231 (1976); 237 (1977); 246 (1978).

DIX, GREGORY, *The Treatise on the Apostolic Tradition of St Hippolytus of Rome* (London: The Alban Press, 1992).

Epicurea, ed. H. Usener (Dubuque: Reprint Library, n.d.).

Epicurus: The Extant Remains, ed. C. Bailey (Oxford: Clarendon, 1926).

EPIPHANIUS OF SALAMIS, *Haereses* (or *Panarion*), *PG* 41–2.

EUSEBIUS OF CAESAREA, *The Proof of the Gospel*, trans. W. J. Ferrar, 2 vols. (Grand Rapids: Baker Book House, 1981).

GREGORY OF NAZIANZUS, *Sermons*, NPNF, 2nd ser. 7 (1955).

GREGORY OF NYSSA, 'Address on Religious Instruction', in E. R. Hardy (ed.), *Christology of the Later Fathers* (London: SCM, 1972).

—— *Contra Eunomium libri* (Leiden: Brill, 1960).

—— *Gregorii Nysseni Opera*, ed. W. Jaeger (Leiden: E. J. Brill, 1921).

GREGORY THAUMATURGUS, *De passibili et impassibili in Deo*, in J. B. Pitra (ed.), *Analecta Sacra*, pt. VI (Farnborough: Gregg, 1966).

HAHN, AUGUST, HAHN, G. LUDWIG, and VON HARNACK, ADOLF (eds.) *Bibliothek der Symbole und Glaubensregeln der alten Kirche* (Breslau: Grass, Barth, 1842).

HERODOTUS, *The History of Herodotus*, trans. G. Rawlinson (New York: Tudor, 1928).

HILARY OF POITIERS, *The Trinity*, trans. Stephen McKenna, FC 25 (1954).

HIPPOLYTUS OF ROME, *Contra Noetum*, trans. R. Butterworth (London: Heythrop College, 1977).

—— *Refutatio omnium heresium*, ed. P. Werdlard, GCS 26 (1916), 1–293.

HOMER, *The Odyssey of Homer*, trans. R. Latimore (New York: Harper & Row, 1965).

IGNATIUS OF ANTIOCH, '*Letters*', in Michael W. Holmes (ed.), *The Apostolic Fathers* (Grand Rapids: Baker Books, 2002), 128–201.

JOHN CASSIAN, *The Seven Books on the Incarnation*, in NPNF, 2nd ser., 11 (1955).

JOHN OF DAMASCUS, *Orthodox Faith*, trans. F. H. Chase, Jr., FC 37 (1958).

JUSTIN MARTYR, *Apologia*, in G. Krüger, *Die Apologieen Justins de Märtyrers*, 3rd edn. (Tübingen: J. C. B. Mohr (Paul Siebeck), 1904).

—— 'Exhortation to the Gentiles', in C. C. Richardson (trans.), *Early Christian Fathers* (Philadelphia: Westminster, 1953).

—— *Dialogus cum Triphone*, in Edgar J. Goodspeed (ed.), *Die Ältesten Apologeten* (Göttingen: Vandenhoeck & Ruprecht, 1914).

MAXIMUS THE CONFESSOR, *Selected Writings*, trans. G. C. Berthhold (New York: Paulist Press, 1985).

MELITO OF SARDIS, *On Pascha and Fragments*, trans. G. S. Hall (Oxford: Clarendon, 1979).

METHODIUS OF OLYMPUS, *Three Fragments on the Passion of Christ*, trans. R. Clark, ANF 6 (1899).

Nestoriana. Die Fragmente des Nestorius, ed. F. Loofs *et al.* (Halle: Niemeyer, 1905).

NESTORIUS OF CONSTANTINOPLE, *The Bazaar of Heracleides*, trans. G. R. Driver and L. Hodgson (Oxford: Clarendon, 1925).

OPITZ, HANS GEORG, *Urkunden zur Geschichte des arianischen Streites, 318–328* (Berlin: W. de Gruyter, 1934).

ORIGEN, *Contra Celsum*, ed. Henry Chadwick (Cambridge: Cambridge University Press, 1980).

PARMENIDES OF ELEA, *Fragments*, trans. D. Gallop (London: University of Toronto Press, 1984).

PHILO OF ALEXANDRIA, *The Works of Philo*, trans. C. D. Yonge (Peabody, Mass.: Hendrickson, 1993).

PROCLUS OF CONSTANTINOPLE, 'Tomus ad Armenios', *ACO* 4/2 (1914), 187–95; 196–205.

PSEUDO-DIONYSIUS THE AREOPAGITE, *Pseudo-Dionysius: The Complete Works*, trans. Colm Luibheid (New York: Paulist Press, 1987).

RICHARD, MARCEL, *Asterii Sophistae Commentariorum in Psalmos quea supersunt* (Oslo: A. W. Brøgger, 1956).

SALLUSTIUS, *Concerning the Gods and the Universe*, ed. A. D. Nock (Cambridge: Cambridge University Press, 1926).

SANDBACH, F. H. (ed.), *Plutarch's Moralia*, 16 vols. (Cambridge, Mass.: Harvard University Press, 1969), xv. 38–71.

SCHNEEMELCHER, WILHELM, and WILSON, R. McL. (eds.), *New Testament Apocrypha* (Cambridge: John Knox, 1991–2).

SCHWARTZ, E. (ed.), *Acta Conciliorum Oecumenicorum*, 5 vols. (Berlin: 1927–32).

SEVERUS OF CONSTANTINOPLE, *Letter to Sergius the Monophysite*, trans. Ian R. Torrance (Norwich: Canterbury, 1988).

TERTULLIAN, *Contra Noetum*, ed. Robert Butterworth (London: Heythrop College, 1977).

—— *Treatise Against Praxeas*, trans. E. Evans (London: SPCK, 1948).

The Lenten Triodion, trans. Mother Mary and Kallistos Ware (London: Faber & Faber, 1984).

THEODORE OF MOPSUESTIA, *Opera*, *PG* 66: 9–1020.

THEODORET OF CYRUS, *Eranistes*, ed. Gerard H. Ettlinger (Oxford: Clarendon, 1975).

THEOPHILUS OF ANTIOCH, *Ad Autolycum*, ed. Robert M. Grant (Oxford: Clarendon, 1970).

VAGGIONE, RICHARD P., *Eunomius: The Extant Works* (Oxford: Clarendon, 1987).

XENOPHANES OF COLOPHON, 'Fragments', in G. S. Kirk and J. E. Raven (eds.), *The Presocratic Philosophers* (Cambridge: Cambridge University Press, 1957).

Modern Authors

ABRAMOWSKI, L., 'Die Schrift Gregors des Lehrers "Ad Theopompum" und Philoxenus von Mabbug', *Zeitschrift für Kirchengeschichte* 89 (1978), 273–90.

ADAMS, MARILYN M., 'Redemptive Suffering: A Christian Approach to the Problem of Evil', in *Rationality, Religious Belief and Moral Commitment* (Ithaca: Cornell University Press, 1986), 248–67.

ANASTOS, M., 'Nestorius was Orthodox', *Dumbarton Oaks Papers* 16 (1962), 117–40.

ARMSTRONG, A. HILARY, 'Platonic Elements in St. Gregory of Nyssa's Doctrine of Man', *Dominical Studies* 1 (1948), 123–5.

—— 'Gnosis and Greek Philosophy', in B. Aland (ed.), *Gnosis: Festschrift für Hans Jonas* (Göttingen: Vandenhoeck & Ruprecht, 1978).

BABCOCK, WILLIAM S., 'The Christ of the Exchange: A Study in the Christology of Augustine's *Enarrationes in Psalmos*', Ph. D. thesis (Yale University, 1971).

BAILLIE, DONALD, *God Was in Christ: An Essay on Incarnation and Atonement* (New York: Charles Scribner's Sons, 1955).

BALOIAN, B. E., *Anger in the Old Testament* (New York: Peter Lang, 1992).

BANNING, JOSEPH VAN, 'The Critical Edition of the *Opus Imperfectum in Matthaeum*', *Studia Patristica* 17/1 (1982), 382–7.

BARDY, GUSTAV, 'Monarchianisme', *Dictionnaire de théologie catolique* 10/2 (1927), 2193–209.

BAUCKHAM, RICHARD A., 'Only the Suffering God Can Help: Divine Passibility in Modern Theology', *Themelios* 3 (1984), 6–12.

—— *God Crucified* (London: Paternoster Press, 1998).

BAYES, JONATHAN, 'Divine *Apatheia* in Ignatius of Antioch', *Studia Patristica* 21(1987), 27–31.

BETHUNE-BAKER, J. F., *Nestorius and his Teaching: A Fresh Examination of the Evidence* (Cambridge: Cambridge University Press, 1908).

BOMAN, THORLEIF, *Hebrew Thought Compared with Greek* (Philadelphia: Westminster, 1960).

BOREHAM, LESLIE, 'The Semantic Development of πάσχω', *Glotta* 49 (1971), 231–44.

BRASNETT, B. R., *The Suffering of the Impassible God* (New York: Macmillan, 1928).

BRUCE, A. B., *The Humiliation of Christ in Its Physical, Ethical, and Official Aspects* (Grand Rapids, Mich.: Eerdmans, 1955).

BRUEGGEMANN, WALTER, *Theology of the Old Testament: Testimony, Dispute, Advocacy* (Minneapolis: Fortress, 1997).

BURKERT, WALTER, *Greek Religion* (Cambridge, Mass.: Harvard University Press, 1985).

—— *Ancient Mystery Cults* (Cambridge, Mass.: Harvard University Press, 1987).

BURNLEY, WILLIAM F. E., 'The Impassibility of God', *The Expository Times* 67 (1955), 90–1.

Burns, Charlene P. E., *Divine Becoming: Rethinking Jesus and Incarnation* (Minneapolis: Fortress, 2002).

Bushnell, Horace, *The Vicarious Sacrifice* (New York: Scribner, 1877).

Cain, C. C., 'A Passionate God?' *Saint Luke's Journal of Theology* 25 (1981), 52–7.

Cantalamessa, R., *L'omelia 'In s. Pascha' dello pseudo-Ippolito di Roma* (Milan: Vita e pensiero, 1967).

Chadwick, Henry, 'Eucharist and Christology in the Nestorian Controversy', *JTS* 2 (1951), 145–64.

Chadwick, Owen, *John Cassian: A Study in Primitive Monasticism* (London: Cambridge University Press, 1968).

Chagny, André, *Les Martyrs de Lyon de 177: étude historique* (Lyons: Emmanuel Vitte, 1936).

Chenu, Bruno, *et al.*, *The Book of Christian Martyrs* (New York: Crossroad, 1990).

Childs, Brevard S., *Old Testament Theology in a Canonical Context* (Philadelphia: Fortress, 1986).

Christiansen, Peter G., 'Dieu, sa vie, son œuvre: Jean D'Ormesson's Attack on "Apatheia" as a Quality of God', *Literature and Theology* 8 (1994), 405–20.

Coakley, Sarah, '*Kenosis* and Subversion: On the Repression of "Vulnerability" in Christian Feminist Writing', in Daphne Hampson (ed.), *Swallowing a Fishbone?* (London: SPCK, 1996), 82–111.

Colish, Marcia, *The Stoic Tradition from Antiquity to the Early Middle Ages*, 2 vols. (Leiden: E. J. Brill, 1985).

Collins, Adela Yarbo, 'The Worship of Jesus and The Imperial Cult', in *The Jewish Roots in Christological Monotheism: Papers from the St Andrews Conference on the Historical Origins of the Worship of Jesus* (Leiden: Brill, 1999), 234–57.

Cook, D. E., 'Weak Church—Weak God: The Charge of Anthropomorphism', in *The Power and Weakness of God: Impassibility and Orthodoxy* (Edinburgh: Rutherford House, 1990), 69–92.

Cousar, Charles B., *A Theology of the Cross: The Death of Jesus in the Pauline Letters* (Minneapolis: Fortress, 1990).

Creel, Richard E., *Divine Impassibility* (Cambridge: Cambridge University Press, 1986).

—— 'Process Theology: Debate Continues', *Christian Century* 104 (1987), 225–6.

Crousel, Henri, 'La Passion de l'Impassible. Un essai apologétique et polémique du IIIe siècle', in *L'Homme devant Dieu; mélanges offerts au père Henri de Lubac* (Paris: Aubier, 1963), 269–79.

Cullmann, Oscar, *The Earliest Christian Confessions*, trans. J. K. S. Reid (London: Lutterworth Press, 1949).

Danielou, Jean, *Platonism et théologie mystique* (Paris: Aubier, Éditions Montaigne, 1944).

—— *From shadows to Reality: Studies in Biblical Typology of the Fathers* (London: Burns & Oates, 1960).

—— *Gospel Message and Hellenistic Culture* (Philadelphia: Westminster, 1973).

DAVIES, B., 'God, Time and Change', *Word and Spirit* 8 (1986), 3–12.

DAVIES, J. G., 'The Origins of Docetism', F. L. Cross (ed.), *Studia Patristica* 6 (1962), 13–35.

DAWE, DONALD G., *Jesus: The Death and Resurrection of God* (Atlanta: John Knox, 1985).

DE HALLEUX, ANDRÉ, 'La Reception du symbole œcuménique, de Nicée à Chalcédoine', *Ephemerides Theologicae Lovanienses* 61 (1985), 5–47.

DE LABRIOLE, P., 'Apatheia', in *Mélanges de philologie de littérature et d'histoire anciennes offerts à A. Ernout* (Paris: C. Klinsieck, 1940), 215–25.

—— 'Apatheia', *Reallexikon für antike und Christentum* 1 (1950), 484–7.

DEHANDSCHUTTER, B., 'Le Martyre de Polycarpe et le développement de la conception du martyre au deuxième siècle', *Studia Patristica* 17/2 (1982), 659–68.

DIEPEN, H.-M., 'Les Douze Anathématismes au Concile d'Éphèse et jusqu'en 519', *Revue Thomiste* 55 (1955), 300–38.

DILLON, JOHN, *The Middle Platonists* (New York: Cornell University Press, 1977).

—— 'The Nature of God in the *Quod Deus*', in J. Dillon and D. Winston (eds.), *Two Treatises of Philo of Alexandria*, Brown Judaic Studies 25 (Chico: Scholars Press, 1983).

DODDS, E. R., *Pagans and Christians in an Age of Anxiety: Some Aspects of Religious Experience from Marcus Aurelius to Constantine* (Cambridge: Cambridge University Press, 1965).

DORNER, I. A., *Divine Immutability: A Critical Reconsideration*, trans. R. R. Williams and C. Welch (Minneapolis: Fortress, 1994).

DRAGAS, GEORGE DION, *St. Athanasius Contra Apollinarem*, Church and Theology, 4 (Athens: (no pub.), 1985).

DRATSELLAS, C., 'Questions of the Soteriological Teaching of the Greek Fathers with Special Reference to St. Cyril of Alexandria', *Theologia* 38 (1967), 57–608; 39 (1968), 192–230, 394–424, 621–44.

—— 'Questions on Christology of St. Cyril of Alexandria', *Abba Salama* 6 (1975), 203–32.

EDWARDS, R. B., 'Pagan Dogma of the Absolute Unchangeableness of God', *Religious Studies* 14 (1978), 305–13.

ELERT, WERNER, 'Die Theopaschitische Formel', *Theologiche Lehrbücher* 75 (1950), 195–206.

—— *Der Ausgang Der Altkirchlichen Christologie* (Berlin: Lutherisches Verlagshaus, 1957).

FARLEY, EDWARD, *Divine Empathy, A Theology of God* (Minneapolis: Fortress, 1996).

Feitsma, Muus, *Het Theopaschitisme. Een dogma-historische Studie over de Ontwikkeling van het theopaschitisch Denken* (Kampen: Kok, 1956).

Festugière, A. J., *Epicurus and his Gods* (Oxford: Basil Blackwell, 1955).

Feuerbach, Ludwig, *The Essence of Christianity* (Amherst: Prometheus Books, 1989).

Fiddes, Paul S., *Creative Suffering of God* (Oxford: Clarendon, 1988).

Florovsky, Georges, 'Creation and Redemption', in *Collected Works*, iii (Belton, Mass.: Nordland, 1976).

Forster, P. R., 'Divine Passibility and the Early Christian Doctrine of God', in *The Power and Weakness of God* (Edinburgh: Rutherford House, 1990), 23–51.

Franks, Robert S., 'Passibility and Impassibility', *Encyclopedia of Religion and Ethics* xi. 658–60 (New York: Charles Scribners' Sons, 1917).

Frede, Michael, 'The Stoic Doctrine of the Affections of the Soul', in *Norms of Nature*, ed. Malcom Schofield and Gisela Striker (Cambridge: Cambridge University Press, 1986), 93–110.

Fredouille, J. C., 'Sur la colère divine: Jamblique et Augustine', *Recherches Augustiniennes* 5 (1968), 7–13.

Frend, William H. C., *Martyrdom and Persecution in the Early Church* (Garden City, NY: Anchor Books, 1967).

Fretheim, Terence E., *The Suffering of God: An Old Testament Perspective* (Philadelphia: Fortress, 1984).

Fritsch, C. T., *The Anti-anthropomorphisms of the Greek Pentateuch* (Princeton: Princeton University Press, 1943).

Frohnhofen, Herbert, *Apatheia Tou Theou: Über die Affectlosigkeit Gottes in der griechischen Antike und bei den griechischsprachigen Kirchenvätern bis zu Gregorios Thaumaturgos* (New York: Peter Lang, 1987).

Gager, John J., *The Origins of Antisemitism* (New York: Oxford University Press, 1983).

Galot, Jean, 'La Revelation de la souffrance de Dieu', *Science et Esprit* 31 (1979), 159–71.

Galtier, Paul, '*Unio secundum hypostasim* chez Saint Cyrille', *Gregorianum* 33 (1952), 351–98.

—— 'Saint Cyrille et Apollinaire', *Gregorianum* 37 (1956), 584–609.

Gebremedhin, Ezra, *Life-Giving Blessing. An Inquiry into the Eucharistic Doctrine of Cyril of Alexandria* (Uppsala: University of Uppsala, 1977).

George, Stuart, *Melito of Sardis 'On Pascha and Fragments'* (Oxford: Clarendon, 1979).

Gerstenberger, Erhard S., and Wolfgang Schrage, *Suffering*, trans. J. E. Steely (Nashville: Abingdon, 1980).

Goetz, Ronald, 'The Suffering God: The Rise of a New Orthodoxy', *Christian Century* 103 (1986), 385–9.

Goitein, S. D., 'YHWH the Passionate', *Vetus Testamentum* 6 (1956), 1–9.

GONZÁLES, JUSTO L., *The Story of Christianity* (San Francisco: HarperCollins, 1984).

GRANT, ROBERT M., 'Gnostic Origins and the Basilidians of Irenaeus', *Vigiliae Christianae* 13 (1959), 121–5.

—— *The Early Christian Doctrine of God* (Charlottesville: University Press of Virginia, 1966).

GREER, ROWAN A., *Theodore of Mopsuestia: Exegete and Theologian* (Westminster: Faith Press, 1961).

—— 'The Image of God and the Prosopic Union in Nestorius' *Bazaar of Heracleides*', in R. A. Morris (ed.), *Lux in Lumine, Essays to Honor W. Norman Pittenger* (New York: Seabury, 1966), 62–79.

GREGG, ROBERT, 'Centrality of Soteriology in Early Arianism', *Anglican Theological Review* 59 (1977), 260–78.

—— (ed.), *Arianism: Historical and Theological Reassessments: Papers from the Ninth International Conference on Patristic Studies, September 5–10, 1983, Oxford, England* (Cambridge, Mass.: Philadelphia Patristic Foundation, 1985).

GREGG, ROBERT and DENNIS GROH, *Early Arianism—A View of Salvation* (Philadelphia: Fortress, 1981).

GRILLMEIER, ALOIS, *Christ in Christian Tradition*, trans. J. Bowden., 3 vols. (Atlanta: John Knox, 1975).

GRYSON, R., *Scolies Ariennes sur le concile d'Aquilée*, SC (1980).

HALLMAN, JOSEPH M., *The Descent of God* (Minneapolis: Fortress, 1991).

—— 'Impassibility', in *Encyclopedia of Early Christianity* (1997), i. 566–672.

—— 'The Seed of Fire: Divine Suffering in the Christology of Cyril of Alexandria and Nestorius of Constantinople', *Journal of Early Christian Studies* 5 (1997), 369–91.

HANRATTY, G., 'Divine Immutability and Impassibility Revisited', in F. O'Rourke (ed.), *At the Heart of the Real* (Dublin: Irish Academic Press, 1992), 146–8.

HANSON, RICHARD P. C., *The Search for the Christian Doctrine of God* (Edinburgh: T & T Clark, 1988).

—— 'The Source and Significance of the Fourth *Oratio contra Arianos* Attributed to Athanasius', *Vigiliae Christianae* 42 (1988), 257–66.

HARDY, EDWARD ROCHIE, *Christology of the Later Fathers* (Philadelphia: Westminster, 1954).

HARNACK, ADOLF, *History of Dogma*, 7 vols. (New York: Dover, 1961).

—— *What is Christianity?* (Philadelphia: Fortress, 1986).

HEBBLETHWAITE, BRIAN, 'Incarnation and Atonement: The Moral and Religious Value of the Incarnation', in *Incarnation and Myth: The Debate Continued* (Grand Rapids: William B. Eerdmans, 1979).

HEINE, R. E., 'The Christology of Callistus', *JTS* 49 (1998), 56–91.

HELLEMAN, W. E. (ed.), *Hellenization Revisited: Shaping a Christian Response within the Greco-Roman World* (London: University Press of America, 1994).

Hengel, Martin, *Judaism and Hellenism, Studies in Their Encounter in Palestine in the Early Hellenistic Period* (Philadelphia: Fortress, 1974).

—— *Crucifixion* (London: SCM, 1978).

Henry, P., 'Kénose', *Dictionnaire de la Bible: Supplement* (Paris: Letouzey et Ané, 1957), v. 92.

Heschel, Abraham J., *The Prophets* (New York: Harper & Row, 1962).

Hill, W. J., 'Does Divine Love Entail Suffering in God?', in *God and Temporality* (New York: Paragon House, 1984), 55–71.

Hoaas, Geir, 'Passion and Compassion of God in the Old Testament: A Theological Survey of Hos 11: 8–9; Jer 31: 20, and Isa 63: 9, 15', *Scandinavian Journal of the Old Testament* 11 (1997), 138–59.

Hogan, Joseph, 'Our Bodily Union with Christ', *Diakonia* 16 (1981), 10–15.

House, Francis H., 'The Barrier of Impassibility', *Theology* 83 (1980), 409–15.

Hryniewicz, Waclaw, 'Le Dieu Souffrant: réflexions sur la notion chrétienne de Dieu', *Eglise et Theologie* 12 (1981), 333–56.

Hughes, H. M., *What is the Atonement?* (London: James Clarke, n.d.).

Inbody, Tyron, *The Transforming God: An Interpretation of Suffering and Evil* (Louisville: Westminster John Knox, 1997).

Inwood, Brad, *Ethics and Human Action in Early Stoicism* (Oxford: Clarendon, 1987).

—— 'Rules and Reasoning in Stoic Ethics', in *Topics in Stoic Philosophy*, ed. K. Ierodiakonou (Oxford: Oxford University Press, 1999).

Jacob, Edmond, 'Le Dieu souffrant: un theme théologique vétérotestamentaire', *Zeitschrift für die Alttestamentliche Wissenschaft* 95 (1983), 1–8.

Jarrett-Kerr, M., *The Hope of Glory: The Atonement in Our Time* (London: SCM, 1952).

Jeanes, Gordon, 'Baptism Portrayed as Martyrdom in the Early Church', *Studia Liturgica* 23 (1993), 158–76.

Jonas, Hans, 'The Concept of God after Auschwitz: A Jewish Voice', *The Journal of Religion* 67 (1987), 1–13.

Joussard, G., 'Un Problème d'anthropologie et de christologie chez saint Cyrille d'Alexandrie', *Recherches de Science Religieuse* 43 (1955), 361–78.

—— 'Impassibilité du Logos et impassibilité de l'âme humaine chez saint Cyrille d'Alexandrie', *Recherches de Science Religieuse* 45 (1957), 209–24.

Jugie, M., 'La Primauté romaine d'après les premiers théologiens monophysites', *Echos de l'Orient* 33 (1934), 181–9.

Jüngel, Eberhard, *God as the Mystery of the World: On the Foundation of the Theology of the Crucified One in the Dispute between Theism and Atheism*, trans. Darrell L. Guder (Grand Rapids, Mich.: Eerdmans, 1983).

Kamp, Jean, 'Présence de Dieu Souffrant', *Lumière et Vie* 25 (1976), 54–66.

Kannengiesser, Charles, 'Holy Scripture and Hellenistic Hermeneutics in Alexandrian Christology: The Arian Crisis' (Berkeley: The Center for Hermeneutical Studies, 1982), 1–40.

KANNENGIESSER, CHARLES, 'Athanasius' so-called Third Oration against the Arians', *Studia Patristica* 26 (1993), 375–88.

KANT, IMMANUEL, *Religion Within the Limits of Reasons Alone* (London: Open Court, 1934).

—— *Groundwork of the Metaphysics of Morals* (New York: Harper & Row, 1964).

KÄSEMANN, ERNST, 'Eine urchristliche Taufliturgie', *Festschrift Rudolf Bultmann: zum 65. Geburtstag überreicht* (Stuttgart: W. Kohlhammer, 1949).

KEARSLEY, ROY, 'The Impact of Greek Concepts of God on the Christology of Cyril of Alexandria', *Tyndale Bulletin* 43 (1992), 307–29.

KEATING, D. A., 'The Appropriation of Divine Life in Cyril of Alexandria' (D. Phil. Diss., Oxford University, 2000).

KELLY, J. N. D., *Early Christian Creeds* (New York: Longman, 1985).

KERRIGAN, A., *St. Cyril of Alexandria: Interpreter of the Old Testament* (Rome: Pontificio Istituto Biblico, 1952).

KESICH, VASELIN, 'Hypostatic and Prosopic Union in the Exegesis of Christ's Temptation', *St. Vladimir's Seminary Quarterly* 9 (1965), 118–37.

KIERKEGAARD, SØREN, *Christian Discourses*, trans. W. Lowrie (Oxford: Oxford University Press, 1939).

KINZIG, WOLFRAM, *In Search of Asterius: Studies on the Authorship of the Homilies on the Psalms* (Göttingen: Vandenhoeck & Ruprecht, 1990).

KITAMORI, KAZOH, *The Theology of the Pain of God* (Richmond: John Knox, 1965).

KLEIN, M. L., *Anthropomorphisms and Anthropopathisms in the Targumim of the Pentateuch, with Parallel Citations from the Septuagint* (Jerusalem: Makor, 1982).

KOEN, LARS, *The Saving Passion: Incarnational and Soteriological Thought in Cyril of Alexandria's Commentary on the Gospel according to St. John* (Stockholm: Almqvist & Wiksell, 1991).

KOPECEK, THOMAS, 'Neo-Arian Religion: the Evidence of the *Apostolic Constitutions*', in *Arianism: Historical and Theological Reassessments* (Cambridge, MA: Philadelphia Patristic Foundation, 1985), 153–79.

KRAFT, H., *Early Christian Thinkers: An Introduction to Clement of Alexandria and Origen* (London: Lutterworth, 1964).

KRIVOCHEINE, BASIL, *In the Light of Christ: St. Symeon the New Theologian* (Crestwood: St Vladimir's Seminary Press, 1986).

KUSHNER, H. S., *When Bad Things Happen to Good People* (New York: HarperCollins, 2001).

KUYPER, LESTER J., 'The Suffering and the Repentance of God', *SJT* 22 (1969), 257–77.

LAMIRANDE, EMILIEN, 'Hypatie, Synésios et la fin des dieux: l'histoire et la fiction', *Sciences religieuses* 18 (1989), 467–89.

LEE, JUNG YOUNG, *God Suffers for Us: A Systematic Inquiry into a Concept of Divine Passibility* (The Hague: Martinus Nejinoff, 1974).

LIDERBACH, DANIEL, *Christ in the Early Christian Hymns* (New York: Paulist Press, 1998).

LIETZMANN, HANS, *Apollinaris von Laodicea und Seine Schule* (New York: Georg Olms, 1970).

LONG, A. A., *Hellenistic Philosophy* (New York: Charles Scribner's Sons, 1974).

LOOFS, FRIEDRICH, *Nestorius and His Place in the History of Christian Doctrine* (Cambridge: Cambridge University Press, 1914).

LORENZ, RUDOLF, *Arius judaizans?: Untersuchungen zur dogmengeschichtlichen Einordnung des Arius*, (Göttingen: Varderhoeck & Ruprecht, 1979).

MCCABE, H., 'The Involvement of God', *New Blackfriars* 66 (1985), 464–76.

MCCARTHY, BRIAN RICE, 'Response: Brueggemann and Hanson on God in the Hebrew Scriptures', *Journal of the American Academy of Religion* 68 (2000), 615–20.

MCCOY, JERRY D., 'Philosophical Influences on the Doctrine of the Incarnation in Athanasius and Cyril of Alexandria', *Encounter* 38 (1977), 362–91.

MCFAGUE, SALLIE, *Models of God* (Philadelphia: Fortress, 1987).

MACGREGOR, GEDDES, *He Who Lets Us Be, A Theology of Love* (New York: Paragon House, 1987).

MCGUCKIN, JOHN A., 'The "Theopaschite Confession" (Text and Historical Context): A Study in the Cyrilline Re-interpretation of Chalcedon', *JEH* 35 (1984), 239–55.

—— *St. Cyril of Alexandria: The Christological Controversy. Its History, Theology, and Texts* (Leiden: E. J. Brill, 1994).

MCKINION, S., *Words, Imagery, and the Mystery of Christ* (Leiden: Brill, 2000).

MCLELLAND, J. C., *God the Anonymous, A Study in Alexandrian Philosophical Theology* (Cambridge: Philadelphia Patristic Foundation, 1976).

MCWILLIAMS, WARREN, *The Passion of God: Divine Suffering in Contemporary Protestant Theology* (Macon: Mercer University Press, 1985).

MAHÉ, JOSEPH, 'Les Anathématismes de saint Cyrille d'Alexandrie et les éveques orientaux du patriarchat d'Antioche', *Revue D'Histoire Ecclésiastique* 7 (1906), 505–42.

MAIER, BARBARA, 'Apatheia bei den Stoikern und Akedia bei Evagrios Pontikos: ein Ideal und die Kehrseite seiner Realität', *Oriens Christianus* 78 (1994), 230–49.

MARTIN, R. P., *Carmen Christi: Philippians 2: 5–11 in Recent Interpretation and in the Setting of Early Christian Worship* (Grand Rapids: Eerdmans, 1983).

MARTIN, R. P., and B. J. DODD (eds.), *Where Christology Began* (Louisville: Westminster John Knox, 1998).

MATHEWS, THOMAS F., *The Clash of Gods* (Princeton: Princeton University Press, 1993).

MAUSER, U., 'Image of God and Incarnation', *Interpretation* 24 (1970), 336–55.

MEIJERING, E. P., 'Some Reflections on Cyril of Alexandria's Rejection of Anthropomorphism', in *God Being History: Studies in Patristic Philosophy* (Amsterdam: North-Holland, 1975), 297–301.

MESLIN, MICHAEL, *Les Ariens d'Occident* (Paris: Éditions du Seuil, 1967).

MICKA, E. F., *The Problem of Divine Anger in Arnobius and Lactantius* (Washington: Catholic University of America Press, 1943).

MICHAELIS, WILHELM, 'Πάσχω', *Theological Dictionary of the New Testament* (Grand Rapids, Mich.: Eerdmans, 1993), v. 925–6, 935–6.

MILLER, JEROME A., 'The Way of Suffering', *Second Opinion* 17 (1922), 21–33.

MOLTMANN, JÜRGEN, *Theology of Hope* (New York: Harper & Row, 1965).

—— *The Crucified God*, trans. M. Khol (London: SCM, 1974).

MOZLEY, J. K., *The Impassibility of God* (Cambridge: Cambridge University Press, 1926).

MULLER, R. A., 'Incarnation, Immutability and the Case for Classical Theism', *Westminster Theological Journal* 45 (1983), 22–40.

NAUTIN, PAUL, *Trois homélies dans la tradition d'Origène*, SC 36 (1953).

—— 'L'*Opus Imperfectum in Matthaeum* et les Ariens de Constantinople', *Revue d'Histoire Ecclésiastique* 67 (1972), 381–408.

NEUFELD, VERNON H., *The Earliest Christian Confessions* (Grand Rapids: Wm. B. Eerdmans, 1963).

NEWMAN, JOHN HENRY, *The Arians of the Fourth Century* (London: Longmans, 1876).

NGIEN, DENNIS, 'God Who Suffers: If God Does not Grieve, Then Can He Love at All? An Argument for God's Emotions', *Christianity Today* 41 (1997), 38–42.

NICOLAS, JEAN-HERVÉ, 'Aimante et Bienheureuse Trinité', *Revue Tomiste* 78 (1978), 271–92.

NIETZSCHE, FRIEDRICH, *Human, All too Human*, trans. Helen Zimmern (Cambridge: Cambridge University Press, 1986).

NNAMANI, A. G., *The Paradox of a Suffering God: On the Classical, Modern-Western and Third World Struggles to Harmonize the Incompatible Attributes of the Trinitarian God* (Frankfurt am Main: Peter Lang, 1994).

NOCK, ARTHUR D., 'Gnosticism', *HTR* 57 (1964), 255–79.

NORRIS, RICHARD A., *Manhood and Christ: A Study in the Christology of Theodore of Mopsuestia* (Oxford: Clarendon, 1963).

—— 'Christological Models in Cyril of Alexandria', *Studia Patristica* 13/2 (Berlin: Akademie Verlag, 1975), 255–68.

—— 'The Problem of Human Identity in Patristic Christological Speculation', *Studia Patristica* 17/1 (1982), 157–70.

—— 'Chalcedon Revisited: A Historical and Theological Reflection', in Bradley Nassif (ed.), *New Perspectives on Historical Theology: Essays in Honor of John Meyendorff* (Grand Rapids: William B. Eerdmans, 1996), 140–58.

NUNN, H. P. V., *Christian Inscriptions* (Eton: Savile, 1952).

NUSSBAUM, MARTHA C., *The Therapy of Desire: Theory and Practice in Hellenistic Ethics* (Princeton: Princeton University Press, 1994).

—— *Upheavals of Thought: The Intelligence of Emotions* (Cambridge: Cambridge University Press, 2001).

O'KEEFE, J. J., 'Impassible Suffering? Divine Passion and Fifth Century Christology', *Theological Studies* 58 (1997), 39–60.

—— 'Kenosis or Impassibility: Cyril of Alexandria and Theodoret of Cyrus on the Problem of Divine Pathos', *Studia Patristica* 32 (Leuven: Peeters, 1997), 358–65.

OWEN, O. T., 'Does God Suffer?', *Church Quarterly Review* 158 (1957), 176–83.

PALMER, DARRYL W., 'Atheism, Apologetic and Negative Theology', *Vigiliae Christianae* 37 (1983), 234–59.

PANNENBERG, W., 'The Appropriation of the Philosophical Concept of God as a Dogmatic Problem of Early Christian Theology', in *Basic Questions in Theology: Collected Essays* (Philadelphia: Westminster, 1971), ii. 119–83.

PELIKAN, JAROSLAV, *The Christian Tradition: A History of the Development of Doctrine*, 5 vols. (Chicago: University of Chicago Press, 1971–91).

PETERS, F. E., *Greek Philosophical Terms: A Historical Lexicon* (New York: New York University Press, 1967).

PINNOCK, C. H., *The Most Moved Mover* (Grand Rapids, Mich.: Baker Academic, 2001).

PIRE, D., 'Sur l'emploi des termes Apatheia et Eleos dans les œuvres de Clément d'Alexandrie', *Revue des sciences philosophiques et théologiques* 27 (1938), 427–31.

PLACHER, WILLIAM C., 'Narratives of a Vulnerable God', *The Princeton Seminary Bulletin* 14 (1993), 134–51.

POLLARD, EVAN T., 'The Impassibility of God', *SJT* 8 (1955), 353–64.

PRESTIGE, GEORGE L., *God in Patristic Thought* (London: W. Heinemann, 1952).

QUASTEN, JOHANNES, *Patrology*, 4 vols. (Allen, Tex.: Thomas More, 2000).

RAMSEY, IAN, *Religious Language: An Empirical Placing of Theological Phrases* (New York: Macmillan, 1957).

RASHDALL, HASTINGS, *The Idea of Atonement in Christian Theology* (London: Macmillan, 1920).

RAVEN, CHARLES E., *Apollinarianism: An Essay on the Christology of the Early Church* (Cambridge: Cambridge University Press, 1923).

REINHARDT, KARL, *Kosmos und Sympathie* (Munich: C. H. Beck, 1926).

RICHARD, LUCIEN J., *A Kenotic Christology in the Humanity of Jesus Christ, the Compassion of our God* (New York: University Press of America, 1982).

RIST, JOHN M., 'The Stoic Concept of Detachment', in *The Stoics*, ed. J. M. Rist (Berkeley: University of California Press, 1978), 259–72.

——, *Stoic Philosophy* (Cambridge: Cambridge University Press, 1989).

ROBINSON, WHEELER H., *Suffering, Human and Divine* (London: SCM, 1940).

ROMANIDES, JOHN, 'St Cyril's "One Physis or Hypostasis of God the Logos Incarnate" and Chalcedon', *Greek Orthodox Theological Review* 10 (1964–5), 82–107.

ROWE, W. V., 'Adolf von Harnack and the Concept of Hellenization', in *Hellenization Revisited: Shaping a Christian Response within the Greco-Roman World* (Lanham, Md.: University Press of America, 1994), 69–98.

RUSSEL, NORMAN, *Cyril of Alexandria* (New York: Routledge, 2000).

RUTHER, T., *Die sittliche Forderung der Apatheia in den beiden ersten Christlichen Jahrhunderten urd bei Klemens von Alexandrien: ein Beitrag zur Geschichte des Christlichen Vollkommenheitsbegriffes* (Freiburg: Herder, 1949), 3–19.

SAGNARD, F. M. M., *La Gnose Valentinienne et le Témoignage de Saint Irénée* (Paris: Librarie Philosophique J. Vrin, 1947).

SANDERS, JACK T., *The New Testament Christological Hymns: Their Historical Religious Background* (Cambridge: Cambridge University Press, 1971).

SAROT, MARCEL, 'Patripassianism, Theopaschitism and the Suffering of God. Some Historical and Systematic Considerations', *Religious Studies* 26 (1990), 363–75.

—— *God: Passibility and Corporeality* (Kampen: Pharos, 1992).

SCHAFF, P., and WACE, H., *Ante-Nicere Fathers* (Grand Rapids: Wm. B. Eerdmans, 1952).

—— *A Select Library of Nicere and Post-Nicere Fathers of the Christian Church* (Grand Rapids: Wm. B. Eerdmans, 1952).

SCHELER, M., *The Nature of Sympathy*, trans. P. Heath (London: Routledge & Kegan Paul, 1970).

SCHLATTER, FREDERIC W., 'The Pelagianism of the *Opus Imperfectum in Matthaeum*', *Vigiliae Christianae* 41 (1987), 267–85.

—— 'The Author of the *Opus Imperfectum in Matthaeum*', *Vigiliae Christianae* 42 (1988), 364–75.

SCHOPENHAUER, A., *On The Basis of Morality* (Indianapolis: Bobbs-Merrill, 1965).

SCHWARTZ, E. (ed.), *Cyrill und des Mönch Viktor* (Vienna: Hölder-Pichler-Tempsky, 1928).

SELLERS, ROBERT Victor, *Two Ancient Christologies: A Study in the Christological Thought of the Schools of Alexandria and Antioch in the Early History of Christian Doctrine* (London: SPCK, 1954).

SIMONETTI, M., *Studi sull'Arianesimo* (Rome: Studium, 1965).

—— *La crisi ariana nel IV secolo* (Rome: Institutum Patristicum Augustinianum, 1975).

SLUSSER, MICHAEL, 'Theopaschite Expressions in Second-Century Christianity as Reflected in the Writings of Justin, Melito, Celsus and Irenaeus', D. Phil thesis (Oxford, 1975).

—— 'Docetism: A Historical Definition', *The Second Century* 1 (1981), 163–72.

—— 'The Scope of Patripassianism', *Studia Patristica* 17/1 (1982), 169–75.

SMITH, RICHARD, 'The Modern Relevance of Gnosticism', in *The Nag Hammadi Library in English*, ed. J. M Robinson (San Francisco: Harper & Row Publishers, 1992), 532–49.

SOELLE, D., *Suffering*, trans. E. R. Kalin (Philadelphia: Fortress, 1975).

SOLOMON, ROBERT S., *The Passions* (Notre Dame: University of Notre Dame Press, 1976).

SOMOS, ROBERT, 'Origen, Evagrius Ponticus and the Ideal of Impassibility', *Origeniana Septima* (Louvain: Peeter, 1999), 365–73.

SONG, CHOAN-SENG, *The Compassionate God* (London: SCM, 1982).

SORABJI, RICHARD, *Emotion and Peace of Mind: From Stoic Agitation to Christian Temptation* (Oxford: Oxford University Press, 2000).

SPANNEUT, M., 'L'apatheia Chretienne', *Proche-Orient Chretien* 52 (2002), 165–302.

ŠPÍDLIK, TOMÁŠ, *The Spirituality of the Christian East: A Systematic Handbook* (Kalamazoo, Mich.: Cistercian Publications, 1986).

SPOERL, KELLEY MCCARTHY, 'Apollinarian Christology and the Anti-Marcellan Tradition', *JTS* 45 (1994), 545–68.

—— 'The Liturgical Argument in Apollinaris: Help and Hindrance on the Way to Orthodoxy', *Harvard Theological Review* 91 (1998), 127–52.

STEAD, CHRISTOPHER G., 'The Platonism of Arius', *JTS* 15 (1964), 14–31.

—— 'Rhetorical Method in Athanasius', *Vigiliae Christianae* 30 (1976), 121–37.

STREETER, BURNETT H., 'The Suffering of God', *Hibbert Journal* 12 (1913/14), 603–11.

STROUMSA, G. A. G., *Another Seed: Studies in Gnostic Mythology* (Leiden: E. J. Brill, 1984).

SULLIVAN, F. A., *The Christology of Theodore of Mopsuestia* (Rome: Gregorian University, 1956).

SURIN, KENNETH, 'The Impassibility of God and the Problem of Evil', *SJT* 35 (1982), 97–115.

TAKÁCS, SAROLTA A., 'Hypatia's Murder—the Sacrifice of a Virgin and its Implications', in *The Formulation of Christianity by Conflict Through the Ages*, ed. K. B. Free (Lewiston: Edwin Mellen Press, 1995), 47–62.

TELEPNEFF, GREGORY, 'Theopaschite Language in the Soteriology of Saint Gregory the Theologian', *Greek Orthodox Theological Review* 32 (1987), 403–16.

TEMPLE, WILLIAM, *Christus Veritas* (London: Macmillan, 1924).

TIRLEMONT, ANTONIN DE, 'Apatheia', *Dictionnaire de spiritualité ascétique et mystique, doctrine et histoire* (Paris: Beauchesne, 1937), i. 727–46.

TON, JOSEPH, *Suffering, Martyrdom, and Rewards in Heaven* (Lanham, Md.: University Press of America, 1997).

TURNER, HENRY E. W., *The Pattern of Christian Truth, A Study in the Relations between Orthodoxy and Heresy in the Early Church* (London: AMS, 1954).

—— 'Nestorius Reconsidered', *Studia Patristica* 13 (1975), 306–21.

VAGGIONE, RICHARD P., *Eunomius of Cyzicus and the Nicene Revolution* (Oxford: Oxford University Press, 2000).

van Banning, Joseph, 'The Critical Edition of the *Opus Imperfectum in Matthaeum*', *Studia Patristica* 17, pt. 1 (1982), 382–7.

van Beeck, F. J., "The Weakness of God's is Stronger" (1 Cor 1: 25): An Inquiry Beyond the Power of Being', *Toronto Journal of Theology* 9 (1993), 9–26.

von Campenhausen, Hans, *The Fathers of the Greek Church* (New York: Pantheon, 1959).

von Hügel, Baron F., 'Suffering and God', in *Essays and Addresses on the Philosophy of Religion*, 2nd ser. (London: Dent & Sons, 1926), 165–213.

Wallis, R. T., *Neoplatonism* (London: Duckworth, 1972).

Ware, Kallistos T., 'The Meaning of *Pathos* in Abba Isaiah and Theodoret of Cyrus', *Studia Patristica* 20 (1989), 315–22.

Weinandy, Thomas, *Does God Change?* (Still River: St Bede's Publications, 1985).

—— *Does God Suffer?* (Notre Dame: University of Notre Dame Press, 2000).

Welch, L., 'Logos-Sarx? Sarx and the Soul of Christ in the Early Throught of Cyril of Alexandria', *St Vladimir's Theological Quarterly* 38 (1994), 271–92.

Wheeler, D. L., 'The Cross and the Blood: Dead or Living Images', *Dialog* 35/1 (1996), 7–13.

Whitehead, Alfred N., *Process and Reality: An Essay in Cosmology* (New York: Free Press, 1978).

Wickham, L. R., *Cyril of Alexandria: Select Letters* (Oxford: Clarendon, 1983).

Wiles, Maurice, *The Spiritual Gospel* (Cambridge: Cambridge University Press, 1960).

—— 'In Defense of Arius', *JTS* 13 (1962), 339–47.

—— 'The Nature of the Early Debate about Christ's Human Soul', *JEH* 15 (1964), 139–51.

—— *The Making of Christian Doctrine* (Cambridge: Cambridge University Press, 1967).

—— *Archetypal Heresy: Arianism Through the Centuries* (Oxford: Clarendon, 1996).

Wiles, Maurice, and Robert C. Gregg, 'Asterius: A New Chapter in the History of Arianism?', *Arianism: Historical and Theological Reassessments* (Cambridge: Philadelphia Patristic Foundation, 1985), 111–51.

Wilken, Robert L., 'Pagan Criticism of Christianity: Greek Religion and Christian Faith', in William R. Schoedel and Robert L. Wilken (eds.), *Early Christian Literature and the Classical Intellectual Tradition* (Paris: Éditions Beauchesne, 1979), 117–30.

—— *The Christians as the Romans Saw Them* (New Haven: Yale University Press, 1984).

Williams, D. D., *What Present Day Theologians are Thinking* (New York: Harper & Bros., 1959).

Williams, Rowan D., 'The Logic of Arianism', *JTS* 34 (1983), 54–81.

—— *Arius: Heresy and Tradition* (London: Darton, Longman & Todd, 1987).

WILSON, O. R., 'A Study of the Early Christian Credal Hymn of I Timothy 3: 16', Ph. D. thesis, (Louisville, 1954).

WINSTON, DAVID, 'Philo's Conception of the Divine Nature', in Lenn E. Goodman (ed.), *Neoplatonism and Jewish Thought* (Albany: State University of New York Press, 1992), 21–42.

WOLF, W. J., *No Cross, No Crown, A Study of the Atonement* (New York: Doubleday, 1957).

WOLFSON, HENRY A., *Philo*, 2 vols. (Cambridge, Mass.: Harvard University Press, 1947).

—— 'Negative Attributes in the Church Fathers and the Gnostic Basilides', *Harvard Theological Review* 50 (1957), 145–56.

—— 'The Negative Attributes in Plotinus and the Gnostic Basilides', *Vigiliae Christianae* 13 (1959), 121–5.

WOLTERSTORFF, NICHOLAS, 'Suffering Love', in *Philosophy and the Christian Faith* (Notre Dame: University of Notre Dame Press, 1988).

WONDRA, GERALD, 'The Pathos of God', *Reformation Review* 18 (1964/5), 28–35.

YAMAUCHI, EDWIN M., 'Anthropomorphism in Hellenism and in Judaism', *Bibliotheca Sacra* 127 (1970), 212–22.

—— 'The Crucifixion and Docetic Christology', *Concordia Theological Quarterly* 46 (1982), 1–20.

YOUNG, FRANCES M., 'A Reconsideration of Alexandrian Christology', *JEH* 22 (1971), 103–14.

—— *The Use of Sacrificial Ideas in Greek Christian Writers from the New Testament to John Chrysostom* (Cambridge, Mass.: Philadelphia Patristic Foundation, 1979).

—— *From Nicaea to Chalcedon* (Philadelphia: Fortress, 1983).

INDEX OF SELECT BIBLICAL REFERENCES

GENERAL INDEX